Software Methods for Business Reengineering

Springer
New York
Berlin
Heidelberg
Barcelona
Budapest
Hong Kong
London
Milan
Paris
Santa Clara
Singapore
Tokyo

Alfs Berztiss

Software Methods for Business Reengineering

With 29 Illustrations

 Springer

Alfs Berztiss

Department of Computer Science
University of Pittsburgh
340 Alumni Hall
Pittsburgh, PA 15260
USA

and Institute of DSV
Stockholm University
Electrum 230
S-16440 Kista
Sweden

Library of Congress Cataloging-in-Publication Data
Berztiss, Alfs T.
    Software methods for business reengineering / Alfs Berztiss.
        p.   cm.
    Includes bibliographical references and index.
    ISBN 0-387-94553-9
    1. Software engineering.   2. Organizational change—Data
processing.   I. Title.
    QA76.758.B47   1995
    658.4'063—dc20   95-19289

Printed on acid-free paper.

Production managed by Frank Ganz; manufacturing supervised by Jacqui Ashri.
Typeset by Best-set Typesetter Ltd., Hong Kong.
Printed and bound by R.R. Donnelley & Sons, Harrisonburg, VA.
Printed in the United States of America.

9 8 7 6 5 4 3 2 1

ISBN 0-387-94553-9 Springer-Verlag New York Berlin Heidelberg

Preface

Business reengineering is a term that is being heard more and more often, and lately with a negative connotation. Although much already has been written about it, both its nature and its purpose often are misunderstood, and the result is disenchantment. This is particularly noticeable in discussions on the support that software engineering and information technology are to provide for business reengineering. Either too much or too little hope is put on software. This book attempts to remedy the situation by introducing modern principles of process-oriented software development to management. Technical personnel in information systems departments also will benefit from our survey, in which we aim to make software development more scientific without becoming too formal, and to outline a management view of business reengineering to developers of information systems. Thus, two classes of readers can benefit from this book—managers and information systems personnel. Ed Yourdon addresses himself to the latter: "Not only do we need to be experts in people-ware . . . , systems development methodologies, . . . and software re-engineering, but we also need to know business process reengineering . . ." [Cw93a].

Business reengineering is part of our transition to a postindustrial era. Some barely feel the revolutionary forces shaping the future; for others, the transition is traumatic. The knowledge revolution that characterizes our times is one of three major upheavals in human history—first came the transition to an agricultural age, then to the industrial age, and now to a postindustrial age. We cannot stop the revolution. All we can do is make the transition to a postindustrial society smooth and rapid, so that everybody comes to enjoy the benefits of the transition as early as possible.

Revolutions change the way we function. The knowledge revolution makes us take a fresh look at our organizations, their basic purpose, their structure, their management, their operation, and their interaction with other organizations. Such examination should result in a restructuring that allows an organization to perform its basic functions in a more effective way. When the effectiveness of an organization is being at least doubled, we can speak of business reengineering.

Management is being bombarded with suggestions of how to improve an organization—total quality management, theory Z, cost centers, outsourcing, intrapreneurship, a host of Japanese business practices with exotic names. All of these suggestions have merit, and all should be considered when an organization is being put together. But first the organization has to be taken apart, redefined *as a set of processes*, and reassembled according to the new definition. For this radical reorganization there is no simple recipe.

Although there is no recipe, there is a preferred approach. This is to base all reengineering activities on sound engineering principles. The discipline of software engineering, which over the past 20 years has evolved into a legitimate branch of engineering, can provide the analytical expertise for defining business processes, and the notations and tools to help transform process descriptions into support software systems. Ideally, software engineers in information systems (IS) departments would assume key roles in reengineering teams in which they would closely cooperate with personnel outside of IS. By being outside traditional departments, such as sales, marketing, and personnel, IS people can view their organization with neutral eyes. More importantly, the IS people know much about the organization, but they must realize that there is much more that they do not know.

Moreover, the changes to be implemented will be much more radical than the changes ISD has had to deal with in the past. In fact, in order to deal with these changes, the processes of information systems have to be reengineered first. And herein lies a problem. Information technology is perceived as not having paid off. Partly this is due to information systems personnel being unprepared to carry out major changes, which partly is due to a reluctance by top management to authorize radical changes based on information technology. Management reluctance is understandable—the fairly low level of technical preparedness of some American software developers is cause for concern [Yo92]. Considerable opposition can therefore be expected to placing the ISD in a central position of the reengineering effort. Some will say that software people do not understand business; others will point to the expensive failure of this or that software project in the past. Actually, reality is not as bad as the perception. Software personnel can give excellent technical support to reengineering, and their effectiveness would be even greater *if they were willing to become disciplined software engineers*. This book defines some of the things they would have to know or be prepared to learn in order to achieve this.

Much of this book is a selective adaptation of a software requirements course I have given to industry and academic audiences in the Americas, Europe, Asia, and Australia. The course has evolved over 10 years or so, but from the very start it had processes as the basis of study, where a process may be the handling of a purchase order, cash withdrawal from an ATM, the operation of a furnace, or the development of a software system itself. The decision to concentrate on processes turned out well, particularly when we began to consider requirements analysis in the context of business reengineering. Most importantly, we came to realize that a process can be designed and validated without regard to its ultimate implementation. This means that once the essential nature of a process has been established, the process can be implemented under a traditional organizational structure or a reengineered structure. In other words, the essence of a process is independent of the structure of the organization that supports the process. This realization defines our approach to business reengineering: Information technology, such as computer networks and CASE tools, provide essential support for the processes of an organization, but the technology is secondary to a thorough understanding of each process. Our aim is to show how to reach such understanding.

Part I of the book explores the nature of business reengineering, and Part II is a brief introduction to the principles and practice of software engineering. To some extent, these two parts are independent of each other. Although some effort was made to relate software engineering to business reengineering, we consider it important that the picture of software engineering presented in Part II be fairly complete, i.e., that it go beyond the role software engineering is to assume in business reengineering. The essence of a reengineered organization is found in a set of processes that depend on an information base—Parts III through V establish how the processes and their supporting information base are to be defined. There we take a software engineering approach. Although not all of the examples relate specifically to business reengineering, they all deal with techniques that can be directly translated into reengineering practice. In Part VI, we return to the process of reengineering, but now with a software engineering attitude. Some chapters of the book deal with technical matters. This is how it should be. Business reengineering has a technical side, and my aim was to concentrate on the technicalities without becoming too engrossed in them. Readers not directly concerned with the technical side can merely skim through these chapters, but they should not skip them entirely—one of our purposes is to point out the need for greater technical competence. A reading guide contains pointers to literature that will enable readers to follow up on topics they find particularly relevant or interesting.

Alfs Berztiss
(alpha@cs.pitt.edu)

Contents

This is related to teamwork, and two formats for group workshops are contrasted.

A business process is defined as an ordered collection of business tasks that is to achieve a specific goal. A distinction is made between business activities that fit this definition and those that do not.

II. What is Software Engineering

The next six chapters are primarily addressed to managers to give them an appreciation of the nature of software engineering, but software developers will also benefit from this statement of goals. The aim of engineering is to utilize economically the materials and forces of nature. Software engineers do not deal with natural phenomena, but they still follow the same activities as conventional engineers. Many of these activities are relevant to business reengineering.

A software application system can be considered as made up of an information component, a control component, and data transformers. The systems that support the operation of a reengineered organization follow this pattern, and will be called information-control systems.

Software modules are defined, and their history is traced. Each module of a software system is to have a well-defined purpose, and its interaction with other modules is to be minimized. The same objectives hold in the definition of the business processes of a reengineered organization. The definition of modules is an important function of requirements engineering.

Software quality has many facets, including verifiability, robustness, maintainability, reusability, and understandability. One concern of requirements engineering is the ranking of these quality attributes in order of importance for the particular software system under considera-tion, keeping in mind that the most important quality attribute is user acceptance. Special emphasis is given to software performance estimation.

Disciplined system development has to follow a plan. We discuss how the waterfall model for system development, in which requirements determination is a distinct initial phase, is to be replaced by the spiral model or by specification-based prototyping in which requirements determination is to a large degree integrated with system design. The Software Engineering Institute process maturity levels are introduced.

Cost and risk estimation is a highly skilled activity that requires much experience. It is a crucial part of requirements analysis in that it determines whether or not a system is to be developed at all.

III. Business Analysis

Most of the processes with which a reengineered organization will be concerned already exist in some form in the organization. The processes are redefined as requirements documents. A more radical approach is to redesign an organization without any regard for what already exists.

It is good practice to have some rudimentary requirements statement ready before employees of an enterprise are interviewed. Proper interview techniques are crucial to the elicitation of reliable information.

Group sessions can lead to many improvements of a given set of requirements. These sessions should be supervised by trained moderators. Two types of sessions are considered, brainstorming and JAD (Joint Application Development).

A specification must express process requirements unambiguously, and a specification language must facilitate demonstration of whether the system defined by a specification will have a particular property or exhibit a particular behavior. A specification language should preferably be executable. It is then a prototyping language. Interaction of business domain specialists with the prototype is likely to suggest changes to process requirements.

IV. The Reengineering Blueprint

The processes of an organization are dynamic, but they are supported by an information base that has a static structure. This and the next chapter deal with these two aspects of process definition. Most requirements are initially expressed in natural language. The requirements analyst must try to make the natural language statements unambiguous and verifiable. From these statements the analyst develops a graphical representation of the information base for the processes, which in our case is an Entity-Relationship diagram.

The dynamic aspects of the reengineered enterprise are captured in state transition and data flow diagrams.

VI. Implementation of Reengineering

The 16-step reengineering plan in Chapter 4 is reexamined with a software engineering attitude. The five chapters that then follow deal with the most important aspects of the reengineering process.

The actual reengineering of an organization starts with the definition of the organization in terms of processes, and specification of the processes. The costs, risks, and benefits associated with different processes and their implementation variants determine reengineering priorities. Of particular concern is the process that converts research and development findings into products for the market.

The existing software systems of an organization represent a major investment. Moreover, they are reasonably reliable. This legacy software is to be integrated into the process systems of the reengineered organization, but only if the software does not impose heavy constraints on how the reengineering teams are to proceed.

Most reengineered organizations depend on local area and wide area networks for communication. An imaginative use of these facilities can raise significantly the effectiveness of an organization.

Most of the software systems that support business processes interact with human participants in these processes. Although it is difficult to express user-friendliness in quantitative terms, benchmarking allows the quality of a user interface to be measured. Experimental data exist on the effectiveness of different modes of user-system communication.

Maintenance of a process is corrective, adaptive, perfective, or preventive. Maintenance is facilitated if the need for future maintenance is anticipated at the time the process is designed. Software maintenance is sometimes considered as little different from software reuse. A special case of reuse is the adaptation of a product for international markets.

Appendices

This appendix introduces some basic notations of set theory and logic. Its main purpose is to help in the reading of SF specifications.

    The reading guide refers mainly to books in which some of the topics
raised in the text are discussed in detail. For the most part, the organization of the reading guide follows the order in which these topics are
dealt with in the text.

I
What is Business Reengineering

1
The Established and the Reengineered

Business reengineering is made necessary by the movement of our society into a postindustrial era. It is a radical transformation of an organization from a rigid structure defined by departments to a flexible structure defined by processes. Ten myths regarding reengineering are explored.

Business reengineering is an inevitable part of the transition of our industrial society into a postindustrial age. We are living through the third major change in human history. The first was the settling of hunters and gatherers into an ordered agricultural life. Next came the transformation of agricultural society into industrial society. This transformation had an interesting effect on agricultural production: In some industrialized countries, production was lifted to such an extent that today a farmworker in the United States produces 130 times as much cereals as the average farmer in preindustrial Africa [Ke93, p.69].

We do not really know what the postindustrial age will look like. But we do know that it will be based on knowledge. What physical plant was to industry, knowledge bases will be to the new society, a society that is being brought into existence by what is being called the *knowledge revolution*. The shift is already noticeable in a comparison of two companies—on February 28, 1995, the ratio of market value to assets was an amazing 6.14 for Microsoft; for IBM, the ratio was only 0.54 (using data from [Bw95]). Knowledge is the intangible in these valuations, and on February 28, 1995, the market saw Microsoft as better positioned than IBM to put its knowledge pool to good use.

We also know that companies that succeed in making the transition to the postindustrial world will achieve twofold, threefold, or even twentyfold improvements in product development, manufacturing, and customer service. These improvements will be brought about by business reengineering. But, just as the birth of agricultural society was accompanied by wanderings of enormous masses of people, and the industrial revolution changed the lives of millions of people, so, too, the knowledge revolution is not without a social cost.

There is no way back to the supposed golden age of the 1950s. The Luddites tried to stop the industrial revolution, but they did not succeed. We cannot stop the decrease in well-paid unskilled and semiskilled jobs in traditional industries. Even if the borders of the United States were closed to the importation of manufactured products, local competition would favor companies that produce the same goods with fewer workers. As one division manager of an American insurance company put it, "If we succeed, half of us will no longer have a job in this division; if we fail, none of us will" (quoted in [Da93]).

Sometimes I ask myself: Instead of developing software that makes manufacturing and service industries more efficient, should we not try to slow down the transition to the postindustrial age? On reflection, we should see that a slowdown would not help. Keep in mind that the industrial revolution was slow, and that many generations of workers suffered before we finally saw the benefits. Let us learn from this. Let us make the transition to the new age as rapid as possible so that we can see its benefits in our own lifetimes.

Moreover, although reengineering has in many cases resulted in re- duction of personnel, this is not an essential feature of the process. Reengineering can stimulate a company to growth in sales, profits, *and* personnel. Product diversification, quality improvement, and greater attention to customer relations should drive expansion. All that is needed on the part of the company is willingness to introduce new products and services, and to educate its employees in new skills. All that is needed on the part of employees is flexibility and willingness to acquire these new skills. An example that this approach works is provided by Hewlett- Packard: In three years this company reduced operating expenses from 38.4 to 31.1% of revenues without firing any employees [Fo94], and 70% of their orders are for products introduced or redesigned within the past 2 years [Fo94c].

Reengineering raises a few problems of terminology. First, reengineer- ing can be effective in many different settings, such as private companies, corporations, nonprofit organizations, sports teams, and government agencies. In referring to these entities I prefer the blanket term *organi- zation*, but, to break monotony, I shall also use the terms *enterprise*, *company*, and *corporation*, more or less interchangeably. Second, a reengineered organization depends on large amounts of data stored in computers. Structured aggregates of such data are being referred to as data bases, but, as deductive capabilities and ways of dealing with un- certainties in the data are being developed, it becomes more appropriate to speak of information bases or even knowledge bases. Our preferred term will be *information base*. Third, a reengineered organization is defined in terms of processes, and we think of each process as being ultimately supported by a software system. We shall therefore use the terms *process*, *software system*, and *process system* more or less interchangeably. Similarly, *process personnel* and *system users* will be regarded as nearly synonymous, but sometimes *users* will take on a broader meaning, and will refer collectively to the process personnel and others who interact with the process without belonging to the process personnel. Sometimes users in this broader sense will be called *process participants*.

Reengineering can be defined operationally or by the effect it has on an organization. Operationally, business reengineering is the identification of basic business processes, the specification of these processes, and the implementation of the processes. By effect, business reengineering is the structural redesign of an organization to allow it to carry out its basic business processes at a dramatic improvement in performance. These definitions are complementary, and they allow different groups to concentrate on those aspects of the total reengineering effort that concern them most. For us, the operational definition is of greater concern.

Let us dissect the definitions. We consider an organization to be defined by a set of processes that this organization carries out—typically, 10 to 20 processes define the activities of an organization, but, for a company operating in a complex business domain, such as the carrying of goods by rail, there can be many more processes. One example of a process is the introduction of a new product, carried out by a team assembled for just this purpose. The team disbands after the project has been completed. Another example is mortgage approval. In contrast to a project process, this process has many instances, and a permanent mortgage approval team is associated with this process.

In the specification of a process we are interested in just the essence of the process. Thus, as regards mortgage approval, we define the steps of the process and the order in which the steps are to be carried out, indicating also which steps can be carried out simultaneously. But in such a specification we do not care whether each step will be carried out by a separate individual, or all steps by the same individual, or some steps by humans and others by expert systems.

Only when we come to implementation do we define in detail an information base that is to support the process, and set up a computer software representation of the structure of the process. A program steps through this structural representation and issues prompts at the right times, e.g., "Use the valuation of the property to determine the maximum amount of the mortgage loan." At this stage, our implementation is rather schematic, i.e., we determine what prompts will be needed, but we do not care whether the prompts go to persons or expert systems. Let us use the term *schematic implementation* for this stage.

In the definition by effect, the important terms are *structural redesign* and *dramatic improvement*. During schematic implementation, we are not interested in who is doing what. But, in order to make an implementation efficient, we have to bring in the players, and this is linked to the structural redesign of the organization. Under the old system, a mortgage application may well pass through three different departments of the bank, with some employee in each department making a contribution to the ultimate decision. In the reengineered bank, everything relating to mortgage approval is to be handled by a single organizational unit, which may be located at bank headquarters or be physically distributed over different branch buildings. Having decided on a single organizational unit, our next task is to make sure that this unit will dramatically improve the mortgage approval process, where improved performance relates both to the cost of the process to the bank and to the time a customer has to wait for a decision. To do so, the reengineering team may have to evaluate three options: a team handles the mortgage application, a single person handles it throughout, or a knowledge-based support system is developed to help this person reach a decision. The option selected is likely to vary from one bank to another.

As we shall see in the next chapter, the call for reengineering is not a new phenomenon. What is new is that the call is at last being widely heard, and that it generates a response. The response can range from critical acceptance to bizarre faddishness. Numerous myths have arisen that may make some executives suspect the legitimacy of the claims for reengineering.

Reengineering is a permanent process. Reengineering is often confused with the incremental improvement of business processes. Instead, reengineering is a radical one-time effort. Its aim is to improve dramatically the performance of an organization. For example, Asea Brown Boveri set its aim at reducing its total product development time by 50% for each new product [Pe92, p.52]. Clearly such an improvement cannot be obtained over and over again, but, after the initial reengineering of product development, the development time can still be incrementally improved.

If It Ain't Broke . . . Break It. This is the title of a recent book [Kr92], and its advice can be taken too literally. The goals of what reengineering is to achieve must be clearly stated. If these goals are realistic, a reengineering plan can be developed that will lead to their attainment. However, a start-up company may have evolved in full accordance with all of the principles that reengineering attempts to inject into moribund mature organizations. Such a company is as healthy as can be, and to carry out radical changes in such a company just for the sake of doing something is to invite disaster. Of course, employees in the start-up company should always be on the lookout for opportunities for incremental improvement. Davenport [Da93, p.15] suggests an exception: "well-funded government organizations" should not reengineer. With this, as a taxpayer, I find it hard to agree. We should note, though, that governments have many functions, and one such function may be to provide employment to a disadvantaged group in the population so that this group can improve its economic and social standings—this need not imply that employment of the disadvantaged cannot be cost-effective.

Reengineering is a real money-saver. It is, but only if it is done properly. American Express estimates that business reengineering has saved it 1.8 billion dollars in operating expenses in just 2 years [Cw94d]. Other companies have become disillusioned because they expected too much too soon. It may take a while for the savings to appear. In the short term, for reengineering to succeed, a lot of expensive technology may have to be put in place. Also, positions may have to be eliminated, and typically this translates into a large one-time charge. However, as we have already noted, reengineering need not result in lost jobs. The effectiveness of downsizing has not been established—loss of experienced employees and collapse of employee morale may outweigh the savings in wages and benefits. The biggest danger arises when downsizing is carried out in an irrational manner, and this activity is believed to be reengineering. Far too often the result is that employees who add value to products and services are let go, and those who do not add value stay. The most valuable resource of an organization is the collective knowledge of its personnel. Great care is to be taken that it is not squandered. In a healthy organization, this knowledge is like the picture that results when a jigsaw puzzle is properly fitted together. As pieces are removed from the puzzle, the picture loses definition.

Business is war and reengineering is our secret weapon. The total war metaphor goes beyond "us against them" to "us or them." However, the aim of reengineering is not to destroy the competition—without healthy competition, one's own company easily may become stagnant. Instead, the aim is to make the entire industry a vital contributor of goods and services. It is therefore curious to see Sun Tzu, Attila the Hun, and other ancient warriors turned into "management gurus" [Ho91, Ro93].

Reengineering is incompatible with other business improvements. Because reengineering should take precedence over everything else, organizations are warned against attempting reengineering and some other major initiative at the same time. This is good advice, but only if the two initiatives are regarded as totally separate activities. Suppose an organization considers introducing reengineering and, say, TQM (total quality management). Both should actually be introduced simultaneously, but with the TQM effort a subordinated part of the reengineering plan. Indeed, process teams, which are an essential part of reengineering, can function as quality circles in a natural way. Reengineering is not a sharply defined isolated endeavor. Rather, it is concerned with the definition of a set of processes that should be implemented with full regard for every technique that can contribute to the effectiveness of the processes. Effectiveness here means reduction of costs, *and* cost-effective reduction of process time, *and* cost-effective improvement of quality. Effectiveness is not achieved by expending much effort on incremental improvements to a process already selected for reengineering—if such improvements are made to those parts of the process that will no longer exist in its re-engineered version, we foster waste.

Reengineering reduces specialization. We could say that the exact opposite holds. The reason for the confusion is that the term *specialization* can be interpreted in two different ways: as the execution of a simple task over and over and over again, or as the acquisition of large amounts of highly specific knowledge, as required by, say, a specialist in organ transplant surgery. Reengineering tends to eliminate specialization in the first sense, but specialization in the second sense becomes all-important. In a re-engineered organization, a team carries out a process. One such process may be the assembly of an automobile. It is bound to turn out that some members of the assembly team are better at some tasks than at others and a natural specialization (in the first sense) develops. However, should one or other member be absent, the rest of the team must be able to cover for the absent team member, implying specialization in the second sense. In other words, employees of a reengineered company have to become specialists at more than one task. The need for specialization (in the second sense) is even more marked in the development of a software system. Here, highly specialized technical knowledge is needed to deal with the performance and reliability properties of the software system, and, to a lesser extent, with the design of the user interface to the system. As regards the latter, in addition to having a user interface specialist as a permanent member of the team, a color specialist may have to be called in on temporary assignment. It should be noted that this type of specialization is as yet rarely practiced in software development, with detrimental effects on software quality.

In a reengineered organization, management withers away. There are two kinds of management activities: those that add value to products and services, and those that take it away. Only the latter activities need to be eliminated. As specialist functions in an organization became identified with separate departments, there arose a need for managers to coordinate the work of the separate departments. In addition, management has come to use various expensive checks and balances to prevent wrongdoing. Often, the cost of prevention far exceeds any possible potential loss. Coordinators and policers do not add value to products. However, a manager who carries out a risk-benefit analysis on a new product and, on the basis of this analysis, decides not to make the product, performs a value-added task. If the product were marketed, and this caused a loss, the loss would have to be carried by all of the other products of the company. The manager has "added" the amount of the projected loss to the value of the other products. Further, in a process-oriented organization in which the processes correspond to separate projects of limited duration, personnel allocation to projects continues to be an important management task. Peters [Pe92] advocates increased dependence on freelancing specialists called in to participate on a particular project. A management task then is to find the right people for the right job. Unfortunately, the experience most people will have had with roofers, plumbers, and physicians suggests that freelancing be approached with caution—the real experts are booked out for months ahead; the ones available may do more harm than good. Finally, although reengineering encourages empowerment of process personnel, this does not imply total lack of controls. A European automaker suffered very large losses when an employee hoped to enrich the company by currency speculations; an employee who guaranteed a supply of nuclear fuel at a fixed price for many years ahead caused substantial losses to a major U.S. corporation. Confusion remains as to who was responsible for a 1.6 billion dollar oil-trading loss by a German metals conglomerate. Proper controls protect a company; excessive controls stifle it.

Reengineering must be done quickly. Dragging out the reengineering effort is the best way to lose initial momentum, but we also should note that reengineering changes the entire culture of an organization, and a cultural change cannot be effected overnight. In particular, two aspects have to be watched very carefully. One, employees who are or who feel threatened by the reorganization brought about by reengineering have to be accommodated. Two, the day-to-day business of the organization cannot be stopped by reengineering. Hence there is a need to start with a carefully orchestrated conditioning of employees, and the changeover has to be planned in great detail. One approach is to carry out the changeover in stages. Thus, when Sweden switched from left-hand to right-hand traffic, the changeover took two days: on the first day, a Sunday, only buses drove on the right; on the next day, everybody did. As a safety measure, only buses were allowed out on the first day. Note, though, that reengineering times are measured in years rather than days or months. Al Gore, Vice President of the United States, estimates that a partial re-engineering of the U.S. federal government will take 8 to 10 years [Bw93].

Reengineering is guaranteed to cause resentment in all. People losing jobs will be unhappy. So will others who may feel demoted in the reengineered organization. However, the resentment is not going to be as universal and as deep as one may think. This is shown by companies that have gone through reengineering. It is also a myth that older employees cannot adjust [Bw93c]. They can if enough of an effort is made to convince them of the benefits of change, and if the change does in fact make their life more interesting. When Australia went decimal, everybody was apprehensive about the effect of this move on pensioners. It turned out that the pensioners went along with the change most enthusiastically of all.

Reengineering will solve all of our problems. Reengineering is no insurance against general economic downturns—even a reengineered company can go into the red. Any external change can have a detrimental effect on an organization. A particularly dangerous situation arises when an irresponsible, even suicidal, price war makes an entire industry suffer enormous losses. However, a reengineered company has the flexibility to react rapidly and effectively to detrimental changes. Hence, all other things being equal, a reengineered company will always be better off than a company that has not reengineered.

Can every organization be reengineered? Yes, it can, but only in some cases will the existing organizational culture assist the effort. In others it will be a hindrance. Then the first step toward reengineering will be to bring about a cultural change. The primary effect of the change should be an understanding that management has to take a scientific attitude. Science aims at establishing cause–effect relationships, but the determination of such relationships is not always easy. It is easiest in the natural sciences, where controlled experiments can exclude all that is irrelevant. In the social sciences, even effects are not always clearly defined, and, when they are, they could have any number of causes, that act either singly or jointly. I like to think of technology as the application of natural science in a social setting, and of business reengineering as a technological activity. This implies that success in business reengineering depends on the recognition that two kinds of skills are needed: strictly technical skills and people skills. Successful management brings together staff with these two kinds of skills, sees to it that they learn each other's language, and ensures that they cooperate for a common good.

This view of reengineering explains why it has been most successful in manufacturing. There the natural science component is strongest, and we can get some idea of what works and what does not work, e.g., it is fairly easy to establish what effect an innovation has on manufacturing cost, but social effects cannot be totally eliminated even there. For example, given that a manufacturing innovation has resulted in reduced absenteeism, we could show that the reduced absenteeism is a consequence of the innovation, but we could not tell with any degree of confidence whether this is a permanent or merely a temporary novelty effect.

At this point we have to ask ourselves several questions. First, we have made process orientation basic to our operational definition of business reengineering, but is process orientation necessary? Second, if it is, how are the processes of a business to be identified and defined? Third, how is a smooth transition to be made from the current way an enterprise does its business to a new process-oriented way?

Of course, the all-important question is the first. In the next chapter we shall explore George Huber's view that the operation of organizations can be explained in terms of four paradigms. We shall see that in the two earlier paradigms emphasis is put on social organization, but that emphasis is on processes in the two more advanced paradigms. This shift of emphasis from static social structures to dynamic processes is conditioned by the rapidity of the changes that occur all around us. Only an enterprise that has a dynamic organizational structure can respond adequately to dynamic changes in its environment. In Chapter 6 we shall discuss the nature of processes in some detail.

Turning now to the second question, let me emphasize that this book is primarily about the support software engineering technology can provide for business reengineering, and this relates almost exclusively to processes. The rigorous definition of processes has always been a concern of software engineering; hence software engineers should be best equipped for this activity. But software engineers need to be told by business experts how the business operates, and then together they may determine what changes should be made. Most of the book deals with notations for defining processes, and with examples of use of the notations.

Process orientation is necessary for success in business reengineering, but it is not sufficient. Unfortunately, in many organizations process orientation is regarded as an alternative to people orientation. People are as important under process-oriented paradigms as they are under the earlier paradigms. Every process is composed of tasks, a time–space structure into which the tasks are organized, role assignments to personnel associated with the process, and the tools and techniques that are to assist the personnel in carrying out the process. In answer to our third question, the transition to a process-oriented enterprise will be only as smooth as people can make it, and, after the transition, the success of the operation of a process will depend on the people in charge of it, i.e., success will be determined by how well the role assignments are made. The importance of its people to an organization will be taken up in Chapter 5.

Most importantly, management must be ready for change if change is to be effective. It has to provide the impetus for the business reengineering effort, has to coordinate people-oriented and process-oriented aspects of this effort, and has to introduce a reengineered process structure with minimal disruption of the day-to-day operations of the enterprise. Business reengineering can succeed only when the importance of both people skills and technical skills is fully recognized, and both are properly applied. Many attempts at reengineering have failed because this has not been understood.

2
Business Reengineering is Not New

Serious beginnings of business reengineering are traced back to around 1973. Particular attention is given to the interpretation of business reengineering as the application of a decision-making paradigm to the design of organizations. Some guidelines for introducing this paradigm into an organization are listed.

In the United States, the realization that we are moving into a postindustrial world arose more or less simultaneously with the start of stagnation in the standard of living of many Americans, around the middle of the 1970s. In 1973, Daniel Bell's *The Coming of the Post-Industrial Society* [Be73] was published. An article by Herbert Simon that links the structure of postindustrial organizations with information technology appeared in the same year [Si73]. The two crucial points had been made: We are entering a postindustrial era, and this era will be characterized by imaginative uses of information technology. In the same year, the oil embargo caused Japanese companies to reexamine their mode of operation. Many companies adopted a process-based, energy-conserving, quality-oriented structure. To use a single word, these companies were *reengineered*.

Ten years later, George Huber described what a postindustrial organization would look like [Hu83]. His basic premise was that postindustrial society will be characterized by accelerating increase in knowledge, complexity, and turbulence, and that postindustrial organizations therefore will have to be qualitatively different from the organizations of the industrial age. The qualitative differences are to be most noticeable in decision making, innovation, and the acquisition and distribution of information. Much earlier, Simon had defined three phases of decision making [Si60]: an intelligence-gathering phase that indicates problems or opportunities for an organization, a design phase that results in the development of several strategies for dealing with the problems or opportunities, and a selection phase in which an effective strategy is selected for implementation. Putting all of this together, we arrive at a coherent description of business in the postindustrial world: (1) a turbulent environment creates complex problems and opportunities for an organization; (2) these problems and opportunities are recognized by the organization in an intelligence-gathering effort that is supported by increasingly knowledgeable information systems; and (3) the organization decides rapidly on its responses, with this decision-making process again supported by information systems. In other words, we need stimulus-response systems in which response to a stimulus is immediate; but the many-layered management structures of the industrial age are not well-suited for immediate responses. The management structures must therefore be reengineered.

The Huber article of 1983 was followed in 1986 by the description of a decision-making paradigm for the operation of organizations [Hu86]. The 1986 paper discusses three earlier paradigms, and then elaborates on the decision-making paradigm. The main characteristic of this fourth paradigm is the explicit provision of structures and processes that facilitate the making of decisions in the operation of an organization. We shall look at all four paradigms in some detail because in our view they correspond to a greater or lesser extent to the four stages of development of society—preagricultural, agricultural, industrial, and postindustrial.

Under a *paternalistic/political* structure, a tribal leader controls all resources, and they are allocated in a way that strengthens the leader's authority. The leader makes all decisions, and there is very little room for subordinates to carry out actions for which they assume responsibility. Features of this archaic structure persisted in China over thousands of years, and it is a characteristic of most planned economies. Elsewhere it is seen in situations in which a leader's authority is deemed necessary for effective operation, as in units at the bottom level of a military hierarchy.

The second paradigm, designated an *accountability/authority* paradigm, is quite pervasive in modern organizations. It could also be called an actor/role paradigm—in designing an organization, roles or responsibilities are allocated to various actors, i.e., the personnel of an organization, and each actor receives sufficient authority to carry out the responsibilities. The most complex political structure of the agricultural age was the Roman Empire, and it functioned precisely according to this paradigm. The paradigm is enshrined in modern-day chains-of-command charts. However, while Roman chains of command had very few links, in many of today's companies the chains have become excessively long.

With industrialization came the workflow paradigm. Instead of emphasis on personnel, as in the accountability/authority paradigm, emphasis is now put on flow of work—an assembly line transforms components into a finished automobile, a purchasing process transforms an outgoing order into additions to the inventory of components, specifications for a machine are transformed into an operating manual for the machine. A workflow diagram defines a process, but the chain-of-command structure has not disappeared—the workflow diagram defines a process structure orthogonal to personnel structure. The chain-of-command charts define departments, and work flows from department to department, i.e., the process structure is superimposed on an existing personnel structure. Such superpositioning can make management extremely complex. An attempt to rationalize management functions in this situation is *matrix management*—each department has its management, each process has its management, and the two management teams are supposed to collaborate.

Unfortunately, matrix management doubles management overhead without generating an appreciable reduction in process costs. Moreover, the objectives of the two sets of managers may be in conflict with each other. Thus, the manager of a process is interested in the fastest possible completion of a particular project, but department managers are interested in utilizing their personnel in the most effective way. The resolution of this conflict can call for a complicated decision process. On the one hand, it is important to keep the personnel of a department fully occupied; on the other, a particular project may have such a high priority that non-optimal personnel utilization is justified.

The way out is to switch from a departmental structure to a process structure. A single process team is then allocated to a process from beginning to end. Priorities are assigned to projects from the very start, and the composition of the team allocated to a project reflects the priority of this project. The initial team allocation is based on complex management decisions in which costs and schedules are balanced against benefits, and process execution can be regarded as a string of decisions that the process team has to make. In particular, the team has to decide when and how to reorganize the process itself: major adjustments will have to be made in response to the specifications of a new product that the team is to produce, which may be quite different from anything the team has dealt with in the past; lesser changes will be suggested by day-to-day practical experience. All of these decisions led Huber to speak of a *decision-making* paradigm. Reengineering is to introduce this paradigm into organizations.

The change of emphasis from departmental structures to process structures is the main characteristic of business reengineering. The change is made in the realization that existing departmental or matrix organizations are not properly positioned for decision making. There is just too much management. Layers of management have arisen to deal with the mismatch that arises when the operation of an organization is defined by processes, which are not always well understood and give rise to crises, while its personnel structure is defined by departments. In addition, management groups established to deal with highly specific problems tend to persist after the problems no longer exist. Business reengineering is essentially the application of the decision-making paradigm to the design of organizations, but effective decision making cannot be achieved until this overload of bureaucracy has been removed. We conclude by adapting some guidelines from [Hu86], which are intended to facilitate introduction of the decision-making paradigm into an organization.

• Assign decision-making authority to the hierarchical level best suited for the type of decision. In broad terms, decisions relate to (a) organization-wide strategy, (b) operational tactics required to implement the strategy, and (c) the day-to-day operation of processes. This suggests that a management hierarchy needs no more than three levels—top executives to formulate organizational strategy and policies, managers of operations, and self-managing process teams.

• Ensure that all decision makers have the specialized knowledge needed to make the decisions appropriate for their level of decision making. This has two aspects. First, the decision makers may need specialized skills, e.g., skills to interpret properly the results of statistical analyses. Second, the decision makers have to be given access to all information and tools needed for this decision making.

• Regard the situations that processes have to deal with as standard or nonstandard. Decision making with regard to standard situations is to be standardized, and automation of decision making is to be considered. Nonstandard situations require process teams to show initiative and flexibility, and much of the training of the teams is to be directed toward dealing with nonstandard situations. This is not to be confused with *anticipated* deviations from the normal flow of control in a process. For example, when X uses a telephone network to contact Y, the normal flow of control ultimately has X and Y engaged in a conversation. Deviations arise when X dials an invalid number, Y's phone is busy, X hangs up after dialing just a few of the digits of Y's number, etc. These deviations are all anticipated, and standard procedures have been developed for dealing with them. Indeed, all of these procedures have become automated. The phoning process becomes nonstandard when an unanticipated situation arises, e.g., an earthquake destroys much of the network hardware. More common nonstandard situations arise in the evaluation of mortgage applications or of insurance claims. The main purpose of empowerment of process teams is to allow them to deal with unanticipated situations rapidly. If the unexpected situation is likely to occur again, the process team is to standardize its course of action for dealing with the situation. Moreover, instead of freezing its standards, an efficient reengineered organization tries to improve them whenever an opportunity to do so presents itself. A combination of a nonstandard process with a standard process arises when an existing product is to be replaced. The changeover to the manufacture of the new product results in a nonstandard process, which is nonstandard because it is a new process, but the process for transforming an existing process into the new process should itself be standard.

• Realize that the flow of information within an organization consists of routine messages and indicators of exceptional conditions. The organization is to provide means of identifying the two kinds of messages, of automating responses to routine messages, and of rapidly channeling nonroutine messages to appropriate decision centers. The nonroutine messages typically indicate unanticipated conditions. As we pointed out above, process teams are empowered to deal with such situations, but they can only do so after they have become aware of them.

• Manage decision making. Under the decision-making paradigm, the making of decisions is the central activity of an organization, which cannot be left to chance. What this means is that the processes that define an organization are to be formally defined, that all points at which routine decisions are made are to be supported by appropriate software support systems, and that an organization as a whole can rapidly change into an exceptional mode of operation when truly unanticipated important decisions have to be made. The changeover into exceptional modes must not be permitted to throw everybody into a panic. Just as airline pilots have to go through regular "disaster drills", management should train itself so that it will respond quickly and effectively to unanticipated events. Such training should become a regular business activity in all organizations.

This discussion should have shown that business reengineering is not something that has just been invented. It is a response to fundamental changes in society that have been recognized for quite some time. Only a sense of urgency is new, and book after book is emphasizing the urgency. Some popular books that emphasize different aspects of our move into the postindustrial age are discussed at the start of Appendix B. Together they provide a balanced view of what we face, and how we are to cope with what we face.

3
The Purpose of Reengineering

The way a reengineered organization copes with the complexity and volatility of the postindustrial business world is expressed in the form of seven goals. The goals are discussed in some detail.

We touched on some reasons for reengineering in the preceding chapters. They all have one main cause: the business environment in which organizations operate has become very complex and volatile. The complexity is caused by an interrelation of effects—interest rates in Germany affect the amount that Japanese invest in U.S. Treasury Bonds, which in turn affects the amount a bank will lend a corporation in my home town. The volatility is largely the result of instant communications. Volatility has made business riskier, but instant communications also should raise awareness of new business opportunities. A reengineered organization is to cope with complexity and volatility by following a three-phase pattern.

Phase 1: Intelligence evaluation. An organization should be aware of all of the changes in its environment that either threaten it or provide it with new business opportunities. For example, a drop in the value of the Italian lire is a threat to a company exporting to Italy because its products may become too expensive for Italian customers. On the other hand, a restaurant chain may regard the predicted introduction of battery-powered cars as an opportunity for planning new restaurants that are combined with battery charging facilities—you have a meal while your car gets its batteries charged. These examples show that a business organization responds to changes in its environment in two modes, an *active* pursuit of an opportunity or a *reactive* response to a threat.

Phase 2: Risk analysis. Reckless risks must become calculated risks. The exporters to Italy may respond to the threat to their company by downsizing, reducing waste, searching for new markets, or a combination of all three. All of these alternatives put the profitability of the company at risk, and a careful risk analysis has to be performed. Similarly, the restaurant business must be careful that at any stage of the exploration of the new opportunity it does not move too fast and thus assume too much risk.

Phase 3: Timely action. Once risk analysis has indicated what action the organization is to take, the selected course of action is to be implemented very rapidly. If the exporters decide to look for new markets, the new markets have to be found and opened before the company is smothered by a buildup of excess inventory. Once the battery-powered cars are on the road, the restaurants should be ready to open so that a habit of combining battery recharging with a restaurant visit becomes established from the very start, and so that competition is locked out.

These three phases leave the impression that a business organization merely responds to changes in its environment. However, such a view is incomplete in that it neglects the broader strategy goals that an organization should have set for itself. For example, when the restaurant company considers combining its restaurant business with battery recharging, it is likely to follow some broader goal, such as reaching three billion dollars in yearly sales.

In discussing decisions in Chapter 2 we found that they relate to organization-wide strategy, operational tactics, and the day-to-day operation of a process, and that each type of decision was to be entrusted to a particular level of management. Combining the active and reactive aspects, we have top executives setting organization-wide strategy goals and interpreting data obtained by intelligence gathering. Managers of operations perform risk analysis to evaluate tactical options, which may have been formulated by both levels of management in consultation. When we get to the process level, there is no longer any distinction between being in an active or reactive mode, and management is not a separate activity—a self-managing process team looks after a process in the same way, irrespective of whether the process has resulted from an active-mode or a reactive-mode decision. The two upper levels are not always defined in our terms. For example, as defined at Pepsi-Cola, their purposes are to create and to enable [Bw93b]. However, despite the difference in the words, the intent is the same: reduce the slowdown of processes by reducing management.

This discussion leads us into defining seven goals that reengineering is to reach. Some goals are broad, sweeping away long-maintained business principles, while others are quite specific.

• The management structure of any organization is reduced to three levels: executive level, operational level, and process level. This implies replacement of functional departments by process teams as the basic organizational units.

• The primary purpose of the two upper levels of management is to continue to change the reengineered organization. A secondary purpose of operational management is the determination of priorities for instances of processes, allocation of personnel to process teams in accordance with the priorities, exercising of fiscal controls, and the hiring and compensation of personnel. Note that these activities are themselves processes, and that operational management can be given a process team structure.

• Intelligence gathering is recognized as most important for the effective operation of an organization. Further, an organization keeps extensive records of its day-to-day operations to allow incremental improvements of these operations.

• Training gives way to education. The purpose of training is to develop a specific skill; education enables people to acquire skills on their own. In a reengineered organization, process personnel must acquire a broad range of skills. Traditional training courses are of limited help because they rarely match the exact needs of the personnel and rarely can be set up precisely when needed. For an example we take a software engineering team. Suppose that in three weeks the team will have to switch to programming in the Prolog language, but that only one team member knows Prolog properly. There is no time to bring in an outside instructor, but, if all members of the team have attended courses on logic and on features of programming languages in general, the Prolog expert on the team can guide the other team members through a self-teaching exercise. This does not mean that training is irrelevant. If time would permit, sending our team to a training course on Prolog would be the preferred solution.

• Physical location is determined by convenience rather than hierarchical considerations. For example, if a process requires personal contact with customers, then the process team should be so located that customers have easy access to members of the team. If customers are widely dispersed, the team may have to be geographically split up, which is made possible by the availability of fast means of communication. A team that processes customer orders may be located in the warehouse, and teams that design manufacturing processes in factories. Indeed, a reengineered company has little justification for a large headquarters building. There seems to be even less justification for fixed field offices. A mobile telephone and a portable computer with suitable attachments for fax communication suffice to turn a car or a hotel room into a field office. Perhaps, though, a securely anchored home base is needed for psychological reasons—we just do not know.

• Customer satisfaction is the guiding principle for an organization. One way of obtaining it is to make customer interaction an explicit component of every process in which such interaction is feasible. An organization can make all of its processes more effective by listening to customers. This applies also to companies that do not sell directly to customers, such as advertising agencies—they have to listen to the customers of the companies that hire them to promote their products. However, customer input is not to be the only source of intelligence for the organization—customers are unlikely to ask you for a totally new product, but they may easily desert you when a competitor introduces such a product. In a for-profit organization, customer satisfaction translates into profits, and profitability is a strong driving force in such organizations. In a nonprofit private organization or a government agency, customer satisfaction should become an end in itself. It should be closely monitored, and, in evaluating the effectiveness of an organization of this type, customer satisfaction and cost containment should be the principal measures.

• Each process is a cost center. As many a Chief Executive Officer and many a shareholder has found out, there is often little relation between the predicted performance of a corporation and the actual results. When processes become the dominant structural components of an organization, the cost of the products of a process becomes fairly easy to estimate. Moreover, with indirect costs due to management overhead significantly reduced, there is a much closer relation between the direct cost of a product and the income generated by the product. For example, if the direct cost of a product is $8, and the indirect cost is $7, a decrease in the direct cost of $3 reduces the total cost by 20%. However, if the indirect cost is just $1, the same decrease of $3 reduces total cost by 33%.

Achievement of these seven specific aims of reengineering requires dismantling nearly all of the existing management structure, and making sure that all employees become linked to an organization-wide comprehensive information system. This has led to two mistaken views. First, reengineering is regarded as the automation of middle-management functions. Middle-management functions are not automated; most of them simply disappear in the reengineered organization. The second mistaken view is that reengineering is defined by electronic communication and information systems, and that an organization is reengineered if it generates a lot of traffic on electronic networks. The real purpose of business reengineering is to define a business in terms of processes from which every task that does not add value is removed, and this has nothing to do with technology. In fact, companies could have been reengineered before computers came on the scene, and they probably would have been if there had been enough competitive pressure. Before computers, insurance companies and banks survived quite well with manual information systems, and so did the Library of Congress and the Social Security Administration, and they all were handling huge amounts of data. Technology merely provides a means of dealing rapidly with rapid changes, and the rapidity of change is itself a consequence of new technology. In other words, technology is needed to keep up with the effects of technology. Of course, technology does provide improvements, but the improvements are only marginal unless processes have been made central to everything else. Confucius has said that rotten wood cannot be carved (Analects 5,

9)—for us this means that first we have to put a solid process structure in place; only then can we do the fine tuning.

Which organizations should be reengineered? The answer is simple: *every organization that is not structured according to the seven goals of reengineering discussed above.* This raises a natural follow-up question: But why these seven goals and not some others? The answer is that they capture in succinct form the essence of reengineering as seen by a wide group of business analysts. The goals as stated are not just the result of my own observations. They are distilled from the observations of many advocates of change. Indeed, every serious definition of business reengineering that I have come across is consistent with the seven goals. The next question: How will a profitable company benefit from reengineering? Of course, a corporation that is highly profitable does not feel the need to change as strongly as a corporation that is not. Still, the profitable corporation may have lost its competitive edge, or may never have had to develop it under the protective umbrella of some regulatory agency. Such a corporation is not well positioned when competition arises in the form of a new company that from the very start engineers its business activities according to the goals of reengineering. The established corporation can now very rapidly slip into the red, and then it may be too late to start reengineering. Still, instead of folding up without a fight, an attempt should be made to reengineer.

Finally, will attainment of the seven goals guarantee success? No, because no important business decision is without risk, and this also holds for reengineering. In the first place, note that a change to a process-centered organization, while essential for ultimate survival, is not sufficient. Intelligence gathering has to take place as well. Products can become irrelevant, e.g., telegrams, typewriters, perhaps even mainframe computers. A healthy reengineered company can thus suddenly find its products without a market. Appropriate intelligence gathering would have predicted this turn of events, and made the corporation diversify while there was time to do so. Further, the inertia of managers and other personnel may be so strong that no real change takes place. The enterprise goes through the motions of reengineering, but internal resistance makes the effort futile. Every organization needs to progress if it is to survive, from the corner newsstand to a nation state. Peyrefitte, in discussing Chinese society in the eighteenth century [Pe92a], uses an escalator metaphor that can be applied to any organization. An organization is like a child trying to move up a down escalator. The movement of the escalator represents all the adverse effects to which an organization is exposed. Standing still can end in catastrophe. Matching the speed of the escalator never gets one ahead. Only by moving faster than the escalator can the top be reached.

4
Steps in the Reengineering Effort

The reengineering of an organization is defined as a 16-step process. Some of the steps are the selection of executive and operational managers of reengineering, setting up educational services, specification of processes, a cost-benefit study of implementation plans, and automation of processes.

Business reengineering is reviving the spirit that operations research had in its beginning. One of its early successes was in improving the performance of British artillery during World War II. One member of each gun crew appeared to have nothing to do, and in fact had nothing to do—at Waterloo he would have held the officer's horse. It should be emphasized that to recognize this required no deep mathematics. However, later on more attention came to be given to developing algorithms for doing a task than to the question of whether the task needed to be done at all. This should be a warning for us today—business analysis is not to become preoccupied with deriving marginal improvements from technology, but should search out horse holders in high places.

The reengineering initiative typically originates at the very highest levels of management. This has several reasons. First, a reorganization that is to replace existing departments with a new structure has to be initiated at a level above these departments. Second, reengineering cannot succeed without a clear indication that top management is seriously committed to it. Third, reengineering is initially a major drain on the budget. Fourth, a plea for reengineering that originates at operational levels is unlikely to find supporters on existing chains of command—after all, reengineering is a threat to the existence of most links of these chains. After the initial decision has been made, the reengineering process should be composed of the following steps:

- Commitment by top management (1)
- Selection of the executive and operational managers of reengineering (2)
- Selection of reengineering teams (3)
- Initial education phase (4)

- Identification of the processes of the organization (5)
- Specification of each process (6)
- Development of alternative implementation plans for each process (7)
- Cost-benefit study for each plan and selection of an appropriate plan (8)
- Infrastructure definition based on the selected plans (9)
- Setting of priorities for the implementation of processes and infrastructure (10)
- Second education phase (11)
- Pilot implementation of one or two processes (12)
- Reexamination of the reengineering effort (13)
- Implementation of the remaining processes (14)
- Continuing automation of the processes (15)
- Automatic linkages to the environment (16)

Let us now examine each of these 16 steps in detail. With regard to the application of software methods in business reengineering, step 6 is the most important in the sequence, and this book is primarily concerned with the implementation of step 6, but we must place this step in its proper context.

1. *Management commitment.* The support of top management is essential for reengineering. Indeed, the level of support the CEO gives to this effort determines its success or failure. It may also be appropriate to appraise the board of directors. Top management must be kept fully informed of the progress of the reengineering effort. Reengineering of an enterprise is likely to fail if change is regarded with suspicion. If such is the case, the institutional culture has to modify itself first.

2. *Manager selection.* The executive and operational managers of reengineering must, of course, be enthusiastic supporters of the concept of reengineering, but they have two essentially different purposes, and this must be reflected in their selection. The executive manager serves as liaison between company executives and the rest of personnel. Primary duties: reporting to the CEO on the progress of the reengineering effort, the removal of obstacles to the effort, and instilling enthusiasm about reengineering at all levels of an organization. In other words, the executive manager represents the reengineering teams to the outside. This need not be a full-time position. Selection is to be based primarily on enthusiasm, but the executive manager must have enough authority to remove obstacles when needed, and these obstacles may reside way up on an organizational chart. The operational manager is in charge of the technical side of reengineering. My view is that the best place to look for a suitable candidate is in the information systems (IS) department. The position would best be filled by the Chief Information Officer (CIO), but the CIO must understand business in general, and must have a strong

second in command to oversee the reengineering of ISD itself. Operational management relates both to the reorganization of existing departments into process groups and to the setting up of information systems to support the reengineered organization. The one department that may survive as a provider of services to the rest of the organization is ISD, but, as the organization as a whole undergoes reengineering, so must ISD. To be really effective in supporting the reengineering effort, the ISD must have reached at least Level 2 in terms of the software process maturity model developed by the Software Engineering Institute (see Chapter 11). Since reaching this level presupposes that the ISD has been measuring its software process performance over an extended period of time, an ISD that has not given thought to software process measurements requires at least 3 or 4 years to gather the required data. Reengineering may still succeed without this degree of preparation, but it is then a very risky undertaking. If it does succeed, the level of improvement, which is determined by the degree of technological preparedness, will not be as marked as it would be otherwise.

3. *Reengineering teams.* In the Preface we suggested that the ISD is a suitable source for members of the teams because ISD personnel are outside the more traditional departments, they know the entire organization, they are used to defining processes, and they are aware of the enabling information technology. Although we stress throughout this book that process definition is best done with no regard for the ultimate role assignments to people, software, and hardware, knowledge of what software and hardware can and cannot do will have some effect on the process definition. Moreover, if a workshop format is used to define processes, as is discussed in the next chapter, then a prototype software process system may be the most effective process definition, and software development skills are needed to build the prototype. In addition, ISD personnel are likely to have had some experience with working in teams. Members from traditional departments also need to participate in the teams as specialist interpreters of current business activities. A typical reengineering team has around five members, and often several teams are in existence at the same time. To begin with, there is just one team, to deal with step 5. We shall call it the *superteam*, and it is the operational manager's staff. Since the team is unlikely to have reengineering experience, just reading literature may not prepare the team sufficiently well. Augmenting the team with outside consultants is a solution. After the individual processes are identified, a separate team is assigned to each process. The superteam sees to the creation of these teams, assists them when needed, and monitors their progress. Since this may not be enough to keep the superteam fully occupied, it may retain "ownership" of one of the processes to be reengineered.

4. *Initial education.* The executive manager should appoint an education officer whose initial task is to design the first phase of an educational

plan. The purpose of this first phase is to acquaint everybody in the organization with reengineering in general. Outside consultants may have to be brought in to develop and present the material.

5. *Process identification*. The number of processes with which a company is concerned typically varies between 10 and 20. Under the workflow paradigm there is some understanding of processes, but a process is seen as the movement of a piece of work from site to site, where the sites are under the control of different departments. Not only is a process defined in terms of a number of sites, but a site may serve more than one process, e.g., a site that checks the credit rating of a customer normally would be used both by order processing and by credit issuance. Therefore, the actual identification of processes can be more difficult than it appears. A process that is essential for the effectiveness of the reengineered organization is intelligence gathering and evaluation. It is unlikely that this process even exists in the old organization.

6. *Process specification*. In this step a process is separated into component tasks, each task is examined to determine whether it is actually needed, unnecessary tasks are eliminated, and the remaining tasks are restructured. In the restructured process specification there has to be a clear indication of the order in which the component tasks are to be performed, and which tasks can be performed in parallel. We recommend the use of a formal specification language for this. The formal specification is to be supplemented with diagrams to help achieve intuitive understanding of the process. We elaborate on this step in much detail in Part IV. Here we will just add the remark that the specification of a process should be sufficiently general to allow a fair degree of implementation freedom.

7. *Implementation alternatives*. Bridge designers have the standard practice of presenting a client with several preliminary designs, and the designer and client decide which design to carry forward [Sp86]. The same approach can be used with a business process, but in this step alternative designs are merely listed, with no decision as to which design is to be adopted.

8. *Cost-benefit analysis*. The costs for each of the alternatives of step 7 are established. This is relatively easy, but it is not easy to determine corresponding benefits because of the difficulty of assigning a definite cash value to an intangible benefit such as customer good will. When an order is filled within 7 hours rather than 7 days, we can measure the reduction in inventory-carrying charges, and the effect of receiving payment 6 or 7 days earlier, but we cannot predict whether this has tied a customer more closely to our corporation, and, if it has, how to express this benefit quantitatively. If one of the alternatives is an improvement over another in every aspect, then we know which to choose; but, more commonly, we have to balance both higher cost and higher intangible benefits of one alternative against both lower cost and lower benefits of

another alternative. The decision then is little more than inspired guess-work, but fuzzy decision theory can reduce uncertainty to some extent.

9. *Infrastructure definition*. The infrastructure consists of a communication system and an information system. A local area network (LAN) costs less to install and maintain than a wide area network (WAN). Also, a distributed system presents more problems than a centralized system. In this step the infrastructure costs are determined for the total set of processes under the implementation alternative selected for each process in step 8. The processes, which we have been considering in isolation, now become integrated. It is possible that a different alternative will now be chosen for some of the processes in order to reduce infrastructure costs.

10. *Setting of priorities*. In deciding the order in which the redesigned processes will be implemented, we have to consider several factors. First, a process for which reengineering brings about a large improvement in the cost-benefit ratio is a good candidate for early implementation. Second, a process that does not interact with other processes is a good candidate. Third, if two processes interact strongly with each other or share a task, such as the credit check of the example discussed in step 5, then the two processes should be implemented at the same time. Fourth, implementation of reengineered processes brings about a change from departmental structure. Disruptions due to this structural change are to be kept low, and this will have a major effect on the ordering of processes in the implementation plan. Fifth, priorities of implementation depend on the effect they have on the infrastructure. Reengineering typically requires that several independent data bases be combined into a composite information system. This integration process has to be synchronized with the implementation of the reengineered processes. Similarly, a process that depends on a WAN cannot be implemented before the WAN is in place.

11. *Second education phase*. The educational effort introduced in this phase relates to the actual operation of the reengineered company. After a process is handed over by a reengineering team to a process team, the process team must be able to look after the process. Not only must the team perform operations that previously were performed in several different departments under close management supervision, but each member of the team is expected to be able to perform every task of the process, and this in a self-managing mode. Self-management also implies that responsibility for improving a reengineered process rests with the process team.

12. *Pilot implementation*. Pilot implementation can be done in two ways. One is to select a process and to run it both in the old and the reengineered modes. Suppose that the process relates to the handling of purchase orders, where in the old mode an order was moved between three departments and in the new mode it is to be handled by a single

member of the order-processing team, and that the company has 5000 customers. Let us split the customers into two groups of sizes 1000 and 4000, respectively, and let orders from the larger group be processed in the old way. The new way is tried on the smaller group. If it results in failure, the effect of the failure is reasonably well contained. This reassures top management, which may still have some doubts regarding reengineering. Note here that there should be no failure—if failure arises, it is due to a misunderstanding of the reengineering process or an obstruction of the process. Another advantage of the split mode of operation is that it allows the process team to become used to dealing with a process before it is exposed to the full customer load. The disadvantage is that for a while two sets of personnel are being maintained. The other way is to switch a process totally from the old to the new mode of personnel organization, but to let the process team adapt gradually to the new process structure. Under this approach, team members brought in from the three old departments continue to perform the same tasks they had before, with a gradual switch to the new mode of operation, under which a single person deals with all tasks relating to a purchase order.

13. *Reengineering reexamined.* Pilot implementations serve two purposes. One is to reassure top management (and possibly also the board of directors) that reengineering is more than just promises. But it may be bad policy to select for pilot implementation the process for which the most spectacular improvement is expected. Everything after this will seem like a letdown. The second purpose is to gain experience in the reengineering process itself, and to use the experience to improve this process. The one or two processes selected for pilot implementation should be moderately difficult. An easy process will not show up problems; a difficult process may discourage the reengineering team—the team is still gaining experience.

14. *Completion of implementation.* The reengineering team that carried out the pilot implementation should be split up, and its members assigned to teams that are getting ready to implement the remaining processes. Each reengineering team then has some experienced members. As these teams carry out the implementation of all processes to completion, care should be taken that this effort is synchronized with the development of the infrastructure. Ultimately, reengineering teams have to be disbanded, with some members returning to the ISD and others assigned to process teams.

15. *Continuing automation.* In Chapter 2 we introduced the decision-making paradigm. In organizations that embody this paradigm, the tasks that define a process should be regarded as decision-making centers. We distinguish between a decision support system (DSS) and an expert system (ES). A DSS assists a person in the making of a decision, an ES makes decisions on its own. The purpose of this step is to introduce DSSs and ESs where appropriate. The utility and cost-effectiveness of DSSs and

ESs are still being questioned, and not all expert systems measure up to human decision-making standards. My own view is that they have proven themselves, but, as with any fairly new development, differences of opinion are to be expected.

16. *Automatic linkages*. Some manufacturing companies have already established electronic linkages between their information systems and those of their major suppliers and major customers. Retailers have such links to suppliers. This allows the participation of suppliers and customers in the development of new processes, speeds up the delivery of goods by suppliers, and simplifies the filling of customers' orders. Such linkages become particularly effective when the decision-making functions that link up processes of the cooperating companies have been taken over by ESs.

We believe that most of the 16 steps are essential. They represent another way of looking at reengineering to that expressed in the seven goals of Chapter 3, and, as was the case with the seven goals, they express a composite view held by most business analysts with an interest in reengineering. However, the order in which we discussed the 16 steps does not always have to be followed. For example, initiation of the two education phases can occur earlier (but not later). Also, work on process automation and automatic linkages to cooperating organizations can begin before implementation of all processes has been completed. More importantly, some steps can be combined. In the next chapter we discuss how group workshops with user participation can be used to define the processes of a reengineered enterprise. At such a workshop, steps 5 (process identification), 6 (process specification), 7 (implementation alternatives), 8 (cost-benefit analysis), and 10 (setting of priorities) could well be considered in combination. A workshop may in fact produce a process specification in the form of a prototype software system. If that is the case, then the process implementation (steps 12 and 14) is to a large extent completed as part of the earlier steps, and all that remains is the conversion of the prototype into a robust operational system, and role allocation to process personnel. As can be seen, the 16 steps should be regarded merely as a checklist of what needs to be considered during business reengineering. The main principle to keep in mind is that reengineering is the specification and implementation of processes as value-adding activities, and that these value-adding processes define the essential purpose of an organization.

A process-structured intelligence-gathering organization produced by reengineering is necessary for survival in a postindustrial world, but process structure and intelligence evaluation are not enough. We also need to consider service to customers. Ideal process teams should provide service with TEETH, which means that service should be

Trustworthy—promises to customers are kept
Efficient—customers are served quickly and nondisruptively
Effective—the process team gets everything right the first time
Timely—customers receive service when they need it
Happy—customers are made to feel well

5
Making the Most
of Human Resources

The wise use of human resources, particularly of the intellectual capital they represent, is an important aspect of business reengineering. Also, a reengineering effort should be adapted to the culture of an organization. This is related to teamwork, and two formats for group workshops are contrasted.

Every year I spend some time in Sweden. It was there that I first became interested in reengineering quite a few years ago—a Swedish company that repaired circuit boards transferred many of the front office functions to the workshop by letting workshop personnel receive repair orders and do customer invoicing themselves. I forget now the exact number of days by which this reduced the time the customers had to wait, but it was enough to make the change a reengineering success. I like much of what I see in Sweden. Swedes enjoy universal health coverage, six weeks of vacations, and liberal *paid* parental leave. With all this, their per capita GNP of $26,800 is 15.8% higher than the $23,150 for the United States, under nearly equal rates of economic participation in both countries (1992 data from [Eb94]).

At first I found it strange that my Swedish colleagues rarely took work home for the weekend, but later on this caused a fundamental shift in my views on productivity. For some 10 years now I have set aside one day a week on which I do not touch professional work—I will not even jot down an idea. The result has been increased productivity, fewer mistakes, and less stress. The Swedish experience has convinced me that there is a limit beyond which stress makes work counterproductive. We have to be careful that reengineering does not create unacceptable stress levels. It is also important that in the reengineering of an organization effective use is made of the intellectual capital of the organization. Insufficient attention to human resources, particularly its intellectual capital, is a health risk for a company at any time. This was first recognized by the Swedish insurance company Skandia AFS—in 1991 it became the first company in the world to appoint a director of intellectual capital [Fo94d]. We shall find that Scandinavian attitudes to human resources have much relevance to reengineering.

The wise use of human resources is important at all times, but it becomes most important during business reengineering. Reengineering is to be initiated, kept on track, and the reengineered enterprise is to be moved ahead. In all this intellect is the most important resource, and it is very dangerous to assume that most of the intellectual capital of an organization is located in its management levels. The reengineering effort should seek itself a broad support base, everybody affected by a reengineered process should be consulted during the specification of the process, and serious thought should be given to the capabilities of the personnel who will take charge of the process. We are just starting to understand how important its intellectual resources are to a company, and our understanding of how best to evaluate and make use of these resources is very limited. Therefore, it should be kept in mind that the suggestions that follow are not a fully tried recipe for success, and that the success of any innovation depends largely on the culture of the organization in which it is tried.

Let us consider first the initial selling of the idea of reengineering. The success or failure of any endeavor in which people have to be convinced depends on how well the suggested change matches the cultural values of those who are to be convinced. Reengineering has quite a few different aspects, such as improvement of product quality, improved intelligence gathering and exploitation, cost reduction, improvement in employee job satisfaction, emphasis on customer service, rapid introduction of new products, ease of customization of products, and simplification of management structures. The relative importance assigned to these aspects will be determined by organizational culture; and in any prospectus outlining the potential benefits of business reengineering to an organization, emphasis should be on those aspects that are considered most important in this organization.

Cultural differences can be very marked between countries. In a comparison of the significance that Canadian and Danish software designers assigned to different values [Ku90], Canadians were found to give greatest importance to the following (at a 1% significance level):

- Participation of managers of users in design decisions
- Clear statement of user responsibilities
- Planning and control of the project by the developers
- Maintainability of the system
- Development within budget

The Danes, on the other hand, put greatest importance (also at a 1% level) on:

- Participation of actual users in design decisions
- Users' autonomy in the use of the system
- Analysts' autonomy in the development of the system
- Job-induced stress on users

- Variety of user responsibilities
- Job security for users
- Interpersonal contacts among users
- Security of access to information

This clearly shows that users are much more important to Danes than to Canadians. The extent of the importance goes beyond the interaction of a user with the system—it includes a broad range of social effects of the system on its users.

Although the comparison of values relates to software projects, the same differences are likely to arise in the consideration of a business process as such. We want to emphasize that these days nearly all business processes do have some form of software support, and also that this is exactly what it is—*support* of a business activity that is also supported by people and hardware. It seems that in the early phases of process definition the allocation of process tasks to people, software, and hardware should not be fixed. But this is so only in principle. In real life, the most economical way of designing a process that fully satisfies the user community is to produce a prototype of the software system, and let the users interact with it. We shall discuss workshops that accomplish this further down. Prototype-based process definition has further implications. Because the process support software interacts with hardware, it is a de facto definition of the hardware requirements as well, although the selection of the exact hardware configuration can be postponed. Moreover, one purpose of the software system is to issue reminders to process personnel, telling them what to do next. This defines the duties of personnel, although the assignment of specific roles to individuals has no urgency. Indeed, it is better to postpone such assignments so that the basic structure of a process can be defined without intrusion of role assignments, which are irrelevant to this structure. What matters is this: the need to validate user requirements implies that early attention be given to the specification of process support software, and this specification is very close to a specification of the process itself.

I have not seen any experimental data that relate job satisfaction, productivity, and product quality of developers of software systems in Scandinavia and North America, but my own nonscientific observations put Scandinavians ahead on all three counts. This does not mean, though, that North American organizations should now import Scandinavian attitudes and methodologies in a big way. A transfer can only succeed where there is reasonable agreement on most social issues between donor and recipient. The use of the terms of transplant surgery is deliberate— just as an organism rejects an implant that does not properly fit in, so an organization rejects an attitude or methodology that is inconsistent with the fundamental attitudes of this organization. Still, reengineering personnel should be aware of how business changes are effected in other countries, and be ready to adapt the changes and the methods of introduction of these changes to their own conditions.

In any case, the cultures of Scandinavia and North America are not too far apart. In both regions users are being involved more fully in the development of prototype software systems—in Scandinavia the method of involvement is participatory design (PD) and in North America it is joint application development (JAD). The two approaches have different motivations and different formats, but their similarities are greater than their differences. The old approach to obtaining information has been to ask users, or, what is more often the case, their managers, in one-to-one interviews, and not to go beyond this. The dependence on what managers tell is risky because managers rarely have direct experience on which to base the information they supply. The reliability of the information that managers supply is therefore suspect. Interviews are still an important source of *initial* information (see Chapter 14), but there is an increasing dependence on group workshops, and both PD and JAD have a group orientation. There is now ample evidence that user participation in group workshops leads to better software systems.

The primary motivation of PD is grass-roots democracy in the workplace, and this is to lead to a more pleasant workplace, for both the introducers of a process and the process participants. The effect of the process on the quality of life of people outside the organization is also to be considered. In Scandinavia, trade unions participate extensively in the operation of business enterprises, and the PD movement was initiated by trade unions. The motivation for JAD is cost reduction by getting a product right the first time. Of course, the participation fostered by JAD should also lead to a better workplace, and the better workplace aimed at by PD contributes to the development of a better product.

Typically, the basic structure of the application that JAD is to develop is fixed at the time the JAD workshop convenes. The workshop participants are merely to determine what needs to be done to achieve the goals defined for the application. Under PD, the goals themselves may be questioned. The objective is to reach consensus on the goals, and then to reach consensus on how best to achieve these goals. The different objectives of JAD and PD have a strong influence on the form of their respective workshops—JAD workshops tend to be more formal, with a fixed agenda and extensive use of preprinted forms, at least at IBM [Au91]; PD workshops are more relaxed, and the agenda can be modified by workshop participants.

It seems that for business reengineering the PD format is more suitable. With a fixed agenda the "re" part in "reengineering" does not get proper recognition: JAD is fine for engineering a well-understood process, but not for defining a process. To put it another way, when the pieces are known, JAD is good at giving the right shape to the pieces, but PD is good at finding out what pieces are needed, and this is exactly what reengineering tries to establish. On the other hand, PD can consume a lot of time and energy in reaching a consensus. It could therefore benefit from the emphasis on workshop structure that characterizes JAD. If there were such a thing as "pure PD" and "pure JAD", the greatest benefits should come from an approach that takes the best from both. Where exactly on the line between the two "pure" extremes an organization would put itself would be determined by the organizational culture. In the North American context, JAD has already proven itself in industry, while PD is still largely a subject of discussion by academics. A North American organization would therefore put itself closer to the "pure JAD" end, but with an understanding that reengineering requires departure from existing structures and methods. We shall return to JAD in Chapter 15.

User-oriented workshops are to define the processes of a reengineered organization and the software support systems for these processes. After this, the processes have to be implemented and handed over to the personnel who will be operating the processes. The participants of a JAD-style workshop consist of a sample of users and of system developers, and the developers are required to produce a system definition that meets the expectations of the users. Here, "users" are the people who will take charge of the system or be affected by the system, and "system definition" can range from a set of annotated diagrams to a formal specification, or even a working prototype. In some versions of JAD there is no developer participation—when JAD takes this somewhat outdated format, the system definition is usually just a set of statements in a natural language.

The developers participating in a JAD workshop come from the information systems department, and they should possess expertise in process definition techniques, representations for process definition, and tools to support the process definition. Having developed information systems within the enterprise in the past, they can be expected to have a fair general understanding of the business, but not necessarily of the detailed business activities that are to be structured into a reengineered business process. The detailed business knowledge is to be supplied by the user participants in the workshop. The process definition is the base on which a process reengineering team can now construct a process implementation. As we noted above, in a modern enterprise a major component of a process is its software support system, which effectively defines the process, i.e., a process definition is the specification of its software support system. If the specification is of high quality, then the implementation will present few problems.

It is natural for the developers who take part in a JAD workshop to become a well-integrated team. At least one member of this team should become a member of the implementation team, thus ensuring continuity between specification and implementation. The personnel who will take charge of the process after its implementation will also be a team. We should therefore look in some detail at what teams are needed, and how the teams should operate for common benefit. First there is the superteam, which we introduced in Chapter 4 as the staff of the operational manager of business reengineering. Next, if the reengineering effort is based on a JAD-style workshop format, there are the teams of developers at the workshops. Let us call them specification teams. After a workshop, an implementation team takes over. An implementation team should maintain links with business experts who are to make sure that the implementation team correctly interprets the specification produced at the workshop. The superteam assigns personnel to specification teams and implementation teams, and provides guidance for these teams.

Despite strong evidence that a workshop is an economical way for arriving at a process specification, management is still reluctant to adopt the workshop methodology. This is due partly to inertia, partly to not knowing of the existence of the methodology, partly to not having the right facilities for a JAD-style workshop, and partly to not having the right people to form a specification team that will perform well under considerable stress. Still, even when a workshop is not used, teams are important.

How does teamwork differ from collective individual efforts? Over a period of 6 years I have observed a total of 320 software engineering students do project work in randomly selected groups of four, with the teams free to choose their own internal management structure. Over the years the results have been roughly the same: about 10% of the students do not fit into teams; the other 90% are much more productive than when working on their own; the work products keep surprising me with their thoroughness and quality of presentation; the weaker students learn much, and have their self-confidence greatly improved. Evaluation has also worked out well. Students are evaluated in two steps: first the work product is evaluated and the team as a whole receives a score; then the score of some individuals may be adjusted up or down, but so that the total team score remains unchanged. The individual adjustments are based on confidential evaluations each member of a team makes of the other members. The evaluation scheme has not raised any complaints. With regard to the 10% of misfits, in nearly every instance the cause was plain laziness—there have been only three cases in which personality clashes caused disruptions that went beyond the trivial, but they still were not significant enough to affect the product in a serious way.

Of course, these findings will not translate to a business enterprise as they stand. Our students were not yet set in their ways, and working in teams was for them a welcome novelty. I do not know what would have happened once the novelty wore off, but there is some evidence that the length of time for which a team has to work together is an important factor [Ha90a]. Also, the teams did not have to interact with other teams. Development work often requires the cooperative effort of numerous teams, and communication breakdown can then become a serious problem.

However, when personnel are organized into sections, and section managers communicate, there is the same danger of communication breakdown [Cu88].

Communication breakdown between teams has two causes—the spokespersons from different teams misunderstand each other, or a spokesperson is unable to communicate effectively with the rest of the team. This can be fixed by electronic conferencing. Although the exchange of information between teams is still primarily the responsibility of the spokespersons of the teams, pertinent information is entered into a computer file, and this file can be accessed by and commented on by all members of the teams. In particular, anybody can ask for clarification.

The entire business reengineering literature supports the concept of self-managing process teams. Still, a team does require one of its members to act as its spokesperson in the interactions of the team with the outside world. There also has to be some internal monitoring that the team is on schedule and within cost estimates. Further, in the interests of efficiency, it helps to set up an agenda for meetings of the team, and to see that a meeting follows its agenda. There are thus three essential roles to fill: spokesperson, auditor, and convener. In many teams, a single leader assumes all three roles for a fixed period of time, and leadership rotates, but the three roles could be identified with three different team members, with or without rotation.

Self-management is one facet of team empowerment, and it is the most important. Other aspects of empowerment relate to authority in customer relations, in purchasing, and in personnel matters. Customer relations are particularly important for teams that actually face customers, and in this setting a team can be exposed to difficult decisions—to what extent is a customer to be kept happy when this imposes much additional work on the team or on other parts of the organization, i.e., such teams must be educated to think in terms of costs and benefits. Purchasing causes frustrations in many organizations: it is quite a common requirement that all purchases be made through a central purchasing department, and that each purchase be authorized by a chain of managers. This can mean that, for the sake of a few discount dollars saved, a team is made to sit idle for days. It makes good sense to establish a purchasing budget for the team and allow the team itself to make purchases within the limits of the budget. Finally, for a team to function well, it should participate in the selection of replacement members.

The self-managed team concept has been successfully tried in numerous organizations. But it is unlikely to succeed where a many-layered hierarchical management structure persists. Management then has to find something to manage, and teams are unlikely to achieve true autonomy in such a setting. Other danger signals to watch: teams that do not want to assume responsibility; teams that spend more time talking than doing; and teams that are uncertain about their exact responsibilities.

6
The Nature of a Process

A business process is defined as an ordered collection of business tasks that is to achieve a specific goal. A distinction is made between business activities that fit this definition and those that do not.

We have been discussing processes without a clear understanding of what a process is. A fairly extensive search through software engineering textbooks revealed that most of the books did not have *process* in the index. When they did, the interpretations fell into three categories: something that converts an input into an output; a bubble in a data flow diagram; or something that results in a software system. Not one of these definitions is particularly informative. Rather unexpectedly, my *Webster's Third New International Dictionary* of 1971 is more to the point: the action of passing through continuing development from a beginning to a contemplated end. This definition tells us that a process has a beginning and an end, that the end is "contemplated", which we take to mean that there is a specific goal that the process is to achieve, and that there is a purposeful progression toward the goal. The dictionary definition is the basis for our definition of a business process: an ordered collection of tasks that is to achieve a value-adding objective within a finite time interval.

Let us use Figure 6.1 to expand on this definition. In the figure, the tasks are represented by arrows, and the circles establish an ordering of the tasks. We have a convention that no task that originates at a circle can start before the tasks that end at this circle have been completed. Thus, denoting a task that starts at circle x and ends at circle y by $<x, y>$, task $<5, 8>$ cannot start before tasks $<2, 5>$ and $<3, 5>$ have been completed. The process starts at circle 1 and ends at circle 8. Now, if we knew how long each of the tasks in Figure 6.1 would take, then, if no tasks were ever performed in parallel, the time for the process would be the sum of the individual task times. But Figure 6.1 allows parallelism—thus tasks $<5, 8>$, $<6, 8>$, and $<7, 8>$ can be performed in parallel. Critical path analysis can then determine the least time in which the entire process could be completed under conditions of greatest possible

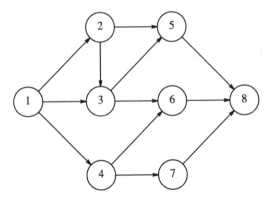

FIGURE 6.1. The structure of a process.

parallelism. The time estimate can next be used to arrive at an estimate of the value the process adds.

However, processes do not always follow the simple structure of Figure 6.1. There we are assuming that all of the tasks have to be performed. But what if only one of <3, 6> or <4, 6> needed to be performed? What if task <2, 5> were replaced by task <5, 2>, and we had to go through the sequence (2–3–5–2) many times, but we could start on task <3, 6> after having passed through circle 3 only a few times? In Chapters 18 and 19 we look at more powerful notations for the representation of processes.

It is not just a matter of notation. Some business activities fit our definition better than others. Some that fit well are product development, product manufacture, product maintenance, order fulfillment, and supplier relations. Some that do not are legal services, information systems, and financial management. The reason for substituting a process structure for a departmental structure is that everything is to be eliminated that does not add value. Under a hierarchical static departmental structure it is very difficult to tell what does and what does not add value, and what the cost-effectiveness of a particular change amounts to. Under a process structure, the cost of each task can be determined rapidly, the cost reduction effected by a change to a task estimated, and the estimate compared to the actual cost after the implementation of the change. The comparisons of estimated to actual costs should in time lead to highly reliable estimation techniques. Now, for our first set of activities it is easy to establish how much value they add. This is not so easy for the second set. Therefore, in a business reengineering initiative, emphasis should be on defining the first set of activities as processes, on eliminating from these processes all tasks that do not add value, and on improving the value-to-cost ratio for those tasks that remain.

Self-management does not mean that processes become totally detached organizational units that float around oblivious of any external managerial constraints. Structure is needed, and some of it is provided by communication links between teams; but this is not enough to allow the teams to pursue coordinated action to advance corporate goals. Actually, the teams will not even know what the corporate goals are unless they are told. A mechanism is therefore needed for letting process teams know what the goals are and what is to be done to achieve them. Such a mechanism is *process ownership*. We noted earlier that two levels of management above the process teams are necessary—the top level establishes strategy, and, in a second level, managers of operations see to the implementation of the strategy. The second-level managers as a group own all of the processes. This group determines what new processes are needed, which existing processes have outlived their usefulness, and which sets of existing processes should be reorganized into new process structures. This has to be a collective activity. There also has to be an individual owner for each process. The owner facilitates intergroup collaboration, checks the accuracy of the team's internal audits with regard to cost and schedule, establishes a purchasing budget for the process team, and represents the interests of the team in general.

Hammer and Chompy [Ha93] give a different interpretation to process ownership. They are more interested in reengineering itself than in the processes that reengineering is to define and implement. In their view, the staff of the reengineering effort should consist of a leader of the entire effort, process owners, reengineering teams, a steering committee consisting of high-level managers, and a reengineering czar. In our terminology, the leader is called the executive manager, the czar is our operational manager, and reengineering teams remain reengineering teams. We have replaced the steering committee with the superteam of step 3 of Chapter 4, but the superteam should be in close consultation with top management. Our reason for this is that IS personnel are accustomed to think in terms of processes, which is not the case with most managers. In [Or94], the set of assumptions, expectations, and knowledge about information technology is called a *technological frame*, and it is shown that conflicts can arise when different groups in an organization have significantly different technological frames. Generalizing the frame concept to that of the entire organizational culture, we can see that most managers will not have as strong a commitment to a process-based organization as IS personnel. The superteam then has the double task of identifying processes and of convincing management of the benefits of a process orientation. The success of this depends on the acceptance of a process view by management at the very top.

We do not see a need for a process to have an individual owner before it has been implemented. It suffices that the superteam "owns" the entire reengineering effort. This is more or less essential if reengineering is to follow the workshop format discussed in Chapter 5, which allows a single workshop to specify several processes, with their precise boundaries unknown before the boundaries are drawn by the workshop participants.

Let us now consider what kinds of processes an organization requires. To begin with, there are two major process groups—one group of processes deals with the creation of a product, the other with the dissemination of the product. Activities that relate to creation are intelligence gathering and use, research and development, product design, inventory management, and manufacturing. Under dissemination we have to consider warehousing and transportation, product marketing, sales, order fulfillment, and customer service. Most of these activities are easily identifiable as processes, or as sets of processes. An exception is intelligence gathering and use, and, to a lesser extent, research and development. By its very nature, intelligence gathering and use does not fit the process model—the information on which strategic decisions are based may be hard data from internal reports, but it may also be rumor heard at informal lunches or on the golf course. A decision, when it is made, takes all this into consideration, but the CEO will not be able to explain how exactly the decision was arrived at. Some of the intelligence gathering can become a process—let us call it "management of the strategic information repository", but much of the gathering, and all of the utilization of the information in strategic decision making does not fit the process pattern. Research and development is in many ways similar to intelligence gathering: months may pass without that "spark" that is to solve a knotty problem, and then suddenly the solution is just there.

When a process is being specified, we should be aware that the process is being specified for the conditions of today, and may be out of date tomorrow. For example, inventory management based on the just-in-time principle achieves low inventory carrying costs, which is important when the cost of capital is high, but just-in-time cannot be recommended when interest rates are low and there are frequent labor disputes at supplier companies. This means that a specification of the inventory management process should be designed for easy modification, and that, as a general reengineering principle, all process definitions should be easy to modify.

In addition to the creation and dissemination processes, we have to consider support services such as legal services, information systems, and resource management. It is very difficult to set a valuation on services. Take information systems—on the one hand we hear that information technology has not improved productivity; on the other, we see all around us that it has kept costs to customers down and improved customer service. Could the current volume and cost of air travel, long-distance telephone calls, and banking services be maintained without information technology? On-line approval of credit card charges now enables supermarkets and drugstores to accept payment by credit card. Electronic mail messages are replacing hard-copy letters that either would not be written at all, or would cost much more—a letter drafted by a manager, typed by a secretary, proofread by the manager, retyped, proofread for a second time, and passed through two mailrooms does cost a lot. We could make a cost reduction estimate here, but how do we value a law library? It seems that the elimination of departmental structure for support services will not lessen the difficulty of determining quantitatively what value these support services provide.

The retention of a departmental structure for the support services does not mean that some of their activities cannot be defined as processes. Software development has been given a process orientation for many years. Lately, much emphasis has been put on the software development process, and we are beginning to understand how to improve the process. Unfortunately, misguided efforts to "make information technology pay" sometimes force software developers to accept unrealistic schedules. In an attempt to meet a schedule, proper software development principles are disregarded. The result is an incomplete and faulty system. Great care should be taken that reengineering schedules are realistic and that process specifications are well thought out. Otherwise, the reputation of business reengineering will suffer.

II
What is Software Engineering

7
Engineering Principles
in Software Development

The next six chapters are primarily addressed to managers to give them an appreciation of the nature of software engineering, but software developers will also benefit from this statement of goals. The aim of engineering is to utilize economically the materials and forces of nature. Software engineers do not deal with natural phenomena, but they still follow the same activities as conventional engineers. Many of these activities are relevant to business reengineering.

If no name had yet been given to the radical reorganization of enterprises in which processes become the central concern, our choice would still be *business reengineering*. This term implies that the reorganization of an enterprise is to be based on engineering principles. Engineers are accustomed to thinking in terms of processes, so they have the right reengineering attitude. However, the processes of a reengineered enterprise will be implemented as software systems, or at least will be supported by such systems. This, and the familiarity of the ISD (Information Systems Department) personnel of an organization with the entire organization, led us to recommend that ISD personnel provide the main technical support for reengineering. Experienced ISD personnel are increasingly being called software engineers, but there is still some doubt as to whether software engineering is a legitimate branch of engineering.

Since the earliest days of computing, software development has been seen to be in a crisis, brought about by high costs, unkept schedules, and unreliable products. This is not a characteristic of traditional engineering, but cost, schedule, and reliability become problems in an established branch of engineering as well whenever a totally unfamiliar project needs to be tackled. The "software crisis" then does not have to do so much with the nature of software engineering, but with the nature of the problems it has to face, and with the reluctance of software developers to take an engineering attitude toward their work.

In his famous "Silver Bullet" paper, Frederick Brooks [Br86] suggested three fruitful approaches to dealing with the essential difficulties of software development. First, spread costs by developing an easily adaptable product, or a product that will lead customers to adapt their practices to the product characteristics. Second, let a software system evolve from a rudimentary prototype. Third, produce great designers. The problem here is that great designers are hard to come by. The rudimentary proto-types, and the software that evolves from them, will therefore have to be developed by good rather than great designers, by competent craftsmen rather than outstanding artists. Competence increases when a systematic approach is taken to software development, and this systematic approach is software engineering.

Although software development is still beset by problems, the situation is improving as software engineering develops into a mature discipline, and a greater number of software developers come to understand its importance. Software engineering is concerned with the adaptation of general engineering principles to software development, and the applica-tion of findings of computer science in this setting. Note that the Engineers' Council for Professional Development (UK) defines engineering as

the profession in which a knowledge of the mathematical and *natural* sciences, guided by study, experience and practice, is applied with judgement to develop ways to utilize economically the *materials and forces of nature* for the benefit of mankind (quoted in [Co86]).

Our italics in this definition highlight a major difference between con-ventional and software engineering—software engineering is the "unnatural" branch. Put another way, conventional enginering produces tangible objects, software engineering produces intangible artifacts. The main characteristic of tangible objects is their lack of permanence: natural materials are subject to wear and tear, and the objects constructed of such materials deteriorate with time and eventually fail. On the other hand, computer software failures are caused exclusively by design errors or clerical mistakes. Hence the expectations of software engineers do differ from those of conventional engineers. Nevertheless, there is a similarity: Software engineers engage in the same activities as other engineers.

Instead of becoming entangled in definitions, it may be more profitable to look at what engineers in the traditional disciplines actually do, or should be doing, and relate this to activities in the software branch. Our aim is to list the activities of engineers, express the list as a set of principles, and show that the set of principles can serve as a basis for a definition of software engineering. This will define one of two supports for software engineering, the other being computer science, as shown in Figure 7.1.

The work of engineers is highly varied, ranging from research through planning and design to on-site supervision of manufacturing processes or construction projects, but every engineer is required to perform at least some of the tasks listed below. Furthermore, it is hard to think of a professional engineering activity not covered by one or another of these tasks:

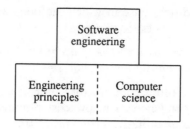

FIGURE 7.1. The foundations of software engineering.

- Definition of requirements and setting up of development plans
- Resolution of conflicts in requirements and setting of priorities
- Use of standards
- Anticipation of changes and allowance for modifications
- Provision for the unexpected
- Transfer of theory into practice
- Scaling up from models or prototypes
- Control of quality
- Selection of tools
- Cooperation with other specialists
- Management of the above
- Engagement in technological adventure

We now examine each of the 12 tasks in detail, and formulate in each case a general engineering principle.

Principle 1: *Engineering development follows a plan in accordance with quantitative requirements, and engineers assume responsibility for carrying out the plan.*

Before an object is constructed, there has to be a clear understanding by all concerned of what is to be constructed, and of the construction process to be followed. The construction process is defined by a plan, the object by requirements. The requirements, which may be functional or nonfunctional, must be verifiable, i.e., they must be stated in quantitative terms. Functional requirements tell what is to be done; nonfunctional requirements add constraints. For example, a functional requirement for a library is that it provide a borrowing service; nonfunctional requirements may state that each borrowing transaction should take no longer than 1 minute, and that in 95% of the cases borrowers should not have to stand in line for longer than 2 minutes. In mathematical language, a functional requirement relates an input x to a result $f(x)$, where f is the name of a function. For example, the value of $cos(x)$ is the cosine of angle x, and the value of *telephone*(*Berztiss*) is my telephone number. (Even the borrowing service of the library can be defined in this way by the rather strange function *borrows*—the "value" of *borrows*(*Berztiss, War and*

Peace) is an altered data base in which the book *War and Peace* is now associated with me as its borrower.)

Principle 2: *Requirements are ranked according to cost-effectiveness, and the development plan has an incremental structure.*

Requirements are often contradictory. For example, a high reliability requirement is in conflict with a low cost requirement. It is therefore essential to develop quantitative estimates of trade-offs between requirements, such as between reliability and cost, or versatility and ease of learning, and to assign priorities to requirements. An effective approach is a cost-benefit ranking. Reliability has a special role in this: It indicates to what extent other requirements may be relaxed. Further, when the object to be constructed is made up of distinct parts, attention to the order in which the parts are constructed can produce a useful product even when the entire project as originally planned cannot be completed. An example is a housing development: If there are uncertainties about financing, houses should be built one cluster at a time rather than all at once. Then, if money runs out, at least some houses will be ready for sale. In any case, the increase in construction costs by building in clusters is likely to be more than balanced by improved cash flow due to early sales.

Principle 3: *Standards are used where available and applicable, with every departure from applicable standards explicitly justified.*

Standards are established to allow engineered objects or their parts to be readily interchanged, thus reducing maintenance costs. Also, the initial cost of an object is reduced if the object can be constructed from standard parts. Standardization is achieved by having an enterprise or an entire industry use the same specification for the object or part, or for the user interface of an object, or for the interfaces of a part with other parts. The notion of standardization has been extended to engineering procedures, such as the writing of requirements, but such extension may be detrimental to progress. As a rule of thumb, we recommend that standardization be limited to entities that can be patented or copyrighted.

Principle 4: *Future changes are anticipated, and engineering design minimizes the cost of modifications.*

Engineers try to anticipate changes, and allow for such changes in their designs. For example, a bridge may start out having a single deck, but with enough strength to allow a second deck to be added should traffic density grow. This is just one example of a change in the environment bringing about a modification of the engineering product. Another type of change arises from design defects—in the automobile industry, such defects result in recalls. Standardization of interfaces localizes the effects of changes.

Principle 5: *Fault and failure tolerance are built into engineering designs.*

Not all conditions can be anticipated. A sudden upsurge of pressure in a gas main can result in explosions that destroy homes. Engineers try to minimize the effects of unexpected conditions by fault-tolerant and failure-tolerant designs. A *fault* is a defect in an object that is due to a design error, a production error, or an imperfection in the material that goes into the making of the object. A *failure* is an observable deviation from requirements. We say *observable* rather than *observed* because sometimes a failure goes unnoticed for a long time, e.g., when a computer program wrongly adds two cents to your electricity bill. Fault tolerance means that the exercising of a fault does not lead to failure; failure tolerance minimizes the effect of failure of an object on the environment in which the object resides. For example, a respirator is fault tolerant if it continues normal operation after a component of the respirator fails; the respirator is failure tolerant if a failure of its main power supply allows emergency power to be switched in before there are serious consequences for the patient.

Principle 6: *Findings of mathematics and the sciences are applied in the solution of engineering problems.*

The primary concern of the more mature engineering disciplines is to adapt the findings of theory to solve practical problems. For example, applied elasticity is a branch of mathematics that deals with stresses in objects; strength of materials is applied elasticity made relevant by being adapted to engineering practice; a stress calculation is the application of strength of materials in a specific engineering design task. The main benefit of theory is that it allows a design to be fully evaluated before it is implemented.

Principle 7: *Efficient techniques are used to scale up size or production.*

Engineering often starts with a *model*, i.e., a scaled-down version of the target object, such as a laboratory model of a chemical plant, a *mock-up*, i.e., a version of the target object that includes only selected features of the target object, such as a user interface, or a *prototype*, i.e., a full-scale version of the product to be manufactured. Each of these three types of experimental versions solves its particular type of problem but creates others. A model establishes feasibility—results from a study of flows in a system of small-bore pipes shows that the chemical plant can be built, but some results have to be scaled up to a system of large-bore pipes. A mock-up tests user satisfaction—the size and form of the external packaging of a device are altered until users are satisfied, but then the device has to be made to fit the packaging. A prototype is used to iron out all remaining problems with a product before manufacturing starts— the product is now ready for release, but, whereas the building of the prototype may have taken 1 week, production now has to be scaled up to a rate of 500 per hour, say. When software people talk about a rapid prototype or a rudimentary prototype, they usually mean just a mock-up. This usage is now so well established that we, too, shall refer to mock-ups as prototypes.

Principle 8: *Quality-control techniques are used to maintain quality at predetermined levels.*

An engineering ideal is to produce objects with zero defects, i.e., objects that fully conform to requirements, both functional and nonfunctional, but this goal may not be cost-effective. Even the lesser goal of eliminating all defective objects before delivery to customers may not be cost-effective in the case of, say, thumbtacks. However, statistical quality control and reliability engineering can be used to impose strict control on quality levels.

Principle 9: *Tools are used to improve productivity, but the use of tools is no substitute for human creativity.*

The nature of tools in engineering has changed dramatically over the past 20 years with the introduction of computer-based tools. The latter have replaced T-squares and other drafting tools, physical mock-ups of packaging, and much other physical modeling. Electronic infrastructures have contributed to the success of concurrent engineering. However, tools can only produce representations of conceptual designs developed by engineers and help engineers make adjustments to such representations. As yet, no tool has replaced human creativity.

Principle 10: *Contributors from many disciplines participate in engineering tasks.*

Engineering practice is not individual-oriented. The design of a large building requires the collaboration of civil, mechanical, and electrical engineers, and design engineers have to interact with architects and builders.

Principle 11: *Effective engineering management is based on a collection of skills acquired by an extensive process of learning.*

Because of the cooperative nature of engineering, not every engineer has to become a manager, but every engineer should have an appreciation of the nature of engineering management. Cost and risk estimation, the matching up of design tasks with personnel, constant monitoring of the progress of a project, and the timely identification of problems require a good grasp of management principles and people skills, broad knowledge of the technical aspects of engineering, and much experience. Only a few engineers have all of these qualifications.

Principle 12: *Technological adventure is good engineering, provided the aim is to add to engineering knowledge.*

Technological adventure has a respectable tradition in engineering. The Roman Pantheon, built in the early second century, has a dome 43 meters in diameter. Its builders did not know much about applied elasticity, but the building still stands after close to 1900 years. Nearer to our time, the Wright brothers initiated heavier-than-air flight without knowing much about aerodynamics. When a technology for an area has not yet been developed, engineers still move ahead, and in so doing develop the technology.

In the rest of this chapter, and in Chapters 8 through 12, we shall outline some of the characteristics of software engineering. In this we shall not restrict ourselves to just those characteristics that directly relate to business reengineering as perceived by the business community. Our motivation for taking a broader view is fourfold. First, although software tools are not essential to support the reengineering effort itself, much can be learned from software engineering about how to specify the processes that reengineering is to introduce. Second, software systems are needed to support reengineered processes, and these systems will be developed by software personnel. It helps therefore for all reengineering personnel to have some exposure to the language of software engineering. Third, not all software developers have given much thought to what they actually do. We hope that our fairly compact outline of software engineering will help them to come to a better understanding of what their work involves, and will stimulate them to adopt more of an engineering attitude. Fourth, the business community is accustomed to thinking of the software in their organizations as *information* systems. Business software systems have increasingly assumed *control* functions as well, and the disappearance of a sharp demarcation between information and control requires going beyond just those concerns of software engineering that relate to information systems. The concurrent engineering movement is accelerating this trend. Under concurrent engineering product design, manufacturing facilities and a marketing strategy are developed in parallel.

Software engineering has the same 12 concerns as the more established engineering disciplines: requirements determination, resolution of conflicts in requirements, use and reuse of standard components, planning for maintenance, provision for the unexpected by building robust systems, transfer of the findings of computer science into practice, scaling up of size, quality maintenance, selection of tools, teamwork, management, and going beyond the tried and tested.

Let us look at these concerns in detail. As we do so, we shall observe that most of the 12 concerns are highly relevant to business reengineering as well. We start with requirements, which we define as a set of verifiable statements. Requirements and a resource allocation schedule define a system plan. Planning is often omitted in software development, with very bad consequences. Only by setting up a system plan can later misunderstandings be avoided. The worst way to squander time is to say "We are so short of time that we will just have to go ahead without a plan." Of course, a system as initially envisaged by the sponsor or the software engineer need bear little resemblance to the final product. However, the discussions between sponsor and software engineer that lead up to the plan, and the need to express requirements in quantitative terms, lead to a better understanding of the product domain by both parties. There is also no great harm in early changes of mind because these changes merely change the system plan rather than the system itself. The success of business reengineering depends to a great extent on how well the reengineering process is planned. A major concern in planning the process is that the day-to-day operation of the business is not seriously disrupted during reengineering.

Suppose we have arrived at a plan with which everybody is happy, but then discover that the cost of building a system according to the plan is $2,000,000, while the budget provides only $1,000,000. Without a plan, we would have charged on in any case, only to find ourselves with just 20% of the system, perhaps, and all of the money gone. Planning permits us to scale down the system in a meaningful way. By stripping away the costlier features, we may manage to keep 80% of the initially planned system capabilities and still remain within the $1,000,000 budget. If priorities are set properly, the 80% capability may satisfy the most urgent needs of all users.

The balancing of cash against user needs is quite common. Another common occurrence is the situation in which the sponsor wants, say, a highly flexible system that is also easy to learn. Unfortunately, these are conflicting requirements, and the sponsor has to choose between a versatile system that is difficult to learn to use, but after a tough initial learning period fulfills the user's every need, and a system that can be understood at once, but has an inflexible structure. In business reengineering terms, priority is to be given to processes that will have the greatest impact on costs, user satisfaction, or future growth of the organization.

Another way to save is to use existing standard components. The ultimate under this approach is to buy a ready-made system rather than build one from scratch. How many of us would have our apartments surveyed and a special set of vacuum cleaner nozzles designed just for the one apartment? The use of existing components requires that the components be standardized. There has been a fair amount written about software reuse, but the conclusion has tended to be that we do not as yet have much to show in a tangible way. This conclusion is debatable in that it is both too pessimistic and too optimistic. To begin with, we already have achieved a fair degree of standardization with program control structures and program libraries in mathematics and statistics, and libraries of operations on priority queues and the like have also been developed.

However, we should not put too much hope in the reusability of software components. The difficulty is that there is not all that much that can be standardized, and all that can be has already been standardized or will be shortly. The problem is that an application software system is a model of an application domain, that there are many application domains, that the application domains bear little resemblance to each other, and that the behavior of the entities that make up the application domains is difficult to formalize. The registration of students at different universities follows the same basic pattern, but even in this limited domain the registration system of one university is difficult to adapt to the needs of another. Of course, here we are back at the vacuum cleaner nozzles. Why should a university adapt an imported software system to its current registration practice instead of changing its practice to fit the software system? Retraining personnel is often easier than changing the software. How does this relate to reengineering? When a utility company reengineers its billing procedures, it may well consider buying existing billing software from some other utility company. On my electricity bill there is a month-by-month graph showing how our electricity usage for the past 12 months compares to that of the 12 months before. I would like to see such a graph on my gas bill as well.

The anticipation of change is a very difficult problem, and maintenance is regarded to be the most expensive component of system development [Li80], but little practical advice can be found in the literature on how do deal with the problem. Maintenance activities are primarily caused by misunderstanding of sponsor requirements, by changes in the domain in which the system operates, and by a wish to add capabilities to a system. Good engineering practice requires that misunderstandings be avoided, that the effects of domain changes on the software be proportional to the magnitude of the domain changes, and that the addition of new capabilities have little effect on the parts of the system that already exist. Exactly the same objectives hold for business processes. A reengineered process should correctly embody the expectations that management has about the process, and the process should be easy to modify in case changing business conditions make modifications necessary. A special problem arises with business mergers. Suppose one airline absorbs another. Are its software systems so designed that they easily absorb the information base of the other airline, or will the software merger take 6 years, as has been the case with USAir and Piedmont [Cw94b]?

Provision for the unexpected means that software has to be robust. We refer to this as fault and failure tolerance. Fault tolerance masks the effects of faults in software, i.e., faults are prevented from causing failures. Hardware fault tolerance is achieved by duplicating components. If you are afraid that your alarm clock will stop during the night, you could buy another and set both clocks. If you are still anxious, you could buy one more. With software, fault tolerance is more difficult to achieve because of the so-called common-cause faults—two software developers may misinterpret requirements in exactly the same way, and both versions will fail in exactly the same way. Failure tolerance lessens the effects of a failure. For example, a software engineer, alone or in collaboration with a domain expert, has to specify how an elevator system is to be restored after a power failure so that passengers on the elevator experience the least inconvenience. Failure tolerance should be built into every reengineered organization. To this end we suggested at the end of Chapter 2 that management in a reengineered business should undergo regular training in how to deal with unexpected situations.

In the transfer of theory into practice, one important aspect is the sequencing of concerns. In engineering, applied elasticity or strength of materials tells how stresses are distributed in bodies subjected to forces. Materials engineers then take over and determine whether a body made of a particular substance can take the stresses. The analogy here is to algorithms and their implementation. A software engineer needs to know and be able to apply the fundamental algorithms of sorting and searching, and algorithms that relate to computer systems, such as scheduling. But the software engineer does not have to know all kinds of inventory-control algorithms or the algorithms that designers of elevator systems use to determine where to place empty elevators. Let the experts in the other disciplines supply the specialized knowledge. Then, under sequencing of concerns, algorithms are developed by domain experts, these algorithms are introduced into designs of software systems by software engineers, and the software systems are implemented as code by programmers. As was discussed in Chapter 1, business reengineering encourages specialization of this kind.

Scaling up of size is intimately related to the transfer of the findings of computer science to software engineering. Computer scientists understand very well how to develop dependable small programs, which is often called "programming in the small", but they have not paid much attention to the development of large software systems. The latter is the concern of software engineering. The transition from programming in the small to programming in the large is a big step, but when a software product is partitioned into modules of manageable size, the techniques of programming in the small can be applied as they stand to the modules, and then the step no longer seems so big. The business processes that reengineering identifies are comparable to large modules, and the tasks that make up processes are comparable to smaller submodules. Indeed, the software that is to support reengineered processes should have a modular structure that corresponds to the tasks of the business processes.

The training of software developers has tended to interpret software quality primarily as having to do with the functional aspects of software. The result is that insufficient attention is given to nonfunctional attributes, which will be discussed later on. Requiring that testing be done with respect to *all attributes of the software system throughout the software development process* ensures that quality will be maintained with respect to all of these attributes. Such an attitude is cost-effective because both development and maintenance costs are greatly reduced if faults are prevented in the first place or, when they do occur, are detected and removed as early as possible. A driving force of business reengineering is that an organization can only survive if it produces products of high quality or provides high-quality service, and it will not be able to do so if the software that supports its processes is of low quality. Quality consciousness is thus an important characteristic of business reengineering.

Tools can make the software developer's life much easier, and more and more excellent tools are coming on the market. First, there are tools relating to management, such as Gantt charts, Pert networks, etc. Second, software developers require tools for creating representations, for managing the representations, and for communication. It has been estimated that, with the proper use of software development tools, the productivity of software developers increases by 50–100% [Jo91, p.173]. But too much is sometimes expected of tools. Tools do not design software, people do. Just as text processing tools do not write books, but merely manipulate the text that authors create, so software tools merely manipulate representations of processes and information structures that software engineers define. So, if a software engineer produces poor designs, tools are actually detrimental because they amplify the negative effects of the designs. The tools in a reengineered business relate to decision making—they are decision support systems and expert systems. Also, if management of a business is to have a proper understanding of what does and what does not work, there have to be measurements. The taking of measurements is rather boring. So, unless the measurements are taken by automated tools, there will be a reluctance to introduce a proper regime of measurement into an organization.

Software engineers, who should have professional competence in their own discipline, have to cooperate with professionals in other disciplines. They simply cannot be expected to know everything. We see the work load of technical personnel growing while there is serious underemployment elsewhere. It seems that after reengineering has been completed in every workplace, the length of the work week will in general go down. But the need for top professionals to keep up with new knowledge keeps increasing the length of their work week. Also, downsizing is equated by some companies with the overloading of their remaining employees. This is false economy—tiredness leads to reduced quality. A way to escape this anomalous situation is increased collaboration between experts, with narrower focusing of the speciality of individuals within a collaborating group, thus allowing the top professionals to have more leisure time as well. This requires, however, that collaborating personnel speak a common language, and in technical fields this tends to be the language of mathematics. Computer science therefore puts much emphasis on mathematics, and software engineers need to expand their mathematical knowledge as well, particularly in statistics and control theory. Parnas goes as far as to say that software developers should start out in control engineering [Pa90].

We will not put that much emphasis on control engineering, but the control aspects of software systems must be taken more seriously. One problem with business reengineering is that too often the participants have too narrow an outlook. The control of baggage handling at a new airport, a new composite travel reservation system for an airline, and a new air traffic control system for the Federal Aviation Authority can all be regarded as business processes. A full realization is long overdue that there are no pure business information systems and no pure control systems. A process system has both information components and control components, and their proper integration requires cooperation of experts from different fields. The relative importance of the two kinds of components will vary, but no process system will be entirely satisfactory unless software engineers and various application domain specialists cooperate freely and fully in its specification.

But far too often, when process systems are being developed, high walls seem to separate various interest groups. Now and then a narrow door opens in a wall and information passes through, but this information should have been available months earlier. In the reengineering of "pure" business processes, such as order fulfillment, the business specialists will try to specify the processes on their own with little regard to what software engineers have to offer. With control systems, the reverse problem arises in that now software engineers are put in full charge of development, but not enough of what domain specialists have to offer gets to them, at least not when there is the greatest need for this information.

Next let us consider management. We see as the ultimate function of management a delicate balancing of profitability and market share, both in the short and the long term. Profitability suffers when there are cost overruns, industrial unrest, or inadequate attention to new technology. Market share in the context of professional software engineering relates to the question "Will the sponsor choose our team again for the next software development project?" This relates to risk analysis. Risk cannot be avoided. The objective is to weigh risks against benefits, which is a positive attitude to risk. For purposes of risk-benefit analysis, it is necessary to know costs, and the importance of cost estimation has been recognized by engineers for thousands of years—"For which of you, intending to build a tower, sitteth not down first, and counteth the cost, whether he have sufficient to finish it?" (Luke 14, 28). But risk analysis goes beyond cost estimation, and we shall deal with risk in detail later on.

As regards specifically the management of software projects, in 1981 Thayer, Pyster, and Wood [Th81] published a ranking of the major problems in software project management. The approach had been to gather a list of 20 problems from the literature, and to have a group of people select the problems they found particularly important. Software project managers found the following 10 problems most significant, ranked by the percentage who listed them.

1. Requirements are incomplete, ambiguous, inconsistent, and unmeasurable (100%).
2. Delivery time schedules are inaccurate (97%).
3. The system plan is generally poor (92%).
4. Costs, i.e., resource estimates, are inaccurate (92%).
5. Reliability measures are unavailable, making software failure predictions impracticable (90%).
6. Test strategies are not based on meaningful selection criteria (85%).
7. Programmer performance with respect to both quality and quantity is difficult to estimate (77%).
8. Maintainability is difficult to measure (76%).
9. Quality criteria, such as maintainability, ease of use, and reliability, are not given enough weight (75%).
10. Accountability structure can be very poor (75%).

The respondents were also asked to make suggestions as to how the situation could be improved. It is significant that there were no suggestions on how to improve system plans or maintainability, but it was suggested that requirements be developed iteratively, i.e., by what today is called prototyping.

Finally, it has to be realized that sometimes we have to proceed without a plan. This applies in particular to artificial intelligence software. Technological adventure has always been in the engineering tradition. We noted earlier that Hadrian's builders of the Pantheon constructed a dome with a diameter of 43 meters without the appropriate mathematics, and the spirit of adventure of the Wright brothers opened up an essential component of modern life. Computer scientists sometimes tell us not to build software systems that we do not fully understand. If this advice had been followed, we probably would not have had a landing on the Moon. Some large systems with components that interact in very complex ways will always remain beyond our full understanding. We will have to continue to develop such systems by trial and error. But when we proceed without a plan, our aim should be to come to a better understanding. This is good engineering; just hacking away is not.

The most important principle that underlies all software engineering activities is the partitioning of a large undertaking into manageable components. One approach is to separate the system development process into a sequence of well-defined phases. An alternative is to partition the system that is being developed into appropriate modules. Ideally, we would like to partition both the product into modules and the process into phases. We shall see in Chapter 11 that there are a number of problems associated with a phased process model. Still, whatever form the software development process takes, it has to have a structure. This structure depends in part on the type of software that is to be developed, how and when modularization is to be undertaken, and what software quality attributes are considered most important. In the next three chapters we shall discuss types of software, modularization, and quality attributes. In Chapter 11 we will look at several software process models, and in Chapter 12 at the costs and risks of software.

8
Classification of Software

A software application system can be considered as made up of an information component, a control component, and data transformers. The systems that support the operation of a reengineered organization follow this pattern, and will be called information-control systems.

The business of a reengineered organization is defined by a set of processes. The proper execution of the processes is supported by software. Modern business depends on programs that refer to information bases, and by software we mean both programs and information bases. We shall see that at a sufficiently high level of abstraction there is no real difference between the two, but often it is convenient to make a distinction. Our task in this chapter is to look at some classifications of software and at the different challenges presented to software engineering by the different classes of software. The classifications will help us to determine how software engineering may assist business reengineering. We shall see that the assistance can be of two kinds.

First, the methods of software engineering can help define business processes. Increasingly, the task of defining requirements for a software system is being seen as the most important task of software engineers. However, when the requirements are being formulated, there is nothing that says that the system being described has to be computer-based—it could equally well be human-based, except when the requirements impose time constraints for which humans are too slow. This suggests that the methods that have been developed for the specification of software systems can be used in the definition of any business process, independent of how it is ultimately implemented.

Second, the representations of processes, both graphical and textual, that have been developed as part of software engineering can aid in the understanding of business processes. Even better understanding develops when the definition of a process is partitioned into separate information and control components. We regard a methodology based on such partitioning as our main contribution to software specification. We believe that, by looking at the information and control concerns separately, the implementation of the processes of a reengineered organization will proceed more smoothly than it would otherwise.

Software systems are being classified according to a variety of criteria. The earliest was by the *size* of the software system, usually expressed as the number of Delivered Lines of Code (DLC) or thousands of DLC (KDLC, where the K is short for kilo). Related to these length measures is the number of person months (or person years) that it takes to produce the software product ready for delivery. However, given two programs of the same size, one may take much longer to develop than the other. This is a function of the *complexity* of the program. For example, a system made up of tightly coupled subsystems is much more complex than a system in which the subsystems are close to being fully decoupled.

Delivered source instructions are relatively easy to estimate, and a comparison of estimates against direct measurements after implementation leads to more accurate estimates as experience is gained. Development time is much more difficult to estimate because it relates to software complexity. Various metrics have been proposed for measuring complexity, but no metric appears to give a fully adequate quantitative indication of software complexity. However, since the late 1970s, function points have been gaining in popularity. The function point metric is quite well suited to business information systems, and we shall return to this metric in Chapter 12.

Software engineers have to deal with various kinds of application software, with software tools that help in the development of application software, and with the software that supports the execution of application programs. For example, Boehm [Bo81] has classified software development processes as organic, semidetached, or embedded, and we shall apply this same terminology to the software that results from the respective development processes. *Organic* software has relatively small size, and system requirements are essentially all functional, i.e., they simply describe the output $f(X)$ that the system is to generate from a given input X. *Semidetached* software has larger size, and some nonfunctional requirements are included. For example, the system may have to generate outputs that satisfy given accuracy requirements, and the system interface may have to be designed for unsophisticated users. *Embedded* software has stringent nonfunctional requirements. The available memory may be limited, the system may have to respond to every external stimulus within a given time limit, and it must be robust with respect to invalid inputs and other external influences, such as power failures.

Our classification here will relate to applications software alone, and in discussing this classification we will put emphasis on business systems, i.e., on systems that are to provide support for reengineered business processes. We classify components of application software according to purpose into *information* components, *control* components, and *data transformers*. An information component responds to queries, which are answered by the examination of a persistent data base. The data base is subject to updates, and the maintenance of the integrity of the data base has to be addressed in system requirements. Examples are a library catalog or an account management data base of a bank. Control components drive processes that are external to the controlling software. Here, the specific concerns are temporal effects—the control component has to respond to external stimuli within a strictly limited time period. Representative of control components are an elevator controller and a climate controller for a building, but, as we shall see, business systems have control components as well. A data transformer typically changes individual data elements or a structure into which the data may be organized. Alternatively, we can say that a data transformer implements an algorithm, i.e., a computational rule that generates a useful result. Examples of data transformers are a text formatter, a spelling checker, and mathematical and statistical software. Most application systems are hybrids that contain components of all three classes. For example, the banking system maintains information about accounts (information activity), sends out overdraft notices (control activity), and prepares monthly statements for the customers (a rather trivial instance of data transformation).

Let us look at data transformers. Computer scientists have long recognized that a good way to specify data transformers is in terms of data types [Pa72]. Under this orientation a data type is considered as a set of objects and a set of operations or functions that relate to the objects of the type. To take a simple example, the data type of integers is defined by the objects $\{0, -1, 1, -2, 2, \ldots\}$ and operations of addition, subtraction, multiplication, division, and remaindering. Thus, $plus(5, 9) = 14$, $minus(5, 9) = -4$. Additional operations can be defined: a sample value of the prime function is $prime(7) = $ true; $gcd(14, 77) = 7$ shows 7 to be the greatest common divisor of 14 and 77.

In mathematics, a function is a collection of argument-value pairs. Thus the function or collection *plus* contains element $<<5, 9>, 14>$, which corresponds to $plus(5, 9) = 14$, as well as $<<3, 7>, 10>$, $<<-6, 3>, -3>$, etc. The function *prime* has elements $<6,$ false$>$, $<7,$ true$>$, $<8,$ false$>$, $<9,$ false$>$, etc. The function *telephone* has for one of its elements $<Berztiss, $ 624-8401$>$. Values of the three functions are obtained in different ways: *plus* by means of hardware circuits; *prime* by means of a computation defined by a program; and *telephone* by looking up a data base. This difference suggests a classification of software according to the nature of the functions. Figure 8.1 shows the classification. The classes are defined by two orthogonal two-way partitions. The first relates to the determination of function values. The function *telephone* is stored as a table of entries of the form $<$subscriber, telephone number$>$, but the value of *prime* for a given integer is found by application of a computational rule to the integer. In the classification we are not concerned with function values generated directly by hardware—developers of application software simply accept them as given. The other partition separates functions into static or immutable, and dynamic or mutable. An immutable function does not change—for example, the prime function, or a finite function that supplies the times of sunrise in Pittsburgh for the 365 days of the year 2001. A mutable function changes. Thus, before I got my present office, *telephone(Berztiss)* had the value 624-6458. Now, the value is 624-8401.

The classification is not always clear-cut, and at the specification stage one should not have to decide how a function will be implemented. The sunrise function is a case in point—it can be implemented as a table of 365 entries, or as a program that computes the times of sunrises. Similarly, if we were interested in prime numbers never greater than 100,000, the 9592 such primes could be stored as a table. This ability to consider a function either as a component of an information base or as a program is the justification for our statement at the beginning of this chapter that both information bases and programs are software. One reason for our emphasis on functions as mathematical objects is precisely this: To determine whether *prime*(62113) is true or false, we can check whether 62113 is in a table of primes or use an algorithm, but in both cases we are still dealing with a function (by the way, 62113 is not a prime; it is the product of primes 179 and 347). Tables and algorithms are often combined—in looking for the answer to a complicated query, an appropriate algorithm is used to find and to combine information from several tables; when the algorithm implements a system of deduction, we speak of *deductive data bases*.

Most functions belong to the classes LD and RS (see Figure 8.1). The functions based on lookup usually arise as components of persistent data bases. Functions of the class RD arise in artificial intelligence, as in programs that play board games. Given the configuration of pieces on the

	static	dynamic
based on look-up	LS	LD
based on a rule	RS	RD

FIGURE 8.1. A classification of functions.

board, a next-move function evaluates the effectiveness of feasible moves and returns as its value the move of greatest effectiveness. However, the program may be designed to learn from past experience, and it would then try to improve the next-move function, or, what is more likely today, a programmer would change the function. Such learning programs that modify themselves are still experimental. It will probably take decades before they become part of business software systems

The software that supports the operation of a reengineered organization consists of an information base, of programs that effect changes in the information base, and of programs that assist in the exercising of control over the organization itself or its environment. Hybrid information-control systems are therefore our primary concern. Their specifications can be expressed in terms of data types, and the operations or functions of information-control systems belong for the most part to class LD. Moreover, not only are the functions subject to change, but the sets that define the domains of the functions, i.e., the value sets of particular data types, may also change over time. For example, before I moved to Pittsburgh, the telephone function for Pittsburgh had no pair with first element *Berztiss*. A further characteristic of information-control systems is that they operate over extended time periods; the system is continuously available to provide information, or it may control a process continuously.

We shall now identify the information and control components, and the data transformers in a representative process system. First, however, a summary of the properties of the three kinds of components:

• An *information* component allows the system to retrieve factual information. This information may be requested by a user or, internally, by a data transformer.

• A *control* component selects the proper action that is to be taken in response to some external stimulus. This may occur when, for example, a temperature reading or a stock exchange index reaches a boundary value, or at a specific time.

• A *data transformer* implements an algorithm. It may be called on to determine the action that a control component is to take, or to compute an item of information requested by a user. The use of a data transformer may be essential, as for values of most mathematical functions, or its use may be an alternative to retrieval, as in the case of the sunrise function.

We have chosen airline marketing as our process. The analysis will be simpler if the system is partitioned into subsystems and the subsystems looked at separately. We shall look at three such subsystems: customer profiling, frequent flyer programs, and target-group marketing.

Under customer profiling, a behavior pattern is established for each customer that indicates when, where, and under what fare category the customer has been flying. In addition, the subsystem could note how far in advance the ticket was purchased. It could also keep a record of the occasions on which the customer has been a "no-show", i.e., has not used a ticket. Here the information component is straightforward. With regard to data transformers, the data can be analyzed in various ways. One is to use the methods of numerical taxonomy to identify a set of customer classes, and to put customers into these classes. A different marketing strategy can then be applied to each class. The no-show data can even be used by some other process to fine-tune overbooking—they allow an estimate to be made of the probability that individual customers will be no-shows. Customer profiling is a data-gathering activity; consequently, there is no significant control component.

The frequent flyer subsystem imports most of the information it needs from other process systems or subsystems. It is essentially a control system. For the most part, it responds to boundary values and specific times. When particular mileage levels are reached, the system may send out benefit certificates or change membership grades; active members receive updated mileage information once a month. This subsystem should have a direct interaction with software systems of partners of the frequent flyer program—these are usually some other airlines, a bank that issues credit cards, and designated hotel chains and car rental companies. The interaction takes the form of messages sent into the subsystem. This information is a stimulus that causes the subsystem to update the mileage credit of a customer. As part of its data transformer component, the subsystem may use an algorithm to identify inactive members whom it would be worthwhile to reactivate by some kind of a mileage bonus.

The reactivation of inactive frequent flyers could just as easily be part of the target-group marketing subsystem. Other activities that this subsystem can support are special discounts in response to similar initiatives by other airlines or in response to underutilization of capacity on certain flights, and targeting of the business travel accounts of selected corporations. Most airlines arrange complete vacation packages, and much of the marketing of these packages is through travel agents. An information component that tracks the performance of individual travel agencies in various categories, combined with an appropriate algorithm, can identify agencies that are particularly effective, and an incentive plan can be set up that rewards these agencies.

9
Modularization and Requirements Engineering

Software modules are defined, and their history is traced. Each module of a software system is to have a well-defined purpose, and its interaction with other modules is to be minimized. The same objectives hold in the definition of the business processes of a reengineered organization. The definition of modules is an important function of requirements engineering.

The meaning of *module* has evolved over the past 25 years. The closest that *Webster's Third New International Dictionary* of 1971 comes to what software engineers mean by this term is "a unit of size used as a basis for standardizing the design and construction of building parts and materials of articles of furniture," but its Addenda already had "any in a series of standardized units for use together" and "an assembly of components that are packaged or mounted together . . ." and "an independent unit that constitutes a part of the total structure . . .". Putting all of this together and extrapolating a little, we arrive at three properties that software engineers consider crucial to the concept of a module: it is supposed to be coupled to other modules; it is made up of components, i.e., it possesses an internal structure; and it is independent in the sense that it has some well-defined purpose. For software engineers, modules are the building blocks of software systems. It would be impossible to build a software system of say 1000 KDLC as a single unit—partitioning provides the system with structure, and thus improves understanding of the system and aids distribution of the work load while the system is being built.

Let us begin with a brief history of software modularization. Modularization is nearly as old as electronic computation, the subroutine being a very early invention. The initial motivation for modularization was the need to preserve precious space and time. This was essential when a computer occupied a large room, had not much more than 30,000 "words" of memory, and its operating speeds were rated in milliseconds rather than microseconds. But, suppose that square roots were needed at several places in the program. It made sense to have just one copy of the code for the square root and to access this from all of the places at which values of square roots were needed. However, the code for the square root was not yet regarded as an independent component of the program.

With the release in 1957 of Fortran, the first high-level language to find wide acceptance, compilation became an important issue. Given a large program in which changes had been made, it took a prohibitively long time to recompile the entire program. Splitting up the program into units and recompiling the changed units alone would take just a fraction of the total compilation time. This resulted in Fortran systems that allowed separate compilation of such units, and the separate Fortran compilation units became the first instance of modules as independent components of a program.

Another trend soon arose. This was *data abstraction*. It had been found that programming errors are greatly reduced when programmers associate every data object they use with some type, e.g., boolean, integer, array. The next stage was the realization that the programmer needs to know very little about the representation of these objects or about the implementation of the operations that are carried out on the objects. For example, the programmer does not have to know how a negative number is being stored. Similarly, although the programmer does need to know the sign of the remainder in integer division, the details of the division circuit are irrelevant. A change in the internal machine representation of negative integers or in the division circuit should have no effect on existing programs.

A data type soon came to mean not just a set of objects, but also a set of operations on these objects. In higher level languages this already was understood with regard to the built-in standard data types, such as integers and reals. Now this concept came to be extended to data objects defined by users themselves. A well-known device for retrieving stored items in a particular order is a *queue*, which retrieves items in the order in which they are stored. An application is an airline waiting list—the next available seat is to go to the person who has been in the queue longest. The data type of *Queue* comprises objects (individual queues, say one for each flight) and also operations that insert data into a queue, retrieve data from a queue, test a queue for emptiness, etc.

We already mentioned a paper in which Parnas explored the nature of modularization further [Pa72]. He recognized two different purposes of modules. One was to *encapsulate* a data type. Encapsulation means that the user is not told how the data type is implemented and may access an object of the data type only by means of the "official" operations of the data type. Type *Queue* can be implemented in numerous different ways. Suppose that a programmer knows the details of the implementation and, instead of using just the official operations, directly manipulates the representation of the objects. For example, officially the user of a queue has access only to the top element of the queue and, to get the value of the third element, first has to take off the two elements covering it, then read the wanted element, and then put back the two removed elements. The "smart" user can get at the third element much more efficiently. But this has two negative effects. First, a programmer may inadvertently change something so that the queue operations fail after this change. Second, if programmers make deliberate direct use of hidden implementation features, then the substitution of a new implementation for the existing one invalidates the parts of the program in which such use is made. Encapsulation means that access to objects of a data type is *exclusively* by means of operations of this data type. Since the implementation is now completely hidden from the user of the data type, changes to the implementation do not affect the programs that use the data type.

The second purpose of a module is to implement a process. A process is structured from the operations of one or more data types. For example, a spelling checker could operate as follows. A text is read in one word at a time. The word, if it is not already present, is inserted in a binary search tree (*SearchTree* operation). After the entire text has been processed, the words are picked off the tree in alphabetical order (another *SearchTree* operation) and compared against words in a dictionary (*HashTable* operation, assuming that the dictionary is stored as a hash table). Words not in the dictionary are written out

The recommendation that modules should be identified with data types and processes has a theoretical flavor, but practitioners had arrived at more or less the same recommendation. They established two scales for module structure: *cohesion*, which indicates the strength of the interrelation of the components of a module to each other, and *coupling*, which indicates the strength of the interaction between modules. A module should exhibit strong cohesion and weak coupling, and modules that implement data types or well-defined processes do precisely this.

If the coupling between two modules is weak, the modules can be regarded as being close to independent of each other. This means that they can be developed in parallel, which in turn can significantly reduce project completion time. To take a concrete example, consider an elevator system made up of two modules. The first module controls an individual elevator. It deals with floor selection from within the elevator, control of elevator doors, stopping at floors listed in an agenda, etc. The second module is a dispatcher. It picks up calls for service from people who want to get onto an elevator, determines which elevator should respond to a call, and determines the holding floors to which idle elevators should be moved. The dispatcher can tell the location of each elevator by consulting appropriate sensor units. The interaction between the modules is minimal: (1) the dispatcher adds a floor to the agenda of an elevator, (2) it initiates the movement of an idle elevator to a holding floor, and (3) it activates an idle elevator. The interaction can be accomplished by the passing of signals between the dispatcher computer and small computers embedded in the elevators.

Modularization allows system developers to deal effectively with risk factors. In the case of the elevator system, the objective may be very high reliability. Here the individual elevator module is the critical component of the system, but it has a rather simple and straightforward structure, and high reliability is fairly easy to achieve. The dispatcher is more problematic in that some expertise in elevator scheduling practice seems to be called for. On the other hand, the client may be willing to accept a policy of incremental development for this module. For example, to begin with, idle elevators need not be moved to holding floors, and, instead of using a complicated scheduling algorithm, the floor from which service is requested can be added to the agenda of every elevator. Such a policy is quite safe because the incremental changes in the dispatcher module will have no effect on the elevator module. Business reengineering has not been successful when too much has been attempted in too short a time. A schedule for the incremental refinement of the modules that implement process systems avoids undue haste while still defining very clearly what the process systems are to achieve ultimately.

This paragraph is addressed primarily to software engineers, and it points out the significance of a development in software architecture that allows coupling of modules to be minimized. We can recognize three levels of strength of module interaction. An example of the first is the classical call/return paradigm, under which control is passed to a sub-program but then returns to the place from which the call originated. This mechanism closely binds a called software unit to the calling unit. Next comes pipelining, as in Unix, where software unit A passes control to software unit B, and control does not return to A but is passed by B to some further unit C. However, a pipeline is rather inflexible. The third level corresponds to the object-oriented paradigm in which object classes are the modules, and greatest flexibility has been obtained by having control pass around the system in the form of messages. Since modules communicate by messages alone, a very high degree of module autonomy has been attained. This has three major consequences: (1) the possibility of reusing existing modules is improved, (2) a high degree of concurrency can be achieved, and (3) development times can be reduced because structural complexity does not extend over the entire system but is confined to interaction clusters within individual modules.

Our goal is to achieve strong QSC management, where Q stands for quality, S for schedule, and C for cost. It is no accident that we put Q first: with enough thought given to quality throughout the development of process systems, schedule and cost will tend to take care of themselves, mainly because there will be less reworking. The parallelism permitted by increased module autonomy has two effects. First, it has the direct effect of decreasing costs and shortening schedules. Second, weaker coupling leads to simpler systems, and simpler systems are easier to test, their reliability is easier to control, and adverse effects of failures or faults can be confined to just one or two modules. Under proper modularization it is rather easy to identify modules that consume inordinate amounts of resources, and efficiency improvements can be confined to just those modules. It is much easier to understand the operation of a system made up of modules with well-defined individual functions than it is to understand a tightly coupled system in which these same functions are distributed throughout the system. We shall return to quality considerations in the next chapter.

Before one builds a system, there has to be a clear idea of why the system is to be built, what exactly is to be built, how much it will cost, how long it will take to build it, the consequences if it is not completed on time, and the consequences if it fails to perform as expected. Here we can distinguish three concerns: one relates to what the system is to do, another refers to costs and schedules, and the third has to do with risks—the consequences of not building the proposed system have to be weighed against the risks associated with building and operating the system. Strictly speaking, initial requirements analysis should not go beyond the determination of what a system is to do. The rest is the province of cost analysis and risk analysis. However, the results of cost and risk analyses determine whether the system is to be built at all and, if it is, which parts of the system should be built first to ensure that a working core system with at least some of the capabilities of the final system is available for inspection early. This means that these analyses have to be made in parallel with requirements analysis—otherwise, too much effort could get expended on gathering requirements for a cancelled project. We shall use the term *requirements engineering* to indicate a process that goes beyond strict requirements gathering.

There now exists a well-developed methodology for the specification and verification of small programming tasks, and a view prevails that the construction of a large system is merely a straightforward combination of small verified modules. Although this view is justified with regard to, for example, operating systems, it has been unduly optimistic with respect to most large information-control systems. First, it ignores the difficult problem of ensuring that formal specifications correspond to informal intentions. Formal verification can only establish that a program corresponds to its formal specification. If the formal specification has not captured the intentions of the sponsor of the program, then the validation is of little use. Second, there have arisen two essentially separate approaches to specification. One, which is based on abstract data types, derives from programming methodology and has primarily a functional orientation. The other, which was developed in the context of data base management, has entity orientation. However, as we shall see in Chapter 20, an entity-relation model can be given a functional interpretation, i.e., the two approaches are not all that dissimilar.

We therefore have the following stages in the development of large software systems. An initial requirements-gathering phase produces a preliminary requirements statement, which, for the most part, is expressed in natural language. The software engineer augments the natural language text with diagrams, and in time the requirements document becomes transformed into a set of annotated diagrams. Many questions of interpretation of users' needs can be resolved by inspection of the diagrams. A formal textual specification should be generated next. Ideally, it should be executable, and, if it is, the specification is a prototype. Execution of the prototype brings further insights into the nature of the software system under development. These insights help to refine the system further.

With control systems, the focus should be on the system that is to be controlled. Let the latter be called the *target system*. The first task is to come to a thorough understanding of the target system. Here the specification has to be sufficiently detailed to allow various scenarios to be explored. For example, in the case of an elevator system, one should be able to determine whether the elevator doors are open or closed after an idle elevator has been moved from its current floor to a holding floor.

Requirements analysis need not be confined to software. Our whole point is that the reengineering of an organization is to start off with a determination of its purpose, and that determination of purpose is exactly what requirements analysis is concerned with. To take a totally unrelated example, let us examine how this book was initially developed as a set of notes. The primary requirement was that the notes were to serve several purposes. First, they were to be used in a course at the University of Pittsburgh on software and management, supported by extensive additional readings. Second, the notes were to be used in short courses given to industry. These courses were to last either 2 or 3 days. Third, the notes were to become a book manuscript without too much editing. The third requirement has little effect on early development. It relates to implementation, in the sense that the notes were to have a passable English style. We can therefore disregard this requirement in what follows. The second requirement suggested that the "system" be developed as "subsystems" in such a way that the first four "subsystems" could stand on their own. The plan was to present two subsystems on each day of an industry course. This resulted in six main parts of the notes:

I.   What is business reengineering
II.   What is software engineering
III. Business analysis
IV.   The reengineering blueprint
V.   Specification of information and control
VI.   Implementation of reengineering

The 2-day industry course was to use Parts I through IV of the notes. There was much agonizing over the ordering of the third and fourth parts. One part deals with the form in which the results of the process described in the other part are to be presented. Is the form to be discussed first, or the substance? Actually, I believe it makes little difference how the two parts are ordered. As a general rule, whenever it is difficult to make a choice between two alternatives, it may well be that the cause of the difficulty is that either alternative is as good as the other. The next step was to break down each part into "modules". Then the "module" headings were chosen and finally the requirements for each "module" written down. These requirements became the short synopsis paragraphs at the beginning of the individual chapters. Since then, a few chapters have been added and a few chapters taken out, but the titles of all of the original chapters are as they were first defined. Although the synopsis paragraphs have undergone some changes, these have been very minor. The main advantage of the requirements-based development of the notes was that much time was saved—I estimate that working about a week on the requirements saved me at least 30 days of writing.

Some authors suggest that all system requirements should first be written down with little regard to order, and then structured. This is *bottom-up development*. I found here that a structured *top-down* development, starting with the selection of the six main headings, was more effective. This is a bit misleading because the domain under consideration was very familiar to me, which means that I already had an unwritten list of the detailed requirements in my mind before the six main headings were defined. Here we have another instance of the familiar debate on the respective merits of top-down and bottom-up development, and, as usual, the actual development was a mixture of both.

Requirements engineering, then, can begin at two ends. At the top end, subsystems can be identified early. Detailed requirements can then be allocated to the subsystems as these requirements are being formulated. The detailed requirements contribute to a better understanding of the domain in which the system is to operate and the services that the system is to provide, so that the partitioning of the system can be progressively refined. Such integration of requirements gathering and system design has several advantages. First, cost and risk analyses can be carried out on the individual components of the system, and reasonably accurate composite estimates for the entire system may be derived from the component estimates. Second, the component estimates can guide the system developer and the sponsor of the system in setting up a priority list for the system components. Third, for each component, cost-benefit and risk-benefit analyses can establish a priority schedule for the services this component is to provide. Fourth, a framework is established for the gathering of detailed requirements. If we substitute "reengineered business" for "system" and "process" for "subsystem", our discussion becomes a set of guidelines for the early phases of business process definition.

It must never be forgotten that requirements engineering needs to be as well managed as the later stages of system development. Thus, adequate resources have to be provided for requirements engineering. Also, the cost of requirements engineering for abandoned projects becomes a charge against continuing projects. It is therefore imperative that the requirements engineering phase be stopped as soon as it becomes apparent that the project is to be discontinued. In the reengineering context, this means that the implementation of some ideas may be just too risky. For example, referring to the airline marketing process of Chapter 8, the direct targeting of corporate business travel accounts appears very appealing until we realize that it will almost certainly antagonize travel agents, and begin to consider what adverse effect the antagonism can bring about.

10
Software Quality Attributes

Software quality has many facets, including verifiability, robustness, maintainability, reusability, and understandability. One concern of requirements engineering is the ranking of these quality attributes in order of importance for the particular software system under consideration, keeping in mind that the most important quality attribute is user acceptance. Special emphasis is given to software performance estimation.

In most discussions of software *quality*, the term is applied almost exclusively to functional correctness. This, however, is only one aspect of quality. Indeed, there are times when it is advisable to leave a known functionality error uncorrected. A case in point: Suppose that a document preparation system underlines the interposed page number whenever a section of text to be underlined spans two pages. Here, the best solution may be to blank out manually the unwanted underlining. Admittedly this is not an elegant solution. However, a corrective action on the software is unlikely to be cost-effective, and—the crux of the matter—the "corrected" software would probably have become less reliable. Let us list some nonfunctional attributes that all contribute to software quality. Some of these attributes are not particularly important for software that supports a reengineered business, but most of them are.

- *Verifiability* relates as much to the specification of a software system as to the system itself, and it deals with the ability to show that the system is consistent with its specification with respect to all specified quality requirements. This means that the specification must be expressed in quantitative terms, i.e., that the degree of presence or absence of a particular attribute in a software system is to be measurable. Verification is sometimes by proof, but much more often by tests. Quality attribute *testability* relates to the design of test plans. Both the system and its documentation need to be considered in the drafting of test plans. The simpler the structure of the system, the easier it is to test.
- *Modifiability* is the aspect of *maintainability* that relates to the addition of new capabilities to a system (*enhancement* of the system),

changes to the system that redefine at least some of its attributes, changes to the system that improve some aspect of its performance, and the removal of faults. Modifiability depends greatly on proper modularization of the system. In particular, proper modularization helps in the three stages of fault removal: fault location, corrective action, and analysis of the effect of the corrective action on other software components. The transformation of a prototype process system into the implemented system that is actually to support a reengineered business process can be regarded as a modification.

• *Portability*, the other aspect of maintainability, relates to the transfer of a software system from one operating environment to another. Usually this is the adaptation of the software to new hardware or to a new operating system. An important special case arises when machinery controlled by embedded software is modified. Much attention now is being given to international use of software. This has been long overdue. Just as Detroit automakers still barely acknowledge the fact that in some countries people drive on the left-hand side of the road, so American software houses were for a long time ignoring languages other than English. International portability is very important in the reenginerering of multinational corporations.

• *Versatility* indicates to what extent the system can cope with the differing needs of users. For example, a versatile payroll system or student registration system should be usable in more than one setting, and a versatile document preparation system should provide novices and experienced users with different modes of interaction with the system. Besides increasing development costs, versatility tends to increase learning time. A thorough cost-benefit analysis is therefore essential with regard to this attribute.

• *Reusability* relates to the construction of a system from existing components. In designing a system, the interfaces between components of the system should be kept simple in order to improve the reusability potential of the components. Reusability is somewhat related to modifiability because the existing components may have to be adapted to new needs. In the reengineering context, reusability relates to the smooth incorporation of legacy software into the software of the reengineered organization (see Chapter 29), and to the design of process support systems in such a way that parts of this software can be used in other settings.

• *Understandability* relates to the interpretation of the system and of its documentation by the users of the system. This is a component of *human engineering*, which deals with the physiological and psychological aspects of human–machine interaction. It is always a good idea to build on understanding that is already there. For example, in replacing a system with a new system, as much as possible of the old human–machine interface should be preserved (unless, of course, user dissatisfaction with the old interface mandates a change). Understandability contributes greatly to user satisfaction. Some requirements engineering guidelines suggest that a user manual be developed as part of requirements documentation, and that the understanding of the user manual be extensively tested with user representatives. Since the manual has to be a full description of the system as seen by the user, the manual can serve as a substitute for a prototype in eliciting user reactions to the proposed system.

Security, i.e., the protection of a system against unauthorized access, is also often listed as a software quality issue. It is not regarded as such here, because security relates to the management of an entire computing facility. In very special cases, a second level of protection may have to be provided for a particularly sensitive process system—this then would be a requirement specific for this system.

Verifiability and understandability are attributes that every system should possess. Other attributes may be very important for one software system, and of no importance whatever for another. For example, there is no virtue in designing for portability if the likelihood of the system being used in more than one environment is very low. All of the attributes listed above share two characteristics. First, they are not measurable, or at least not easily measured. Second, they are additional restrictions of functional requirements. We now turn to reliability and performance. Both of these quality attributes can be measured, and reliability is a relaxation of the functional correctness requirement in the realization that large software systems that fully satisfy their functional requirements are next to impossible to build.

• *Reliability* relates to the preservation of a software attribute, generally functional correctness, for a stated period of time. If the software contains no faults, then reliability is perfect; but few software systems are without faults. High reliability, particularly with respect to functional correctness, has been the main aim of software developers. Lately we have begun to understand that reliability has to be related to the intended use of a system. In particular, we should clearly distinguish between *correctness* and *risk*. There is no great harm (only annoyance) when a text processor does not cope with quote marks within a mathematical formula. In a different context, a comparable fault could lead to a respirator being switched off or a pension fund selling off hundreds of thousands of shares at a totally inappropriate time. Good engineering practice dictates that sections containing high-risk components should be kept particularly simple. Reliability requirements are stated in quantitative terms, and statistical methods have been developed for showing that a software system meets the requirements. Reliability requirements recognize that software may contain faults that can lead to failures. The next two attributes relate to faults and failures.

• *Failure tolerance* is that aspect of *robustness* that is concerned with criticality of system failure, effect of extended downtime, recovery after downtime, and provision of manual overrides. A robust system preserves as much as possible of the state of the system at the time of failure. If the failure is due to external causes, say a power outage, the system can then be restarted with little effort. If the failure is due to a software fault, the restart can be much more complicated. Moreover, since the cause of the failure is unlikely to be removed until the release of a new version of the system, the failure can recur.

• *Fault tolerance* is the aspect of robustness that relates to the operation of a system under overloading, with invalid inputs, or under exceptional conditions. The system should continue to operate. Good software engineering practice should also protect from accidents. At the time of writing this I had to use two different keyboards each day. My text editor made me hit the "escape" key quite often. Unfortunately, on one of the keyboards, the "break" key was situated exactly where the "escape" key was on the other. Daily I blessed the designers of the Unix operating srystem who had seen to it that the file I was editing was saved before the break took me out of the system.

• *Performance* relates to time. The objective is to get the most done in the shortest time. Actually, these are two objectives—*throughput*, which relates to getting the most done in a given amount of time, and *responsiveness*, which relates to getting a particular task done in the shortest time. In the past, emphasis was primarily on throughput but, with the current widespread use of very powerful personal workstations, performance in this sense is no longer as important. Today we are more concerned with system responsiveness: the user of an information system wants a fast response to a query; a control system must respond to its inputs with a control action within a strict time limit..

Let us now consider performance in some detail. In the early days of computing, nearly everything else was sacrificed in the interests of performance. Then, as hardware costs began their downward slide, performance came to be neglected. This was partly due to the misconception that performance concerns cannot coexist with clear, well-structured, elegant code, that performance improvements require tricky code that nobody understands afterwards. Software developers were advised to work on functionality and hope for adequate performance. If the hopes were misplaced, one supposedly could "fix it later". The fix could be faster hardware or fine tuning of the software. Unfortunately there are limits on hardware speeds, the more serious performance shortfalls are too gross for fine tuning, and, where fine tuning would work, it can easily destroy good structure, elegance, and clarity.

We have come to realize that responsiveness requirements are as important as functional requirements, that both are to to be introduced at the same time, and that compliance to both is to be monitored throughout the evolution of an application system. It can well happen that a prototype built to satisfy functional requirements alone underperforms by a factor of 50 or more. It is unlikely that this kind of problem can be solved with a "fix"; its correction may require costly redesign and reimplementation of the entire system, possibly even a realignment of the hardware–software boundary. It is therefore essential to establish early that one's favorite design can satisfy responsiveness requirements. If it does not, redesign has to take place, which, at this stage of the software development process, should not be too costly.

Every system has a normal mode of operation and exceptions from the normal mode. For example, in withdrawing money from an ATM (automatic teller machine), the normal mode is a sequence of actions that results in the customer receiving the requested amount of money. Under abnormal operation, the customer may ultimately receive the money (after, say, a mistake in typing in the user's PIN has been corrected), but termination of the withdrawal process is more likely. The hardest part in drawing up functional specifications is to think of all that could go wrong, so that appropriate system responses could be specified. A characteristic of a good system designer is a pessimistic outlook—the good designer is good at thinking up anomalous situations.

Fortunately, anomalous situations are comparatively rare, and they are therefore not particularly important in estimating software performance. This means that performance prediction can start as soon as the normal mode of operation of a system has been defined, while functional requirements are still being elaborated as additional anomalous situations are thought up. This does not apply in quite the same way to control systems. The system being controlled operates normally while certain parameters are within given ranges, and the normal mode of operation of a control system is to keep the parameters within their ranges by means of control actions. But responses must be particularly fast in anomalous situations, which are characterized by parameter values outside their normal ranges.

In dealing with performance there are a number of distinct steps to consider. First, responsiveness requirements have to be stated. Mostly they are expressed in statistical terms: "For any 15-minute period of operation of the system, the expected system response time is to be no greater than x seconds, with variance no greater than y," or, to be somewhat less technical, "For any 15-minute period of operation of the system, in 95% of the cases the system is to respond within z seconds." For critical real-time systems, worst-case performance may also have to be stated: "For any 15-minute period of operation of the system, the expected system response time is to be no greater than v seconds, and at no time is it to be greater than w seconds." The worst-case limit is to ensure that corrective action always comes in time to be effective.

Second, an overall system design has to be selected. The initial decision is between a dedicated system and an addition to the load of an existing system. Here, the criticality of responsiveness becomes important. In increasing order of severity the impact of not meeting a worst-case response requirement can be inconvenience, service degradation, service interruption, equipment damage, equipment loss, injury to humans, loss of human life, or major catastrophe. For the last three categories of risk, a dedicated system is essential. When equipment c n become damaged or lost, or when severe service interruption is a possibility, a cost-benefit analysis should suggest whether to invest in a dedicated system.

With a system not dedicated to one specific control function there is the danger that a surge in demand for a competing service will take responsiveness below a safe level. Moreover, even if we can demonstrate that the probability of this happening under *current* operating conditions is much smaller than the probability of the facility being destroyed in a natural disaster, there is the danger that *future* changes in usage patterns will bring about a performance degradation that cannot be tolerated, and this can happen with no prior warning.

Third, several software designs are proposed, which is standard engineering practice. In Chapter 9 we stressed the importance of early modularization, and modules were identified with data types and processes. However, the selection of specific data types and the definition of a process in terms of operations of these data types can have significant impact on performance. To illustrate this we take a toy example—a spelling checker. The bare functional requirements are very simple: Given W, an input text, and D, a dictionary, find all words in W that are not in D, and list them without duplication in alphabetical order. But for performance estimation this is not enough. We need a design. One possible design would define the spelling checker as four sequential tasks: transformation of the input text into a sequence of words, sorting of the words, removal of duplicates from the sorted list, and removal of words that are found in a dictionary from the reduced list. This design need not be the best for all situations. One of several reasonable alternatives would be to compare each word as it is separated out from the text against the dictionary, and put a word that is not in the dictionary into a sorted list if it is not already in the list. The output is this list. A third alternative was outlined in Chapter 9.

The fourth stage starts with the postulation of an operational profile of the system. The performance of each of the competing designs with respect to this operational profile is determined, and the design that gives the best performance is selected for sensitivity analysis in which the effects on performance of changes in the operational profile are examined. Although we may have a realistic understanding of what the operational profile is today, changes over the next few years may be unpredictable. The sensitivity analysis is therefore an essential component of performance estimation. If performance is very sensitive to changes in the operational profile, the alternative designs may have to be reconsidered. Actually, alternative designs do not have to be developed unless the performance characteristics of the initial design prove to be inadequate.

Note here that responsiveness studies do not take place in isolation. Maintainability, reusability, usability, and other nonfunctional requirements are as likely to influence system design as performance. The definition of requirements is therefore intimately linked to system design in an iterative composite process, and after each design change the effects of the change on system responsiveness have to be reexamined.

After performance goals have been established, it has to be shown that they can be reached. During requirements gathering the aim is to avoid serious mismatch between goals and expected performance. If the performance requirement and the corresponding performance estimate differ by less than 25%, say, it is fairly safe to go ahead with the chosen design. First, the estimate may be inaccurate. We can make sure that the inaccuracy is biased in one direction by making consistently pessimistic choices in the performance estimation process. Second, performance requirements can be renegotiated. Third, fine tuning can help. Unfortunately, the scope for fine tuning is limited. The three resources that determine performance are the central processing unit (CPU) and the input/output (I/O) system, which gives access to mass storage devices, such as disks, and, with increasing importance, communication links. Most of our experience with fine tuning has been in trying to reduce demands on the CPU. However, as we shall see further on, the CPU is unlikely to be the limiting resource for most software systems.

The estimate of performance of a software system is determined primarily by the system workload and the characteristics of the environment in which the system will be operating. The workload estimate specifies for each type of process the frequency with which the process is invoked by the system. For example, in a library system, the dominant processes are

- Catalog search
- Borrowing of a copy
- Return of a copy
- Catalog update

The workload estimation is complicated by a nonuniform workload distribution in time. In a university library, return activities peak in the morning and borrowing activities in the afternoon. Returns peak also at the end of the term. This is not so for a conventional lending library where a customer returns a set of copies and, a short time later, borrows a new set of copies. Although the functional specification of the one library can be reused with minimal adjustment in the other setting, differing usage characteristics may require widely differing implementations.

Let us consider an average workload in what follows. Data regarding the average number of copies borrowed and returned, and the number of catalog updates should be readily available. Hopefully, data regarding catalog searches are also available. We consider a large library that holds 3,000,000 copies, with 1% of the holdings out on loan. The average duration of a loan is 7 days. The library is open for 100 hours a week. It is accessed by 50,000 persons, each making an average of 0.5 catalog searches in a week. Users of the library can also find out what they have borrowed. Such enquiries, however, are too rare to matter. Catalog updates are of two types. The status of a copy is updated after each borrowing or return event, and an entry is added to or deleted from the catalog. The status updates will be considered part of the borrowing or return activities, and we shall assume 150,000 catalog additions and deletions in a year. Then we have.

Catalog search	250 per hour
Borrowing	300 per hour
Return	300 per hour
Catalog addition/deletion	30 per hour

Next we have to determine the sequence of more primitive actions that defines each of the activities. Since there are comparatively few catalog additions and deletions, and since such activities can be postponed until the library is closed to the public, we shall ignore these activities.

We assume that a catalog search is by name of author, by title of book, or by a category descriptor. At the first level of search, an index of entries corresponding to the author, the title, or the descriptor is displayed. The index is used to narrow down the search until the search ends in failure (wanted item not in the library catalog or search broken off), or the information pertaining to a particular title appears on the screen. It is highly likely that an interaction that starts with Author=Berztiss will take much less time than an interaction that starts with Author=Smith. Our estimate is therefore an average—we assume that a catalog search requires on the average six accesses to the data base.

Borrowing and return activities also require access to the catalog, but now access is by the identifier of a copy, and the purpose is to update the status of the copy. The sequence of actions for borrowing is

Input of borrower and copy identifiers
Copy id is used to access copy status entry
Status is changed to: On loan to x until date y
Updated status is stored
Borrower id is used to access borrower information
Borrower information is updated
Updated borrower information is stored

The sequence for returning a copy is only slightly different:

Input of copy identifier
Copy id is used to access copy status entry
Borrower id is extracted from status entry
Status is changed to: On shelves
Updated status is stored
Borrower id is used to access borrower information
Borrower information is updated
Updated borrower information is stored

Let us now turn to the characterization of the environment in which the library system is used. It is common practice to think of the environment as a virtual machine consisting of the actual hardware and support software that enhances the hardware, such as the operating system, a data base management system, etc. First consider the CPU. Suppose that it executes 2,000,000 machine level instructions in a second. The average total number of activities in an hour is 880. Since there are 3600 seconds in an hour, we can allocate 8,180,000 instructions to each of our activities. The actual requirements will be measured in thousands rather than millions of instructions executed. Hence we have a safety factor of three orders of magnitude, and contention for CPU access will not be a problem. With CPU speeds what they are today, the only situation in which a CPU fully dedicated to an information-control system becomes a critical resource arises when a complex time-consuming control algorithm is used to determine the correct control response, and the response is required more or less instantaneously.

So our only real concern becomes the number of I/O operations in the accessing of the data base. We assume that each I/O operation in our application requires 100 milliseconds. Our example has been deceptively simple because the workload data were easy to obtain and CPU usage could be ignored. In most situations, estimates are difficult to come by. An appropriate word of advice: "Do not plan a bridge capacity by counting the number of people who swim across the river today." In general estimates tend to be the result of guesswork, but it should be informed guesswork.

One way of arriving at such estimates is by means of a JAD-type workshop (see Chapter 15). The determination of realistic workload estimates by means of JAD is very effective because workload estimates can only be obtained in terms of some sort of design, and the purpose of JAD is to develop rudimentary designs. The initial phase serves to determine the purpose of the project, which allows provisional performance goals to be formulated. The moderator then prepares workshop material that consists of the statement of purpose for the project, typical usage scenarios, one or more high-level software designs, and an overview of performance requirements for different tasks. The user representatives at the actual workshop correct whatever misconceptions the moderator may have had, and system developers change and refine the software designs. Resource requirements to give the required throughput and responsiveness are determined from resource performance data and the performance characteristics of the refined designs.

A strong argument for using off-the-shelf software in preference to customized software is that its performance properties are already known. Since such software, if available and sufficiently reliable, is also likely to be cheaper, its use should be considered first. Only if estimates show that required performance levels cannot be reached with an off-the-shelf product should we investigate the use of customized software for some or all of the functions of this product.

Let us now translate the data base activities into counts of I/O operations. For borrowing and return events, assume that each read from the catalog requires three operations, and each read from the borrower data base requires two operations. In both cases, assume that the address of the data is saved as part of the read, so that the corresponding write requires just a single I/O operation. Then, the total number of I/O operations in an hour is

$$250 \times 6 + 300 \times (3 + 1 + 2 + 1) + 300 \times (3 + 1 + 2 + 1) = 5700.$$

The total time for the 5700 I/O operations is 570 seconds. Considering that there are 3600 seconds in an hour, we are safe with regard to throughput. Next, queueing theory can be used to study the responsiveness properties of our system. Here we merely state that queueing theory analysis of our system shows that responsiveness will not be a problem.

11
The Software Development Process

Disciplined system development has to follow a plan. We discuss how the waterfall model for system development, in which requirements determination is a distinct initial phase, is to be replaced by the spiral model or by specification-based prototyping in which requirements determination is to a large degree integrated with system design. The Software Engineering Institute process maturity levels are introduced.

The most important principle that underlies system development is the partitioning of a large undertaking into manageable components. The first attempt was the "phased life-cycle model". Under this model a system development process is separated into a sequence of well-defined phases. One such model, which has been used at Hughes Aircraft Company, had as many as 17 phases [To79]:

1. Determination of required operational capability
2. Engineering studies
3. Experimental development
4. Concept evaluation
5. System development and allocation
6. Software requirements
7. Preliminary software analysis and design
8. Detailed software analysis and design
9. Coding and debugging
10. Software CPCI (Computer Program Configuration Item) testing
11. Software subsystem integration and testing
12. Software system integration and testing
13. Software/hardware integration and testing
14. System performance testing
15. Acceptance test and evaluation
16. Operational testing and evaluation
17. Operation and maintenance

Note here that this is a model for the development of a composite hardware–software system, where only phases 6–9 deal with the development of *software*, but all six of phases 1–6 relate to requirements engineering. Note further that phases 1–8 produce outputs against which the product of phase 9 is checked in phases 10–17. Thus, part of phase 17 results in a certification that the system satisfies the requirements of phase 1. Similarly, in phase 16, the system is validated against phase 2, in phase 15 against phase 3, and so forth.

Let us extract from the complete life-cycle model just those stages that deal with software alone and modify them somewhat. The result is known as the *waterfall model*. We present this model in Figure 11.1. Unfortunately, several difficulties beset phased life-cycle models.

First, an overlap of phases is inevitable. This mostly relates to requirements elicitation and specification. In principle, these phases should be concerned only with *what* a software system is to accomplish, and not

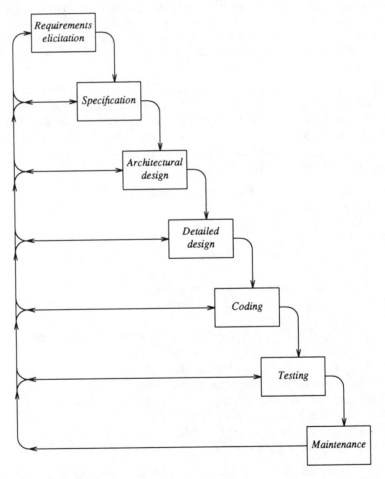

FIGURE 11.1. The waterfall model of the software life–cycle.

with *how* this is to be done. However, often there are additional constraints that force a specification to intrude into the how-to area. Also, as part of the early phases, risk analysis and costing of the project have to be undertaken. It is not clear when and how these are to be done.

Second, the concentration of all testing toward the end of the life-cycle is not particularly cost-effective. Experience shows that the cost to remove faults is much lower in early forms of the software system (the specification) than in later forms (a fully integrated system in operation). The ratio of their costs may be as high as 1 : 1000. High costs arise if the return line in Figure 11.1 has to be followed all the way from "Maintenance" to "Requirements elicitation." This happens when the initial requirements have been misunderstood by the software developers, and the misunderstanding is not discovered before the system has been in use for a while.

Third, since the costs of implementing user-suggested noncorrective changes are also lower when the suggestions are made early, users should be exposed to prototype versions of a system very early, so that they can suggest improvements when the cost of such improvements is not yet very high.

Fourth, the software system itself should be partitioned into manageable components, the modules of Chapter 9. Under the phased life-cycle model modularization occurs in the architectural design phase. But it should take place at the very beginning of the software development process, particularly in the business reengineering context. In the reengineering plan of Chapter 4, process identification is step 5. Each process is normally associated with a software support system, and the support system can be split into subsystems, as was the airline marketing system in Chapter 8. During process identification a vocabulary is established that is shared between the reengineering personnel and process participants. The most important objects that they talk about become the data types that are kernels of modules. For example, in defining banking processes, modules would arise based on accounts, bank employees, bank branches, and so forth. These modules become associated with appropriate processes, and they constitute the information components of the process systems.

To cope with some of the deficiencies of the waterfall model, Boehm has developed and successfully applied a spiral model of software development [Bo88]. The development of a software system is seen as a path that spirals out from a central starting point (point A in Figure 11.2). The model in Figure 11.2 shows three cycles of the spiral: A to B, B to C, and C to D.

Each cycle of the spiral deals with a particular aspect of system development. For example, our three cycles could define, respectively, requirements elicitation, the generation of a formal textual specification, and architectural design. But these are precisely the first three stages of the waterfall model in Figure 11.1. Some critics have taken this to mean

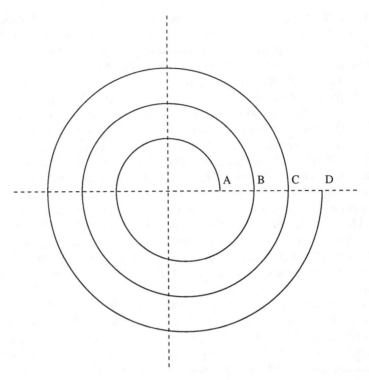

FIGURE 11.2. The spiral model of software development.

that the spiral model is no more than the linear flow path of the waterfall model rolled up, but this is a false interpretation. First, each cycle is a sequence of four distinct phases that require a software team to follow a disciplined cost-conscious pattern of activities. Second, a cycle such as "Requirements elicitation" can be broken down into several consecutive or parallel cycles, each dealing separately with functional, performance, and other requirements. Third, the initial cycle is not requirements elicitation. Instead, it is always a feasibility study, which is to result in a statement of overall system objectives expressed in very broad terms. Risk analysis performed on these objectives provides information that should be sufficient to determine whether or not the project should be pursued further. The four phases of a cycle are as follows:

- *Determination of the specific goals for this cycle*, which includes identification of alternatives for achieving the goals (hardware versus software, reuse of existing software, subcontracting) and identification of resource and quality constraints.
- *Evaluation of the alternatives*, with emphasis on sources of risk. The purpose of this phase is to reduce risk by means of cost-effective

strategies developed by exploratory modeling and simulation studies.
- *The actual development phase*, including validation of the results of this development.
- *Identification of purpose and definition of a plan for the next cycle.* This phase ends with a formal review of the plan for the next cycle.

The spiral model gives excellent structural support for the development of a system that the developers themselves define. Most product software, i.e., software produced in multiple copies for off-the-shelf sale, such as computer operating systems, is in this category. So is the TRW Software Productivity System (an integrated system of 300 tools defined by 1,300,000 lines of code) on which the spiral model was successfully tried out. However, when a custom-made system is developed for an outside sponsor, the spiral model loses some of its effectiveness in that it does not respond well to changing requirements. The software systems that support reengineered processes are prime examples of custom-made systems—the sponsor is the reengineering superteam, and this team cannot freeze requirements for any process system while its understanding of the business aspects of the enterprise continues to be corrected by business domain experts. Three major problems that beset the development of sponsor-defined systems have been identified [Cu88]. Besides inadequate domain knowledge by developers, there is the related problem that requirements keep fluctuating or contain contradictions. The third problem is that software developers are often victims of communication and coordination breakdowns.

The harmful effects of these three problems can be reduced by prototyping. Although exceptional designers are quite good at acquiring domain knowledge in other ways, even they would be helped by a user–developer dialogue supported by a prototype. The information from users is particularly useful when it is in the form of scenarios of system use. Such interaction between users and developers reduces external communication barriers and thus helps stabilize requirements, but internal barriers too are lowered when all members of the development team have the same prototype system to refer to.

Briefly, the main purpose of a prototype process system is to allow users to establish that the developers have a conceptually sound understanding of the process, and to allow developers to determine that user expectations have been met. To this end, a prototype is to provide a user interface and main system components in preliminary versions. A prototype does not in general attempt to satisfy response-time and memory-size constraints, deal with improper inputs and exceptions, provide tolerant responses to system limits being exceeded, or deal cleanly with system crashes and restarts.

Let us note, however, that the term *prototype* has been used with at least three different meanings, none of which corresponds to traditional engineering usage (see Chapter 7). Under the waterfall model, *throwaway* prototypes may have been built in parallel with requirements elicitation, specification, and architectural design, primarily to investigate the feasibility of the system. These prototypes need not have been seen by users, and would have been thrown away at the start of "real" software development. This form of prototyping cannot deal effectively with requirements that remain volatile for a long time, as they may well do during business reengineering, where the understanding of the purpose of a process continues to improve. Under the spiral model, prototypes are used for establishing that the right software functions and user interfaces are being developed, and for selecting between possible alternatives. These prototypes are *evolutionary* in that a prototype constructed in one cycle of the process normally is not thrown away, but is enhanced in the next cycle. But, as was pointed out above, the spiral model is not well suited for the development of systems with volatile requirements. In such a setting we need a *responsive* prototype.

We suggest that a responsive prototype be built early, that it be adapted to user needs, and that the suitably modified prototype be converted into an efficient implementation, preferably by automatic transformations. We regard a requirements document as a program in a very high level language for which an efficient processor does not yet exist. But a requirements document is also a reference base against which the completed system is to be compared. This means that a requirements document and the efficient program that is derived from it must never become inconsistent. The best way of ensuring this is to make all of the changes in the requirements document first. Figure 11.3 is an idealized and grossly simplified overview of this approach.

In Figure 11.3, the "Function allocation" box represents the assignment of process functions to people, software, and hardware. One result of the allocation is an informal software requirements statement that is formalized and structured in the "Requirements documentation" box. The initial input to the "Function allocation" box is from the environment, which is a collective term for various sources of information that we shall look at in Chapters 13 and 14. The outline of the box "Environment" is dashed to point out that the environment is external to the software development process. Some changes to requirements also originate in the environment, and lead to a changed requirements document. Such changes differ from changes suggested by users as part of the prototype test—users are internal participants in the software process.

System specifications are expressed in the form of a "Requirements document". Our recommendation has been that the requirements document be structured in the form of system modules. In general, early modularization serves several purposes. First, reliable cost, risk, and performance estimates can be obtained early. If an estimate is unacceptable, the software project can be canceled while expenditures are

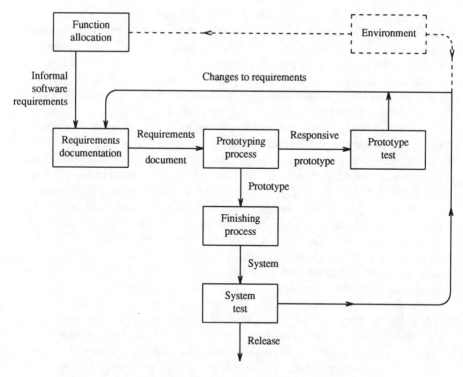

FIGURE 11.3. Prototyping-based responsive software process.

still moderate. Second, the requirements document needs to be given structure, and a modular structure is appropriate for this. Of course, the initial module boundaries can be redrawn later. Third, modularization allows priorities to be set on the order in which different software components are developed. To quote Philip Crosby [Cr84], "quality is conformance to requirements." The requirements documentation process is therefore the most important component of the software development process. It is understood that a technical review of the requirements document is an integral part of requirements documentation. Technical reviews are described in Chapter 22.

The requirements document is submitted to a prototyping process, a prototype emerges from this process, and the prototype is tested. There can be great variability in what the "Prototyping process" and the "Prototype test" boxes contain, and how the two are related. For example, the "Requirements document" may contain an executable specification, i.e., a computer program, in which case there is no need for a separate prototyping process. In some software development processes, the prototype test would be prototype execution with user participation; in others, certain properties of the software system could actually be proven.

The "Requirements documentation"–"Prototyping process"–"Prototype test" loop is iterated until the prototype passes an acceptance review, which we regard to be a part of "Prototyping process". The prototype test assumes particular importance for process systems—such systems are based on conceptual models of the business domains in which they are to operate, and the models cannot be validated without the participation of domain experts and ultimate users of the system.

Testing exposes errors and some oversights, and this leads to changes in the requirements document. Requirements may also undergo modifications when a process system is already in use. Such modifications originate in the "Environment" box, and they represent changes in user needs or in the real-world system that the software system is to model. Examples of real-world changes that will lead to modifications of the requirements are new employee classifications or the elimination of certain tax deductions. With regard to user-suggested modifications, the "Changes to requirements" are actually change *requests*. Each request is reviewed as part of the requirements documentation process, and only approved changes are incorporated into the requirements document.

The accepted prototype moves through the "Finishing process" box in which the prototype is turned into a deliverable system. This may mean the integration of prototypes of several subsystems into a composite system, and the addition of ancillary features such as a help system. We assume that another technical review is part of this process. The composite system is then put through a system test. An alternative is to start with the prototype of a kernel subsystem, perform system tests on this subsystem, and then add prototypes of other subsystems, performing system tests after each addition.

An important characteristic of prototypes of real-time systems is that they rarely provide reliable time estimates. This means that a system that has passed its prototype tests may still fail in the field because its responses are too slow. If the "System test" in Figure 11.3 detects this, then there are three options. First, faster hardware can be introduced. Second, the "Finishing process" can be tuned to improve the program it produces. Third, the specifications can be modified to sacrifice some other properties in favor of improved response times. We hope, though, that early application of performance engineering techniques will have given an accurate estimate of the performance of the system as part of "Requirements documentation".

The one advantage of the waterfall model is that it made each phase of the software process a separate work unit. Each phase in the model of Figure 11.1 is to produce a well-defined work product. This partition of the process is for the greater part lost in the model of Figure 11.3. For example, "Requirements documentation" now encompasses the phases "Specification" and "Architectural design" of Figure 11.1, as well as parts of "Detailed design". However, early modularization replaces the partitioning of the development process with the partitioning of the product that is being developed.

Note that most people use the terms "requirements" and "specifications" interchangeably. We are following this practice to some degree, but, while we use "requirements" to refer to both informally and formally defined properties of a system, we tend to apply "specifications" to formally expressed requirements statements alone. Specifications, then, have to be expressed in precise terms, but precision is difficult to achieve unless the language of specification is a formal language. To emphasize this we often speak of formal specifications rather than just specifications. Nonfunctional requirements, such as reliability, accuracy of results, and response times, are omitted from a formal specification because of the difficulty of expressing them formally and of verifying that the implemented system satisfies these requirements. Often it is impracticable to express even functional specifications formally.

The prototyping-based development plan of Figure 11.3 is at best a generic scheme. Much detail has to be added to define the development plan for a particular software system. The ability to accept a planned process at all, to adapt a generic process structure to actual needs, and to continue to improve the mechanics of how the adaptation is done defines the process maturity level of an organization. Actually, an organization may have reached different maturity levels for different classes of software: A software house may be outstanding at producing computer operating systems for its customers and yet be totally inadequate at developing decision support systems for its own management. Part of business reengineering has to be the determination of the process maturity levels reached by individual reengineering teams and improvement of the process maturity of teams that lag behind the rest of the organization.

The Software Engineering Institute (SEI) has defined five software process maturity levels. At the *initial* level (Level 1) there is no process maturity at all—the "process" is characterized by an unplanned code-and-maybe-test-and-hope-for-the-best attitude. A cost and schedule estimate may be prepared, but, lacking a proper methodology for arriving at reliable estimates, the estimates are nearly always wrong. Unfortunately, software developers at the initial level tend to start each new project in a very optimistic mood. Consequently, they grossly underestimate costs and schedules. This in turn creates a panic when it is no longer possible to ignore the real situation—whatever planning there may have been to begin with is now thrown out, testing is neglected, and documentation of the software is not checked against the software as delivered. Some software developers like this situation—the long hours they put in makes them some kind of folk heroes. Actually, work beyond the limits of human endurance becomes counterproductive. Software development requires a high degree of mental concentration, and such concentration can be kept up for only a limited time. Much software is still being developed by teams at Level 1, and the unreliability of their products is hurting the reputation of software engineering. Teams at this maturity level are obviously unsuitable participants in business reengineering.

To arrive at the lowest respectable maturity level (Level 2), the software process has to become *repeatable*. When presented with two development tasks in the same domain, and of the same size and complexity, an organization at Level 1 can be expected to come up with significantly different cost and schedule estimates. At Level 2, the estimates will not differ by much. In order to reach the repeatable level, an organization has to maintain extensive statistics relating to its past projects.

At Level 3, the process becomes *defined*. To reach this level, an organization has to be able to transform a generic process structure into a detailed definition of the actual process that is to produce a specific software system. An independent software process team is charged with the task of improving the software process. This is an organization-wide unit that assists software development teams in adapting the generic process to their needs and monitors the work of the development teams in order to improve the transformation of the generic into the specific. In a reengineering context, the software process team assists reengineering teams in defining the processes for developing software support systems for their business processes. After the initial reengineering effort, the software support systems will continue to be improved and extended. Each such maintenance task is to be the joint responsibility of the business process team and a software maintenance team, supported by the software process team.

The next step is to arrive at reliable cost and schedule estimates for all projects. Achievement of this aim makes the process *managed*. This is Level 4, and reliable cost and schedule estimates are now available for any system development task, even when the organization has not developed software for the given application domain in the past. In other words, all software development projects can be subjected to adequate management cost controls. This means that the managed level is reached by an organization as a whole. The transition to this level is achieved by defining a set of *standardized* tasks, establishing a costing procedure for each task, and defining the development of a specific software system in terms of the standardized tasks.

At the highest level, the software process has become *optimized*. In order to reach this level, an organization should have automated the collection of process data that are used to improve the software process. For example, these data can indicate that some of the standardized software process tasks are bottlenecks, or that their costs should be reduced. However, optimization is not easy. Different sets of process tasks may have to be defined, and a software process built up in several versions with each version composed of different tasks. Moreover, this merely suggests improvements to a process rather than defining the best of all possible processes.

In the Reading Guide (Appendix B) we discuss some of the literature on the SEI process maturity levels. The model has its critics, and it displays features that could be regarded as anomalies. For example, even a forward-looking company may find it difficult to attain Level 3 if it develops software for a large variety of domains, while a company that produces only computer operating systems may get to Level 5 without great difficulty. But, of course, specialization that improves the process maturity of a company is not against the principles of reengineering. Whatever the critics may say, the SEI model is the most thoroughly engineered contribution to the management of the software development process, and anything that improves the software development process is to be welcomed.

12
Software Cost and Risk Estimation

Cost and risk estimation is a highly skilled activity that requires much experience. It is a crucial part of requirements analysis in that it determines whether or not a system is to be developed at all.

Software costs usually are stated as personnel requirements in terms of person-days, person-months, or person-years. The estimation of costs is a highly skilled undertaking that requires much practice. In the past, estimates tended to be too optimistic, and most projects had cost and schedule overruns. The wider acceptance of software engineering principles, the use of software development tools, emphasis on reusability, structured and object-oriented design and programming, and a greater proportion of the work force with some formal education in computer science or information systems should have eliminated overruns. Unfortunately, this is not the case, for a variety of reasons. First, projects are becoming more ambitious, both in size and complexity. Second, some of the new developments, such as the availability of CASE (Computer Aided Software Engineering) tools and the greater attention given to reusability of software have not yet fully lived up to expectations. Third, the effects of the new developments have been factored into cost-estimation formulas, but with too great an optimism. In particular, since projects have become more ambitious, the observation that the allocation of more personnel to a project in its latter stages may further retard the project is more valid now than ever.

A widely used technique for software cost estimation is Boehm's COCOMO (COnstructive COst MOdel), in which empirical expressions are used to estimate project costs and schedules. The empirical expressions derive from examination of actual completed projects with known costs and schedules.

As was pointed out in Chapter 8, Boehm groups software into classes that are called organic, semidetached, and embedded. The following three expressions indicate the effort (or cost), measured in person-months, required to build a software system estimated to have a size of S thousand delivered lines of code (KDLC):

$$E_{org} = 3.2 \times S^{1.05} \times F$$

$$E_{s\text{-}det} = 3.0 \times S^{1.12} \times F$$

$$E_{emb} = 2.8 \times S^{1.20} \times F$$

The interesting parameter here is F, which stands for a cost-adjustment factor and is the product of cost functions associated with 15 individual project qualifiers. These qualifiers are listed below, grouped into four classes, and each provided with the range of values it may take.

1. Product attributes: required software reliability (0.75–1.40), size of application data base (0.94–1.16), product complexity (0.70–1.65).
2. Hardware attributes: execution time constraints (1.00–1.66), memory constraints (1.00–1.56), virtual machine volatility (0.87–1.30), computer turnaround time (0.87–1.15).
3. Personnel attributes: analyst capability (1.46–0.71), application experience (1.29–0.82), programmer capability (1.42–0.70), virtual machine experience (1.21–0.90), programming language experience (1.14–0.95).
4. Project attributes: use of modern programming language practices (1.24–0.82), use of software tools (1.24–0.83), required development schedule (decrease from 1.23 to 1.00, followed by an increase to 1.10).

By "virtual machine" we mean here the hardware augmented with an operating system, a data base management system, and other ancillary systems. The presence of F makes the model "intermediate" COCOMO; when all cost factors are assumed to have the nominal value of 1, we have "basic" COCOMO. Multiplying first the smallest cost multipliers and then the largest, we see that F can range from 0.0885 to 72.4, the larger value being more than 800 times the size of the smaller and 72 times the nominal value. Despite the quantitative flavor of the figures, they should not be taken too seriously. First, concepts such as "programmer capability" are rather fuzzy, so that one will be hard put to select appropriate numerical values. Second, changes in technology and in our approaches to software development must shift the relative weights of the different qualifiers.

The E-values determined by the formulas given above can be used to compute development times T (in months) as follows:

$$T_{org} = 2.5 \times E_{org}^{0.38}$$

$$T_{s\text{-}det} = 2.5 \times E_{s\text{-}det}^{0.35}$$

$$T_{emb} = 2.5 \times E_{emb}^{0.32}$$

These expressions show that development time cannot be reduced by increasing the size of the development team. For example, if $E = 50$, we would guess that the project could be completed by five persons in 10

months, or by ten persons in 5 months. However, for an organic development process, we get $2.5 \times 50^{0.38} = 11.05$, which means that the project
will take at least 11 months in any case, i.e., that increasing the project
team size above five will not improve matters. The reasons are that it is
difficult to partition a project requiring 50 person-months into more than
five or so subprojects, and a larger team introduces a higher intrateam
communication overhead.

Lines-of-code counts have come under considerable criticism. For
example, they make it difficult to compare programs written in different
languages—some programming languages allow a terse style while others
encourage verbosity. Even when the same language is used for the same
task there can be great variability—in an experiment in which 27 versions
of a program were developed, the size of the programs varied from 327 to
1004 LOC [Kn86]. Just as the volume of an object is not a good predictor
of its weight, so the length of a program is not a good indicator of what it
accomplishes. The search was on for a measure of the "weight" of a
software system, which should lead to more accurate cost and schedule
estimates.

One such measure is function points (FP), which was introduced by
Albrecht in 1979, and has gained wide acceptance, particularly among
developers of business information systems. Under the function-point
methodology, the "weight" of a software system is determined by five
parameters—external input types, external output types, internal file
types, external interface file types, and external query types.

External input types comprise types of inputs that change the information base of the system or exercise some kind of control over the
system, such as an input from a sensor. External outputs can be printed,
such as reports, checks, or work schedules, or they can be displayed on a
screen. Logical internal and external file types measure the size of the
information base of the application. For example, each table of a relational data base that belongs exclusively to the application system
counts as an internal file type. However, if a table in a relational data
base is accessed by several application systems, then the table is counted
as an external interface in all of these systems. Finally, each input/output
combination that does not change the information base is counted as an
external enquiry type. The counting of the different types is relatively
easy, although opinion may be divided on how different the formats of
two reports have to be for the reports to belong to two external output
types.

Next the raw counts have to be weighted, with the weights assigned
according to the complexity of a type. For instance, the weight of an
external input type may lie between 3 and 6, the weight of an internal file
type between 7 and 15, and the weight of an external interface type
between 5 and 10. The sum of the weighted counts is the *UFP* (unadjusted
function points) parameter. This parameter is adjusted to take into

account the technical complexity of the application, and the final adjusted count is given by

$$FP = UFP \times (0.65 + 0.01 \times DI),$$

where DI, the total "degrees of influence", is obtained by assigning a degree of influence value between 0 and 5 to each of 14 application characteristics and adding the values. Typical application characteristics are end-user efficiency, complex processing, and installation ease.

In the past, the internal structure of information systems tended to be very simple, but, if an information system is to make complex decisions, i.e., if it becomes an information-control system, the internal structure gains importance. The "complex processing" characteristic is then no longer an adequate indicator of the structural complexity. Capers Jones [Jo91] has realized this and added a sixth parameter—a count of algorithms.

The DI is similar to the cost adjustment factor F of COCOMO, but there is the major difference that in computing DI its constituents are added, whereas the constituents of F are multiplied. By analogy to other fields in which the composite effect of different influences has to be considered, such as probability theory, a multiplicative adjustment factor appears to be more appropriate than an additive factor. This may be one reason why COCOMO, which has become somewhat antiquated, continues to hold its ground. Even if neither methodology is put to use in cost and schedule estimation, the COCOMO project qualifiers or the processing characteristics of the FP methodology give rise to a useful checklist of factors that affect software productivity. That is why we have listed the COCOMO qualifiers in full.

Even with cost and schedule estimates developed by personnel highly skilled in the use of the FP or COCOMO approach, there remains a risk of cost and schedule overruns. Risk cannot in general be avoided. We cannot prevent all fires, but we can take out fire insurance. We cannot prevent all programmer errors, but we can use reliability analysis to estimate their extent. The objective is to weigh risks against benefits, which is a positive attitude to risks. If we did not take such positive attitude, then surgery, which can result in death, would never be undertaken.

Software risks are of two kinds: those relating to the development of the software and those relating to the effects the software system may have once it is put into use. Let us call them *development risks* and *operational risks*, respectively. Development risks have the following three major causes:

Poor management
Poor user–developer interaction
Project technically impracticable

Since risk identification and analysis are management activities, it is only to be expected that the largest number of the more important risk factors relate to strict management functions. They are (1) unrealistic cost and schedule estimates, which are based partly on unrealistic assumptions regarding the availability and capability of key personnel; (2) inadequate screening and monitoring of suppliers and subcontractors; (3) inadequate monitoring of the performance of in-house personnel; (4) abdication of management control in the face of changing requirements, such as acceptance of a continuous flow of demands for additional features from a sponsor, or nonadherence to requirements by developers, such as "gold-plating", which is the addition of features that are not asked for in the requirements; and (5) no contingency plans or insurance provisions for dealing with disasters such as fires and flooding, industrial actions such as strikes and sabotage, or delays caused by suppliers and subcontractors, or delays caused when sponsors are slow in delivering requirements or do not participate in system reviews and system acceptance tests.

Management should ensure that there is adequate interaction between system developers and the ultimate users of a system. Lack of interaction with users can lead to (1) interfaces that cause psychological or physiological stress in users, or do not adequately correspond to the conventions of the application domain; (2) incorrect system responses in control applications; and (3) information bases that do not contain all of the information needed to support a process or that are cluttered with data for which there is no real need, which we call the "store everything syndrome". Poor user–developer interaction can result in prospective users refusing to have anything to do with a process system, or in extensive redesign after the initial implementation. Both situations are very costly.

Risk due to poor management skills or poor user–developer interaction can be controlled by improved education. Moreover, management should have adequate technical background to cope with the third class of risk, i.e., to realize when a proposed system strains or exceeds physical limits. For example, combinatorial explosion can raise expected process execution time to astronomical levels. Early detection of such a state of affairs will prevent resources from being wasted on process software that cannot succeed.

Risks that relate to development are not explicitly stated in process requirements, but they may suggest that a reengineering project should be scaled down, which would lead to a new set of requirements or possibly even abandonment of the project. Control of operational risks, on the other hand, has to be captured in requirements. In short, operational risks arise from poor quality control, where by quality we mean functional correctness as well as an amalgamation of all of the attributes discussed in Chapter 10. Poor control of operational risks can lead to process participants refusing to make full use of a process system, thus undermining the reengineering effort. Even more serious are system faults that lead to positive damage, e.g., a national telephone network out of service for 12 hours, an air traffic control system that crashes without allowing for a smooth changeover to manual control, an air–defense system that shoots down friendly aircraft. Again, if risks are too high, a project may have to be abandoned.

Just as risks relate to software development and software use, so do software costs. Software engineers usually concentrate on development costs and ignore usage costs and benefits. In the reengineering context, the emphasis should be reversed. Here, the relevant question relates to usage: To what extent will a reengineered process reduce costs and improve benefits? Still, the cost of putting a reengineered process into place is not to be ignored either. The practice of having ISD personnel alone deal with development costs, and personnel of other units with usage costs should be discontinued. Both costs should be considered together, with the participation of all concerned parties.

III
Business Analysis

13
Analysis of Business Activities

Most of the processes with which a reengineered organization will be concerned already exist in some form in the organization. The processes are redefined as requirements documents. A more radical approach is to redesign an organization without any regard for what already exists.

In 1869, John Roebling was competing for the Brooklyn Bridge contract. His strategy was to take a party of 21 engineers and politicians on a tour of inspection of suspension bridges he had already built in Pittsburgh, Cincinnati, and Niagara Falls. The sponsors were turned into believers in suspension bridge technology. The outcome: The Brooklyn Bridge was to be a suspension bridge and Roebling won the contract. Very often, examination of what already exists *and works* can be valuable in suggesting the approach to take.

When we turn to the reengineering of a business enterprise, we may find that the enterprise already has a well-designed set of software systems that define the main processes of the enterprise. For example, the CIO may have always regarded order processing as a single process, but the existing departmental structure has colored the definition of the process and has prevented any real gains to be made from the process view. Then the task may be simply to redefine the process in a way that allows reengineering principles to be followed in its implementation. On the other hand, the conceptual model of the operation of an enterprise may have an extreme departmental orientation under which a department is instructed to perform various tasks, does the required work, and sends the results of the work to other departments. Under this view, the entire organization is seen as a network of flows of forms and materials, and it is difficult to identify individual processes.

When it is clearly understood what processes are needed, there are three ways of identifying the initial requirements for a particular process:

- The process to be defined replaces an existing manual or automatic process in the same organization.

- Similar processes exist in other organizations. Consultants are a good source of information regarding this category.
- A similar process is described in the literature.

The first category is by far the most important, and we shall concentrate on it here. We shall discuss two groups of documentation that the reengineering team should try to obtain or produce for a process in this category.

Group I documents

A clear statement of the purpose of the process.
A list of virtues of the existing process.
A list of deficiencies of the existing process.
Physical models of the environment in which the process operates.

While this material is being gathered, there must be a clear understanding of its purpose. Documents in Group I are basic because they are an informal definition of the existing process. In particular, a radically changed process system should not be forced on users who are reasonably happy with the existing system. Of course, a total change of the process may be needed to improve the effectiveness of the organization. Then the solution is to implement the new process system so that it looks exactly like the old system to its users, i.e., so that the user interface is preserved. Close scrutiny of the statement of why the process is to be reengineered may show that the existing software support system is in no need of change. Often, the clearest indication for this comes from an examination of the operating environment of the process. The solution to a productivity problem may be a simple rearrangement of the physical plant to eliminate bottlenecks rather than new materials-tracing software.

The lists of virtues and deficiencies of the existing system can be obtained by face-to-face questioning or by questionnaires submitted to a well-selected cross-section of users. The proper design of the questionnaire is very important because users, who tend to assume that they will find the good features in the reengineered system no matter what, need to be forced into positive identification of the good features of an existing system. This is essential because it indicates those characteristics of the old system that users will expect the new system to possess, and that the new system must therefore have.

In using questionnaires, much attention has to be given to detail. A short checklist of what to consider is as follows:

- Send out a preliminary notice. Before sending out the questionnaire, warn the sample group that the questionnaire is coming and explain its significance in a sentence or two.
- Express all questions in short sentences, and try to make sure that the answers can also be short.

- Keep in mind that many recipients of questionnaires think that they would have formulated much better questions. Allow, therefore, ample space for the respondents' own comments.
- Test the questionnaire against a small control group to determine that they understand the questions as you do.
- Make sure that a deadline is clearly stated, and make the period to the deadline short. Otherwise, the questionnaire may drift to the bottom of some pile of papers, never to be seen again. Send out a reminder to all nonrespondents the very next day after the deadline has passed.
- Recipients of questionnaires should be identified so that respondents providing particularly thoughtful responses may be targeted for follow-up interviews.

The documents in Group II are to provide an *initial* base on which to build in the interviews and group sessions we shall discuss in Chapters 14 and 15. Let us list these documents and then consider them one by one.

Group II documents
Detailed scenarios for user interaction with the existing process system.
Reports that the existing system has been required to produce.
Sample forms used in the operation of the process.
Incoming correspondence relating to the process, particularly complaints.
Existing procedures manuals or user manuals.
Usage statistics, failure reports, and maintenance files.

Detailed scenarios. The reengineering team itself should try out the existing system. After this orientation they can arrange to obtain traces of actual user interactions with the existing system. This can be by direct observation, video filming, or interface traffic monitoring. Permission must be obtained from management and users for the interaction tracing, and, if several modes of tracing are possible, users should select the mode with which they feel most comfortable. It has to be realized that in most cases a system has different classes of users, and that the system looks quite different to the various users.

Reports generated. Many existing process support systems were designed before interactive computing became widely spread, and the processes they support may have been defined back in the 1930s. Such systems emphasize batching of process instances, and reports rather than ad hoc queries. The times of 4-inch thick monthly sales reports should be past, but reports will still be in use, at least for the next few years. For example, aircraft cabin crews use hard-copy seat assignment reports for the final passenger check. Moreover, the reports generated by the old system will give some insight into the information needs of different groups of process participants.

Sample forms. In most enterprises, paper flow is excessive—while computers should have reduced paper flow, shipments of office paper in the United States nearly doubled between 1982 and 1992, approaching 6 million tons in 1992 [Fo94b]. Reengineerings presents an opportunity to simplify forms, reduce their number, and consider machine-readable forms. In principle, an electronic office should eliminate all passing around of paper *within* the office. Again, however, the information needs of process participants can be deduced from existing forms.

Incoming correspondence. This is paper that originates outside the company. Very useful are complaint files because they suggest what manual procedures should be improved or what software functions need to be overhauled. It is important that such files also contain full details of telephoned complaints.

Existing manuals. Existing manuals are important for three reasons. First, they provide an overview of the different services the existing system provides. Second, they define the existing user–system interface, which should be changed only for the weightiest of reasons. A user who has to relearn how to access the system will not be a happy user. Third, sometimes the main defect of an existing process is that manuals are inconsistent with the process system. If this is the case, the existing process structure may be quite sound; the problem is that no one has a clear idea of what this structure actually is.

Usage experience. Failure reports and maintenance files identify software subsystems to which special attention should be given. Subsystems with an unnecessarily complex structure are most likely to generate problems. One of the reasons for reengineering is to have a process with the simplest possible structure. Usage statistics indicate which parts of the system receive the heaviest use. Additional effort will have to go into streamlining these parts.

As was pointed out above, the primary purpose of all of this information is to suggest starting points for individual interviews and group sessions. For some standard processes in which there is little human–machine interaction, such as a payroll program, which in the reengineered company is to become a payroll process that converts performance figures into electronic funds transfers and salary notices, the information obtained by the analysis of an existing system may lead directly to the formulation of requirements for the reengineered process. But this can be dangerous. When too much emphasis is put on the structure of an existing process, the preoccupation with the existing process can become an end in itself. Even when analysis is not carried to such excess, the new process may inherit too much that is outdated.

The best way of guarding against inheriting too much of the existing structure of an organization is to reinvent the organization. This is a top-down approach that starts with the definition of a few high-level process categories. These categories are refined, and the result is a process hierarchy in which the actual business processes are located at the bottom level. In Chapters 2 and 3 we arrived at a management model consisting of three levels in which executive and operational management facilitate the work of self-managing process teams. In keeping with this management model, the process hierarchy should not exceed three levels—the process hierarchy will inevitably become interpreted as a management hierarchy; hence, every precaution has to be taken that this does not become as complex as the departmental hierarchy that the process-oriented organization is to replace.

We shall take a three-level process hierarchy as standard and try to arrive at an understanding of what each level is to contain. We note that with very few exceptions, such as self-sufficient monasteries, every organization has two main concerns—interaction with the outside world, and its own operation, with the second concern subordinated to the first. However, interactions with the outside world are not processes. Hence, a conception of the top level as made up of an external interface process and an internal process that subsumes all operations, which may seem attractive to begin with, does not fully work out. We propose a model in which the top level still has two components, one of which is operations but the other is strategic planning. Strategic planning moves through the middle level of the process hierarchy unrefined, but operations are refined into second-level processes, such as product design, manufacturing, warehousing, inventory management, marketing and sales, order fulfillment, and customer services. We shall see in Chapter 28 that, although the mission of a manufacturing company is quite different from that of a bank, university, or sports team, all organizations need most, but not all, of the second-level processes on our list. For example, product design is as important to universities and banks as it is to makers of aircraft and breakfast cereals, but universities and banks do not manufacture. Some organizations have to go beyond the list, e.g., utility companies, transportation companies, and communications companies have the specialized need to build and operate transportation networks for the transportation of people, or of natural gas, or of messages.

The external interactions are fairly standard. We have already indicated certain activities that relate to the outside world. They include intelligence gathering, listening to customer complaints, and automatic linkages to other organizations. These important activities eventually will be found in every reengineered organization, although not always under the same names. Note again that they are not processes, but important components of processes that link the outside world to the processes of an organization. Thus, the handling of a customer order relates to inventory control and may trigger a production run in the factory. Also, a customer is to be able to get an immediate answer to a query relating to the status of an order. The linkage is to be provided by information systems, emphasizing the importance of information systems to the operation of reengineered organizations.

Major differences between organizations become apparent when we consider their internal operations. It may appear natural to partition the internal operations into operations that contribute directly to the provision of goods and services, and operations that provide support or exercise control over the organization itself. Among the latter are human resource management, financial management, and legal services. In Chapter 6 we saw that one characteristic of these operations is the difficulty of quantitatively determining the value they add. Although we shall adopt the partition in Chapter 28, the partition is not as natural as it may at first appear. Some organizations will want to keep these operations as central support and control services because queueing theory tells us that centralization allows better utilization of personnel engaged in these services. On the other hand, if these services are distributed among processes, they provide their users with more convenient access, user problems are better understood, and problem situations can be spotted in time for preventive intervention.

A special status should be given to research and development (R&D), which must be separated to some degree from the other activities of an organization so that research is not limited to already existing product lines—R&D should survive as an independent department in a reengineered organization. We may actually consider R&D as a quasi-separate organization, to be reengineered in an effort that is distinct from the reengineering of the organization as a whole. However, R&D must be closely linked with intelligence gathering, and R&D is pure waste if its findings are not translated into products.

The third level in the process hierarchy of an organization, which is the real basis for the reengineering effort of an organization, will differ greatly from organization to organization. In Chapter 8 we took a brief look at the marketing process of an airline. The subprocesses we considered there belong to the third level in the hierarchy, and they are totally different from the subprocesses that define the marketing activities of, say, a construction company. A way to identify the components of the third level is to start with a clear definition of the purposes of the organization and then convert the definition into requirements for the business processes. Numerous business analysis techniques that support this approach have been proposed and tested in practice. Some of the better known are Business Information Analysis and Integration Technique (BIAIT), Business Information Control Study (BICS), Business Systems Planning (BSP), Critical Success Factors (CSF), and Strategy Set Transformation (SST). We shall not discuss them here, except for a brief introduction to CSF.

In Critical Success Factors analysis as it manifests itself in our context, the aim is to develop a process structure that will assist a company to reach its strategic goals. For this, of course, the reengineering team has to be told what the strategic goals are. The determination of the goals is a function of top management, and this is where the strength of the method lies—top management has to become involved in reengineering in a practical way. Under CSF, process definition proceeds in four phases as follows.

- Obtain a general strategy statement for the company. Examples of what the company may wish to achieve are: increase market share, accumulate a cash reserve for overseas expansion, reduce payroll costs.
- Convert the general strategy statement into a list of specific goals and set time limits on the achievement of the goals. Continuing with the above three examples, the market share is to be 50% within two years from now; the cash reserve is to be $150,000,000 within 18 months from now; within the next five years payroll, adjusted for inflation, is to be reduced by 15%.
- From the goals derive critical success factors. For achieving the market share goal, the following software factors may be identified as critical: maximal use of embedded software in all products, reduction of cost to customers by software reuse, and reduction of customer inconvenience by software quality improvements.
- Use the critical factors in process definition. For our market share example, the processes affected could be product design and the development of embedded software. Under product design, special attention would be given to identifying opportunities for software embedding. To achieve this, the product design process could be made to include a mandatory brainstorming session (see Chapter 15). The development process for embedded software could include: (1) a task that searches a software reuse library for software units that could be adapted for this system; (2) a task that determines the reuse potential of all software units being developed for this system; and (3) emphasis on validation throughout. Here, then, we have introduced the highly specific detail that characterizes the third level of a process hierarchy.

There is not much evidence that indicates just how successful business analysis methods are for defining processes. A major problem is that business analysis is inherently difficult. In trying to reduce the difficulty by converting a general statement of intent into a list of specific goals there is the danger of losing sight of the general intent. Indeed, the general statement of intent may be poorly expressed to begin with. Presumably, the objective in trying to reduce payroll is to improve profits. But it is quite possible to achieve payroll reduction and depressed profits simultaneously—employee morale goes down, key experts are forced into early retirement, a hiring freeze leaves key positions unfilled. A way to cope with this problem is to arrange a workshop in which representatives of all levels of management step through the first three phases of CSF analysis. It helps to have nonmanagement personnel participate in such workshops as well.

However, we state without reservation that the most critical success factor for adequate software support of reengineering is the technical competence and the information systems department's will to succeed. If competence is lacking or morale is low, they have to be built up before any serious reengineering efforts are attempted.

14
Individual Interviews

It is good practice to have some rudimentary requirements statement ready before employees of an enterprise are interviewed. Proper interview techniques are crucial to the elicitation of reliable information.

The use of individual interviews in establishing the requirements for processes has to be looked at from five angles. First, however, we have to do something about the incredibly clumsy tongue twisters *interviewer* and *interviewee*. We shall leave *interviewer* alone but substitute *responder* for interviewee. Now for the five aspects, which are (1) selection of responders, (2) homework by the interviewer, (3) the mechanics of the interview, (4) interpretation of what the responder tells, (5) follow up. Also, a distinction has to be made between the gathering of requirements for an existing process (manual or computerized) and for a totally new process. In the latter case, the group sessions to be discussed in Chapter 15 may have to come before individual interviews.

Selection of responders. Here there are four sources. First, if a questionnaire was used, people who showed better than average care in answering the questions should be considered for interviews. Note, however, that the questionnaire was sent out only to samples from various user groups; thus there always will be the danger of some user group being left out. Also, there are groups of people who are affected by a process or who affect the process without being actual participants in the process. The second pool of responders may be recruited by posting appeals for volunteers on bulletin boards. Gause and Weinberg [Ga89] recount the story of an auditor who was the lone respondent to the bulletin-board appeal, but pointed out a flaw so critical in a proposed $20 million purchasing system that the project had to be scrapped. Third, the responders already identified may suggest other responders. Fourth, very dependable information can sometimes be obtained from recently retired employees. Here the advantages are that the retiree has much experience, has the time to reflect on this experience, and is unlikely to be affected by office politics. While the interviews are going on, an organizational chart should be consulted to determine that some important constituency is not missed and that no serious blunders regarding business manners are committed.

Note that some responders may have to be interviewed more than once. As the interviewers' understanding of the process grows, the questioning can become a more probing coverage of the same material. Follow-up interviews are particularly useful after a process system prototype has been built. Their purpose is to resolve misunderstandings that may have arisen in earlier interviews.

Frequently process definition starts without the consultation of important groups because they do not have an obvious involvement. Although the bulletin-board approach can and should be used to get input from such groups, the reengineering team must actively seek input from the accounting and legal departments. Some process systems must have hooks for audit trails built into them, and this falls within the province of accounting. The legal department should check that the system conforms to government regulations, e.g., with respect to privacy. The legal department will also help out when there is doubt regarding copyright protection of some parts of the new process system.

Homework by the interviewer. This we give as a list of items to which the interviewer has to give special attention. The list is by no means exhaustive, and may have to be modified to take into account the corporate culture of the company at which the interviews are carried out. The tasks for the interviewer are as follows:

- Get clearance for the interview from the supervisor of the prospective responder.
- Schedule an interview well ahead of time.
- Ask the prospective responder whether some co-workers should not be interviewed at the same time. People often work in closely integrated teams, and good reactions may be obtained when several members of a team are interviewed together.
- Try to get an interview room where there will be no interruptions.
- Use the information gathered by the techniques in Chapter 13 to define a list of areas to be covered. For each area have a few start-up questions ready. In later interviews, these questions may be suggested by information obtained in previous interviews.

Mechanics of the interview. Here we shall again use a checklist, and again the list is far from exhaustive. The most important principle of successful interviewing is to make the responder feel comfortable throughout the interview, and all of the items in the list relate back to this principle. It has to be faced that some people are better than others at putting responders at ease. Therefore, an important aspect of interviewing is the selection of the interviewers. The do's and don'ts for an interviewer are as follows:

- So that you can concentrate fully on the interaction with the responder, it is a good idea to have notes taken by a third party. You should not take notes yourself.
- This would have already been done when the responder was signed up, but explain again that the information the responder will provide is of crucial importance for coming up with a process to the liking of all participants.
- Do not anticipate answers, i.e., hurry responders along by completing answers. This can lead responders to believe that you know all the answers anyway, and that the responders are not really needed.
- Avoid giving any indication that an answer is what you expected. If the trend in the answers leads you to suspect that the responder is giving "expected" answers, switch to a new area of questioning.
- At times you can become so exasperated with responders' answers that you actually start telling them how they should have used a process system. This will silence them, but information on erroneous use is very important if opportunities for misuse are to be eliminated in the new system.
- When a process spans several departments, responders do not have full knowledge of the entire process system, e.g., a responder may know what outputs a process produces, but nothing about data acquisition. However, they may be unwilling to admit the lack of knowledge. To save embarrassment and to protect yourself from unreliable information, prevent the interview from drifting outside a responder's known area of competence.
- Avoid questions that elicit short answers, particularly yes or no answers.
- Watch the responder very carefully. If there is a marked reluctance to answer a particular question, the reason for the reluctance should be probed, but not in a way that makes the responder uneasy. Perhaps the follow up could go like this: "It seems to me that you expected a different question. What question did you expect?"
- When the responder is a user of the process system, obtain a full picture of this user's interaction with the system. In particular, it is worthwhile to get the user to suggest changes in the user interface. If the user expresses satisfaction with the existing interface, and the satisfaction is genuine, this is an even more worthwhile finding.

Interpretation of responders' answers. Responders will rarely try to mislead the interviewer deliberately. But there is likely to be a cultural barrier between a user and the reengineering team. There may actually be a strong conflict of interests: the user anticipates painful retraining at best and personnel redundancy at worst.

- Some users have unrealistic assumptions about the capabilities of process systems, as in "The computer will think of a way of dealing with this." There is nothing wrong with such statements: simply substitute "software engineer" for "computer" and you have a realistic statement of a user's expectation. The fact that technological limitations may make it impossible to satisfy the expectation is another matter.

• Users sometimes have great difficulty in formulating their real concerns. They may complain about screen layouts, although the real problem may be an indiscriminate use of clashing colors on the screen. Therefore, whatever responders can show, they should show rather than describe. Similarly, a responder may misinterpret an interviewer's question and the interviewer the responder's response, and both may be unaware of this. The solution is to have follow-up interviews after a prototype of the new process system has been built, and to concentrate in these interviews on actual interaction with the system.

• In expressing their dissatisfaction with some feature of a process system, users are often preoccupied with observable symptoms rather than the causes of the symptoms. They should not be blamed for this—it is not their job to deduce the causes, but that of the reengineering team.

15
Group Sessions

Group sessions can lead to many improvements of a given set of requirements. These sessions should be supervised by trained moderators. Two types of sessions are considered, brainstorming and JAD (Joint Application Development).

There are three types of group sessions. First, as was discussed in Chapter 14, responders who interact closely in the workplace may be interviewed as a group. Such group interviews do not differ substantially from individual interviews, and we shall not consider them here. Second, there is *brainstorming*, in which participants egg each other on to come up with ideas for a process definition. Brainstorming can be a very fruitful part of the procedure that defines a new process or product. Third, and somewhere between a group interview and brainstorming, is Joint Application Development (JAD) and Participatory Design (PD), which we introduced in Chapter 5, and the Delphi method. Here we shall discuss brainstorming, JAD, and Delphi.

In the reengineering of an existing process there are the attributes of the old process to look at. In defining a totally new process or product, a list of attributes has to be *created*. This creative effort is the function of brainstorming. Brainstorming has three distinct phases: the first is to identify groups that have or should have something to say about the new process or product; the second is to generate ideas—this is the real brainstorm; and the third is to extract from the list generated in the second phase those attributes that are to be built into the new process or product.

A very effective mechanism for the first phase is a conference set up by electronic mail. A convener starts it all off by identifying a small set of constituent groups, selecting a representative for each group, and sending out to the representatives

- a brief description of the process or product to be developed;
- a list of constituent groups, with the motivation of why each group has been selected;

- a request to add to the list new groups, with motivation, and, if possible, to suggest a representative of the group;
- a request to return the augmented list to the convener.

The convener remains the final arbiter of which new groups are to be be added to the master list and who are to be asked to suggest still more groups. Note that brainstorming teams can be large.

In the second phase, the brainstorming team is assembled in a secluded comfortable room. The convener explains the process or product that is to be developed, states the rules of the game, and starts the team off by suggesting a few attributes for the process or product. Some of these attributes must be outlandish, even downright silly, which introduces the first rule of brainstorming:

Be creative. Original ideas are to be encouraged, even when they seem silly, as long as the session does not degenerate into a competition of who is the better stand-up comic. Many of the most familiar things we see around us started as outlandish ideas. It is a wonder there are automobiles—everyone knew that they were totally impracticable the way they scared horses. Even the inventor of the wheel must have had a hard time—everyone knows that wheels gouge out unsightly ruts in soft ground.

Creativity can be easily stifled, and the only function the convener has after the initial introduction is to prevent such stifling, which takes us to the second rule:

Do not criticize. Both criticism and praise (which is implied criticism of ideas that are not being praised) must be avoided during brainstorming. There is plenty of time afterwards to sort out the ideas that are to be pursued from the ideas that will be quietly dropped.

A ban on criticism does not mean that ideas that have already been presented cannot be modified. Hence, rule three states:

Build on what exists. This is the feature that distinguishes brainstorming from other methods of requirements gathering. The group dynamics encourages participants to improve what is already there, introduce variants, and combine ideas. This means that all of the ideas already generated must be in full view of everybody. They may be written on blackboards, large sheets of paper, or foils to be projected on screens. The writing can be done by the person with the idea, or the idea can be called out to be recorded by assistants designated for this purpose.

The suggestion that ideas be written on overhead projector foils is a brainstorming idea I had while writing this. Probably it is impracticable because of the fourth and final rule:

Produce quantity. Most of the ideas generated in a brainstorming session are discarded, but they must still be produced to help come up with the good ideas. First, an idea may be impracticable as is, but a mutation of it need not be. Second, if the ratio of usable ideas to those that are not is fairly constant, we will generate more usable ideas by generating a greater total number of ideas.

The overhead projector idea has the drawback that the more ideas that are generated, the more projectors are needed. Even if the projectors were available, they would clutter up the room too much.

The next stage is to "validate" the ideas. A mass of ideas is to be converted into a workable initial requirements statement. This task can be carried out by the same group that generated the ideas, preferably at a second meeting. Various voting schemes can be used to come up with a ranking of the ideas. An alternative is to apply previously established selection criteria to the ideas. If this is done, the selection can be made by the convener alone, and then there is no need to call a second meeting. However, it may be politically wiser to have the brainstorming group perform the validation as well.

An interesting exercise in brainstorming is the design of an ideal brainstorming facility. We now have some idea of the brainstorming process, and of some of its shortcomings. One problem is that while some of the participants would have no qualms about calling out the most bizarre suggestions, others would. Even worse, participants can become reluctant to make suggestions that are not bizarre. Examples of product development where brainstorming could assist are novel features for an elevator system, novel features for a telephone, and new services an ATM should provide. In one brainstorming session that I moderated we were to come up with requirements for an updated ATM. One suggestion was that the ATM should handcuff anybody detected using a stolen bank card. This outlandish suggestion led to a variant that was worthy of further analysis: photograph the user of the stolen card and notify the police.

Brainstorming is not well suited for the definition of the processes that are to be reengineered, but it can be made a component of such processes. For example, the marketing process for an airline, which we considered in Chapter 8, could require that the frequent flyer program be subjected to periodic "rejuvenation", with suggestions for new initiatives obtained by means of brainstorming.

Sometimes we have a situation in which we already have a good understanding of the purpose of a process or product, and of what its key attributes should be, but would like to get quick input from many different user constituencies. A reengineered product development process should put much emphasis on this step. An example is a new elevator system for an office building with a restaurant on the top floor. Here we would like to have inputs from representatives of at least the following groups:

children	foreigners	office personnel
cleaners	handicapped people	restaurant patrons
delivery personnel	maintenance personnel	security personnel
elevator inspectors	movers	visitors

Let us look at a few of the groups. Children have to be considered because unaccompanied children do visit their parents' offices, and elevator controls are often out of their reach. (One of the games children love to play in hotels is to get on an empty elevator, press every floor button, and hop off again. This problem does not have to be considered in our case because such games are unlikely to be played in an office building.) Foreigners may not be able to understand instructions. Under the heading of handicapped people we have to consider deaf persons, blind persons, and people in wheelchairs. The three groups may each have their own problems. For example, if there is voiced information, a deaf person will not receive the information. Neither will the foreigner, who has a much better chance of understanding written than spoken language. Office personnel may form several groups as well. The ones with offices on lower floors may have quite different problems from those on higher floors, and they may look at the elevator quite differently depending on where the cafeteria is located relative to their floor.

A technique to use in such a situation is JAD, which we began to look at in Chapter 5. Under JAD, prospective users and developers of a new product to be created or a process to be reengineered meet each other in a moderated workshop that may last several days. Users should outnumber developers four to one or five to one. With regard to process reengineering, the task of getting everybody together is handled by the reengineering team in cooperation with the moderator. However, JAD could also be used at an earlier stage, when it is not yet clear what processes would be needed and where their boundaries should run. At this early stage, responsibility for organizing a JAD workshop belongs to the reengineering superteam. There are several phases to JAD, which we describe with reference to the design of a single process.

1. The moderator establishes, in consultation with the reengineering superteam and high-level business experts, the purpose of the process, obtains some understanding of the assumptions underlying the process, and defines the objectives of the JAD workshop. In defining the purpose of a process, consideration should be given to anticipated benefits and to the relation of the process to other processes of the organization. Part of this is the consideration of the effect of future reorganization of the enterprise on the process, i.e., how easy it would be to adapt it to a new configuration of processes. Key participants for the workshop are also identified. All of this is sometimes done in a preliminary workshop, called JAD-Plan. After this, the moderator can use the electronic mail approach

discussed above to have additional participants identified by the key participants. However, contrary to brainstorming, where the motto is "the more, the merrier," the number of participants in a JAD workshop should be strictly limited. First, the cost of a workshop that runs several days becomes significant. Second, there has to be intensive interaction, but in a well-structured manner, and this is difficult to achieve with a large number of participants. As part of the general orientation, the moderator also collects and gets familiar with a subset of the document-ation discussed in Chapter 13. The moderator may spend 1 to 2 weeks on these activities.

2. The moderator prepares workshop material. The most important component of the material is an initial process model, sketched out with little attention to detail. The model can be expressed using any of the forms of presentation to be discussed in Part IV, alone or together with other forms. The purpose of the workshop is to refine this model by going through several iterations.

3. The workshop takes place. The moderator presents the initial model, and detail gets added piece by piece by the participants. The workshop can have a totally "low-tech" flavor, with the model being expressed entirely as natural language statements. At the other end of the scale there can be a "high-tech" setting in which every participant has a graphics terminal connected to a central data base of diagrams, and the presentation of ideas is by manipulation of diagrams, such diagrams being projected on a screen for everyone to see. The purpose can also vary, from clarification and expansion of natural language requirements to the development of a working prototype of a process system.

A JAD workshop format can be particularly effective for implementing the Critical Success Factor methodology of Chapter 13. The JAD approach is a comparatively recent development, and it is not yet clear at which end of the sophistication scale it is more effective. However, workshops in which effective use is made of groupware (see Chapter 30) are gaining in popularity. Although, as with all sophisticated technology, the tech-nology can do more harm than good if it is used in an unsophisticated manner.

The main advantage of the JAD approach is that it allows instant validation. If the result of a JAD workshop is a prototype, then it would have been built under constant scrutiny of the inputs that define it, and the consistency of the prototype with these inputs would have been checked as work progressed. Moreover, representatives of the various user groups would speak up if they saw the prototype acquiring some unexpected features. But it is not often that the outcome of a JAD workshop is a working prototype. The product is more likely to be a *well-inspected* set of requirements as defined at the beginning of Chapter 22. Since requirements in such a form can be rather easily converted into a prototype afterwards, the use of expensive JAD workshops to build prototypes as actual program code may be inefficient.

We noted that JAD workshops should be well structured. One way to achieve structure is to use the Delphi method. Throughout this book we emphasize cost-benefit analyses, but it has to be admitted that such analyses are hampered by the difficulty of quantifying benefits. This is where the Delphi method can be of great help.

The Delphi method was developed in the early 1960s as a way of reaching a consensus group decision. Let the quantification of benefits be our example. Given a particular business process and a broadly framed statement of what the process is to achieve, the benefits to be derived from the process are to be determined at a JAD-Plan workshop. Its participants are asked to state what they see to be the benefits of the process as defined, and to state in monetary terms how they value each benefit. Reasons have to be given why each benefit is considered important, and a detailed explanation is to support the value estimate. Each member of the group does this independently, the responses are collected and collated by the moderator, and the collated results are circulated to the group again. It is expected that the experts, on examining the reasoning given by the other experts, will modify their estimates. Again, supporting arguments for the modifications are required. The new responses are again collected and collated, and sent out to the group to start a new round of the Delphi process. The expectation is that, after a few rounds, the experts will have reached consensus.

Delphi was originally not intended for workshop use. The participants were to be anonymous, which was to reduce such adverse effects of face-to-face meetings as a tendency to cling to one's initial views, dominance by a single individual, introduction of irrelevancies, and societal pressure. On the other hand, the moderator had to put considerable time into the management of the responses, and the process tended to drag out in time. These adverse effects are eliminated when Delphi is based on groupware and anonymity is preserved. Participants now gather in a room equipped with networked workstations and a large display screen. Their inputs are picked up by the moderator's workstation totally anonymously, structured with the help of groupware tools, and displayed on the screen for all to see. The procedure follows closely a "classical" Delphi process but is compressed from weeks into hours. However, the time compression may lead to estimates that have not been given enough thought.

The network-based Delphi can also be run without the presence of all participants in the same room, looking at a large screen at the end of the room. The participants can be sitting at their own workstations, which may be geographically dispersed, even over several continents. The moderator then flashes the collated responses onto their workstation screens. This can be done in the single-room setting as well, so that there does not seem to be any significant difference between the single-room and the distributed approach. There is one, though: at some point, after the group has gone through a few rounds, the moderator may change the format of the session to a face-to-face discussion, thus introducing group dynamics into Delphi. Note that we already have the technology for distributed "face-to-face" meetings; only its high cost is preventing wider use of this technology. A teleworkshop format is suitable for both the JAD-Plan and the JAD workshop itself.

16
Business Process Prototyping

A specification must express process requirements unambiguously, and a specification language must facilitate demonstration of whether the system defined by a specification will have a particular property or exhibit a particular behavior. A specification language should preferably be executable. It is then a prototyping language. Interaction of business domain specialists with the prototype is likely to suggest changes to process requirements.

The 1981 survey of software project managers that we introduced in Chapter 7 [Th81] found that incomplete, ambiguous, inconsistent, and unmeasurable requirements caused the managers their greatest headaches. The suggested solution was to develop requirements iteratively, that is, to build a prototype. In 1986, Brooks [Br86] outlined three workable approaches to improvement in software productivity: spread costs by developing adaptable products; produce great designers; let a system evolve from a prototype. In 1988, Curtis et al. [Cu88] in interviews with project personnel found that the three main problems were a thin spread of application domain knowledge among system developers, fluctuating and conflicting requirements, and communication and coordination breakdowns. It was suggested that all three problems were to be tackled by prototyping. All of the arguments for the prototyping of software apply in the reengineering context, and in Chapters 5 and 15 we have already given some consideration to prototyping as a component of group reengineering workshops.

The main purpose of prototyping is to establish that the requirements for a process in a reengineered organization are sound. The prototype relates to the software system that is to support the process. This is the most important process component that must be got right—in general, redesigning a software process system is much more difficult and much more expensive than changing the way humans participate in a process (provided, of course, that they have accepted the process concept itself). If a user's interaction with the prototype takes place in the presence of the reengineering team, the latter is to take note of all manifestations of the user's dissatisfaction. As was implied throughout Chapter 14, candidates for initial interviews should be users who have shown special interest in the process system. In selecting candidates for interaction with a prototype, it is important to gather a more representative sample of users. The enthusiastic user will be willing to adapt to features of the system that are less than satisfactory. Not so the disgruntled user, and the reengineering team should pay particular attention to complaints from this class of users. Where possible, causes for their dissatisfaction should be eliminated. Always remember, though, that everybody cannot be satisfied—a feature on which one group of users looks with favor may be thoroughly disliked by another group. For example, the casual participant in a process appreciates being taken through an interaction step by step by an active help system; an experienced member of the process team finds the "help" system unbearably intrusive. But, if they are aware of such user polarization, process developers can design the help system so that it can be switched on or off, depending on each user's particular needs.

The form of the requirements document for a process system will be described in detail in Part IV. Briefly, it consists of unambiguous statements in a natural or formal language, process and information base diagrams, and, possibly, a prototype definition. When several design choices for a prototype are feasible, the reasons for selecting a particular design are preserved for later reference. Prototyping should eliminate obvious contradictions, and all suggestions for changes in the process system requirements should have been acted on, i.e., in terms of Figure 11.3, the prototype is ready to enter the "Finishing process" box.

From that point on, every change to a process system is to become effective only when approved by a change review panel. Changes are submitted to the panel, the panel acts on them, and both positive and negative decisions of the panel, with full motivation, go into a change review file. It should be recognized that there are two kinds of changes: those that are being suggested while a process is still being defined, and those that arise after a process team has taken over the reengineered process. An effective panel for reviewing change suggestions of the first kind is the reengineering team itself; review of change suggestions of the second kind should be undertaken by some or all members of the process team in consultation with an information systems specialist who is to evaluate technical aspects of the suggestion. A change normally belongs to one of the following types:

• Elimination of faults. In designing a complex process with many interacting components, it is impossible to think in advance of all combinations of circumstances that may arise, especially when the process interacts with other processes in a complex way.
• Elimination of subtle inconsistencies, e.g., inconsistencies that

extend across processes. Thus, process participants should not have to adopt different interaction styles with similar processes.

• Essential changes mandated by management, which may arise from changes in government regulations, industry standards, or company policy.

• Nonessential changes. The need to have each change formally submitted, and have it approved by a change review panel should discourage frivolous changes. Although all nonessential changes should be discouraged, it is essential that a process continues to be improved. The owner of the process should assess decisions of the change review panel and step in if the panel becomes too liberal or too conservative.

As a generic definition of a prototype, it should provide a user interface, and the main system components in preliminary versions. As we already noted in Chapter 11, it has two main purposes: to help business domain experts determine that the system is conceptually sound, and to help system developers establish that the expectations of process participants have been met. It does not usually attempt to:

• satisfy time constraints;
• deal with improper inputs and exceptions;
• generate error messages;
• include a help system;
• provide tolerant responses to overloading;
• deal cleanly with crashes and restarts.

However, this simple outline does not give a full picture of prototyping. To begin with, prototypes can be classified along two axes—according to their purpose, or according to what happens to them after the prototyping phase. With regard to purpose, we can identify the following:

• Exploration of a process domain with the participation of domain experts. Some examples of possible misconceptions will be given at the end of Chapter 22.

• Development of user interfaces. A user interface is the point of contact between a process participant and a process system. Participant satisfaction depends to a very large degree on proper interface design. However, interface design should not become the dominant activity of process system developers—the system represents the substance of the process, and the interface merely accesses this substance.

• Feasibility study of a critical software subsystem to determine whether performance constraints can be met. This is extremely important for real-time systems. For example, extrapolation of results obtained in a prototype study of response time as a function of load can determine whether the system will be able to cope with expected loads under operational conditions. This kind of prototype is not normally needed for business processes, but a process for designing products may have to include response-time feasibility studies.

• Trial and error system development when interaction of the components of a system is too complicated to be properly understood by the system developers. Here the main purpose of the exercise is to develop understanding.

The second classification is based on what happens to prototypes after the prototyping phase. Throwaway prototypes (see Chapter 11) are discarded. Evolutionary and responsive prototypes provide starting points for system evolution. For a long time emphasis was on throwaway prototypes because evolutionary and responsive prototypes do away with the clean separation of phases seen in a waterfall life-cycle model. The development of an operational system by a software process in which the early phases are collapsed into a single prototyping stage just was not taken seriously. The sole purpose of the prototype then was to come to an understanding of user requirements. After this was achieved, the real work began. Such duplication of effort is very wasteful. Consequently, throwaway prototypes are no longer popular.

IV
The Reengineering Blueprint

17
From Natural Language to Entities and Relationships

The processes of an organization are dynamic, but they are supported by an information base that has a static structure. This and the next chapter deal with these two aspects of process definition. Most requirements are initially expressed in natural language. The requirements analyst must try to make the natural language statements unambiguous and verifiable. From these statements the analyst develops a graphical representation of the information base for the processes, which in our case is an Entity-Relationship diagram.

Process requirements originate in various ways. An idea that leads to a requirement may relate to a process that already exists:

Perhaps we could increase lengths of employee holidays for those willing to take them when they cost the company less,

or it may conjure up a totally new process:

Perhaps we should start a book club that offers computing books by electronic mail,

or it may state a definite property that a design process is to incorporate into a product:

The A3 has to react to early warning of any unusual activity that the F2 detects.

To begin with, all of this is very vague: we have no idea how big an increase in the holiday period we are talking about, how the book club is to operate, or what F2 is to interpret as unusual activity.

Let us now turn to actual requirements for a library system, expressed in English, that were given to prospective participants in the 4th International Workshop on Software Specification and Design [Ha87].

Consider a small library database with the following transactions:

1. Check out a copy of a book/Return a copy of a book;
2. Add a copy of a book to/Remove a copy of a book from the library;
3. Get the list of books by a particular author or in a particular subject area;

4. Find out the list of of books currently checked out by a particulai borrower;
5. Find out what borrower last checked out a particular copy of a book.

There are two types of users: staff users and ordinary borrowers. Transactions 1, 2, 4 and 5 are restricted to staff users, except that ordinary borrowers can perform transaction 4 to find out the list of books currently borrowed by themselves. The data base must also satisfy the following constraints:

1. All copies in the library must be available for checkout or be checked out.
2. No copy of the book may be both available and checked out at the same time.
3. A borrower may not have more than a predefined number of books checked out at one time.

To begin with, some of the requirement statements are open to more than one interpretation:

(a) In an analysis of this exercise by Jeannette Wing [Wi88] there is a detailed discussion of the exact roles of staff users and ordinary borrowers. For example, the restriction of transaction 1 to staff users can be read to mean that staff users may check out books only to themselves, or that they may check out books to ordinary borrowers as well. The first interpretation is unlikely to be valid because transaction 4 apparently relates to all borrowers.

(b) On the other hand, there may be a distinction between *borrowing* a copy (for use on library premises) and *checking out* a copy (to take home). Then it makes sense for staff users to check out copies to themselves alone.

(c) The requirements imply that there can exist multiple copies of the same "book", and transaction 5 implies that each copy has an identifier. Then, if transaction 5 relates to copies, should not transaction 4 relate to copies as well? Keep in mind that the requirements permit several copies of the same "book" to be checked out to the one borrower.

(d) Who is the "last borrower" of transaction 5? Suppose a copy is currently checked out to X. Is the last borrower X, or is it the borrower before X? In a case like this, the best approach is to have the writer of the requirements resolve the ambiguity. If the writer is unavailable, try to think of a reason for the requirement. Here, unfortunately, there are at least two plausible reasons: it should be possible to recall a currently borrowed copy, and it should be possible to find the culprit when a returned copy is found to be damaged.

(e) What does "remove a copy" mean? Is every removed copy gone forever (because it is lost or damaged beyond repair), or does removal also include taking it off the shelves for repair? In the latter case, it will be added to the library once more sometime in the future, so that we can have different interpretations of what it means to "add a copy" as well.

(f) In "predefined number of *books*," do two copies of the one book count as one or two? Further, does this number relate to the total number of copies held by a borrower, or the number of copies that can be checked out in a single transaction? Is the limit the same for all borrowers?

(g) The requirements leave much to be inferred from general domain knowledge. Thus, presumably, a copy can only be checked out after it has been added to the library, but before it has been removed, and when it is not checked out to somebody else. These constraints are not stated, although they are no more "obvious" than the explicit constraint 2. Further down we shall use a state transition diagram (Figure 17.1) to make explicit some of the domain knowledge.

Our discussion shows that the given requirements need to be clarified. In particular, the use of the term *book* is unfortunate because it has two commonly accepted meanings, as in "last year we published 47 books" and "we have 50,000 books in our warehouse." We also see a need to add to the requirements. The intent of the requirements should become clearer if they were partitioned into two sets:

I. Requirements that define the query-answering capability of the system, i.e, the structure of the information base of the system.
II. Requirements that indicate how the information base of the system may change.

Our task then is to write requirements for an information system that models a library, where the primary objects of interest are *titles* of books (a new term introduced to avoid the book-copy confusion), *copies* of books, *staff users*, and *borrowers*. We have:

Ia. There exists a set of titles where, for each title, the text of the title, the set of its authors, and the set of subject areas this title deals with are known.

Ib. There exists a set of copies. A copy is in one of five states: available for checking out (AV), checked out (CO), being repaired (BR), lost (L), or removed (R).

Ic. The set of copies is partitioned into disjoint subsets. These subsets are in one-to-one correspondence with titles. For each of these subsets of copies there is a title, but it is left open whether there can exist a title for which the corresponding subset of copies is a null set (a situation that can arise when the title information is entered at the time of placement of an order for the first copy of a title, before the arrival of any copies).

Id. There exists a set of borrowers where, for each borrower, the set of copies checked out to this borrower is known.

Ie. For each copy, there exists a check-out history. The extent of this history is left open, but at least the borrower to whom the copy is currently checked out (if any) is known, as is the borrower to whom the copy was checked out immediately before the last return of the copy.

IIa. The copy of a book can undergo state transitions as shown by Figure 17.1, where the circles denote states, and an arrow from circle X to circle Y indicates that the copy can change from state X to state Y. We omit a full description of the conditions under which the state transitions can take place, except to note that a copy enters the system in state AV (hence the double circle), that a copy lost within the library again becomes available if found within a predefined time period, but that a copy lost by a borrower is removed without going through state L.

IIb. There is a predefined limit on the number of copies in the possession of a borrower, which is the same for all borrowers.

This list of requirements has not covered access control, e.g., that the state transitions of IIa may be initiated by staff users alone, and that the information of Ia is accessible to all users. Now, if each copy carries an identifier that is known to staff users alone, then the use of the identifier as an access key allows only staff users to initiate operations that bring about the state transitions of requirement IIa. We therefore add a further requirement:

IIIa. Title identifiers are known to all users, but copy identifiers to staff users alone. Staff users know the identifiers of all borrowers, but ordinary borrowers know only their own identifiers.

This requirement belongs to a new category—category III requirements relate to nonfunctional properties of the system, or to its mode of operation.

A conceptual model of the data base supporting the application is shown as an Entity-Relationship (ER) diagram in Figure 17.2. Here we use the convention that rectangles represent entity types, ellipses stand for attributes of entities, and diamonds represent relationships. An arrow indicates how a relationship should be read, e.g., the two relationships

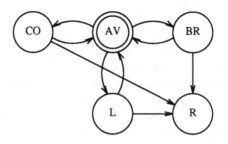

FIGURE 17.1. State transitions of a library copy.

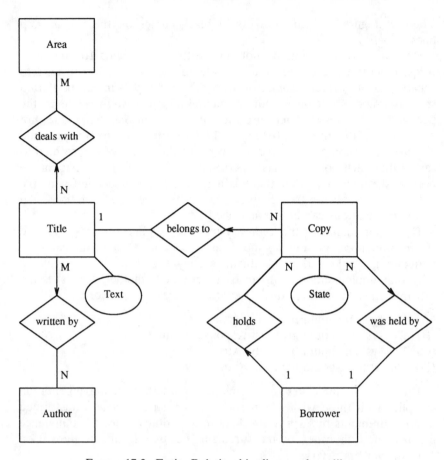

FIGURE 17.2. Entity-Relationship diagram for a library.

linking "Copy" and "Borrower" are read "Borrower holds Copy" and "Copy was held by Borrower." It also indicates how the symbols next to the lines are to be interpreted—our two relations are 1:N (one borrower holds several copies) and N:1 (several copies have had the same previous borrower). The ER diagram, together with Figure 17.1, should make the requirements easier to understand.

In Figure 17.2 we use the traditional conventions for drawing ER diagrams. A more compact drawing that contains exactly the same information is obtained by using conventions developed at the GE Research and Development Center [Ru91]—this is Figure 17.3. Attributes of an entity are now in a box attached to the entity box. Relationships are represented by labeled lines, and the placement of a label indicates how a relationship is to be read, e.g., because "written by" is closer to "Title" than to "Author", we read "Title written by Author." The N and M labels of Figure 17.2 are now small black circles on the relationship lines.

However, our diagrams do not cope with requirements IIb and IIIa. Requirement IIIa does not really relate to the system, but instead to capabilities of different classes of users. The same person can be both a staff user and a borrower, but all queries in our system relate to the person as a borrower. Therefore the entity class of *Staff User* does not even appear in Figure 17.2 (or Figure 17.3). With regard to IIb, we could allocate an attribute *Limit* to *Borrower*, but this could be interpreted as saying that each borrower has a personal limit on the books that can be borrowed rather than that there is a general limit associated with the entire class of borrowers. (However, with extended ER notations, the two interpretations can be distinguished.)

The requirements for the library system as given in categories I, II, and III are now hopefully unambiguous (as far as natural language can ever be unambiguous), and, *if* unambiguous, they are verifiable, i.e., given a particular implementation, it can be determined whether it satisfies the requirements. Let us now turn to a different class of sponsor wishes:

(A) The system should be user-friendly.
(B) The system should give fast responses to queries.
(C) The system should be easily extendible.
(D) The system should have very little downtime.

There is no simple yes or no answer to whether an implementation complies with these wishes, but some such wishes may be transformed into requirements by expressing them in quantitative terms. Compliance can then be established by measurement. Let us reformulate item B on the list. Our first try is

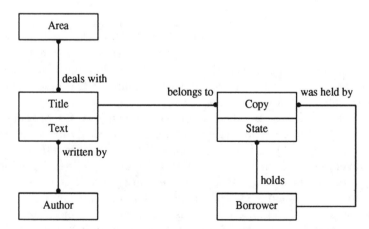

FIGURE 17.3. ER diagram of a library using the GE conventions.

(B_1) The system shall respond to every query within 1 second.

This seems straightforward, but with a system to which many users have simultaneous access it is impracticable to establish compliance by timing analysis of the code. Measurements cannot guarantee compliance either, no matter for how long they are carried out: the day after the tests are broken off in-house, and the system shipped to the sponsor for acceptance tests, a response time of 1.2 seconds may be recorded.
  Let us therefore try

(B_2) In 95% of all cases the system is expected to respond to a query within 1 second.

This is better, because we can now establish compliance by statistical analysis of the test data. Of course, poor sampling procedures can lead to unreliable estimates. The specification of an appropriate sampling procedure should therefore be added to requirement B_2. This is not very difficult because we are dealing with well-established techniques of statistical quality control.
  Statement D is similar to B, but more difficult to deal with. Generating responses to queries is a normal activity of the system, and this activity can provide a large bank of response-time data for statistical analysis. On the other hand, system failures are, we hope, few and far between, so that there are less data to be collected. Moreover, there is essentially just one form of normal operation of a system, but many forms of abnormality. Failure data are therefore difficult to interpret. Reliability analysis, which can predict hardware failures quite accurately, has been adapted for software reliability estimation, but it cannot tell how much time will be needed to restore a failed system to a normal mode of operation. Therefore, although we can change D to, say,

(D_1) System downtime is to be no more than 30 minutes in any 7-day period,

it is difficult to predict whether the delivered system will satisfy this requirement. Consequently, D_1 carries a high risk.

  Statements A and C are still more difficult to cope with. User-friendliness is a particularly dangerous concept: One man's friend is another's enemy. The easiest policy is to ask *the system sponsor* to devise acceptance tests that *the developer* finds reasonable, and not to consider any statement for which the sponsor cannot come up with such a test. However, an ask-the-sponsor policy assigns to the sponsor the role of an expert, whereas the sponsor came to the developer precisely because of the latter's presumed expertise. So, in trying to come to grips with user-friendliness, a lot of sponsor-unfriendliness can actually be generated. A better approach is to explain to the sponsor that statements that cannot be verified should not appear in requirements, and to assist in the conversion of statements that cannot be verified into statements that can, as was done with B.

Statements such as A and C, which we shall call *expectations*, can be included in the requirements document as a nonbinding appendix, and the developer should document the steps taken and the results obtained in all instances in which special attention is given to expectations. For example, improvement in levels of user-friendliness can be documented by means of questionnaires. A benchmark test for measuring usability, which is an important component of user-friendliness, is described in Chapter 31. Extendibility could be demonstrated by giving a step-by-step account of changes brought about by a late addition to requirements. One such addition to the requirements for the library system could be

If. For each copy that is checked out, the staff user who checked out the copy is known.

If the changes to the system caused by the added requirement are easy to make, then it is reasonable to expect that such changes will be easy to make in the future as well. Maintainability relates to the ease of adding to a system, and to the ease of changing a system. A benchmark test for measuring the maintainability of a system in the latter sense is discussed in Chapter 32. Since systems that are easy to change should also be easy to extend, such tests can serve as benchmarks for extendibility as well.

To summarize, a major task of requirements engineering is to transform an initial wish list into a set of unambiguous and verifiable requirements and a set of expectations. The following steps give some structure to the process.

- For each statement on the wish list indicate its source.
- Replace overworked terms (such as "book" in the library example), and define uncertain terms (such as "user") and terms that may have a special meaning in the context of the application (e.g., "age" may mean "age next birthday" in an insurance application). If two terms have the same interpretation, as "borrow" and "check out" seem to have in the library example, then drop one of the terms and consistently use only the other.
- Remove ambiguity by consulting the source of the statement, identifying the underlying reason for the statement, and listening to interpretations provided by colleagues.
- Partition the wish list into (I) requirements that deal with the structure of the information base; (II) requirements that relate to changes of the information base; (III) requirements that define the mode of operation of the system, including access to the system, and the nonfunctional characteristics of the system; and (IV) expectations. During the earlier part of system development, requirements of types I and II are the more important.

- Where possible, convert expectations into requirements of type III.
- Use an ER diagram to illustrate the requirements of type I.
- Make explicit every state change that the objects in the system can go through, i.e., reduce appeals to implicit domain knowledge. As a rule of thumb, use state transition diagrams to indicate all possible state changes whenever an object can be in four or more states.

If the paperwork in this seems excessive, keep in mind that the requirements are meant to be consulted again and again. If the quality of the requirements is low, then so will be the quality of the system.

18
State Transitions and Control Flows

The dynamic aspects of the reengineered enterprise are captured in state transition and data flow diagrams.

A system typically has to deal with two kinds of data, persistent and temporary. For persistent data, the important concept is a state change. An object can be in one of several (possibly many) states, and the requirements tell what these states are. The requirements should also make quite clear which state changes are possible and which are not. Recall Figure 17.1, which shows the permissible state changes of a library book. This state transition diagram is an integral component of requirement IIa. Its purpose is illustrative, but the initial development of a state transition diagram also helps to establish what states are needed.

Moreover, a state transition diagram can relate to the states of an entire system. When it does so, the states relate to tasks that are to be performed, so that the diagram actually defines a process. We shall refer to such a diagram as a *process diagram* or a *control flow diagram*. Keeping to the library example, Figure 18.1 illustrates the process of borrowing a copy of a book. The system is idle in state "start". A transition is made to state "check copy", in which it is determined whether the copy is available for borrowing. If so, a transition is made to "check limit"; if not, there is termination, i.e., return to "start". At "check limit" the borrowing limit is tested—the actual borrowing event takes place if this test is passed.

Our next example would not be categorized as a business process. It deals with the making of a telephone call. It was selected because it has a strong control component, enough complexity to make it interesting, and relates to a domain with which we are all familiar. A true business process of comparable complexity would require a lengthy introduction to the domain. The process has three participants—telephone A, telephone B, and the telephone network. However, we are interested in only those aspects of B and of the telephone network that relate to A. The purpose of telephones is to make calls, and the normal sequence of actions for a call from A to B has the following form:

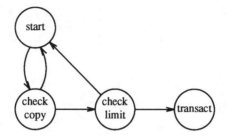

FIGURE 18.1. Borrowing process for a copy of a book.

(a) The receiver of A is lifted off the hook.
(b) The number of B is built up by dialing its digits.
(c) The network establishes a connection between A and B.
(d) B rings.
(e) The receiver of B is lifted off the hook. The connection is open.
(f) The receiver of A or of B is restored to the hook, breaking the connection.

The abnormal situations are as follows:

(i) The sequence of digits dialed this far cannot result in a valid telephone number; an appropriate message should be given.
(ii) All lines are busy; an appropriate message should be given.
(iii) B is busy; a busy signal should be given.

The state transition diagram illustrating these requirements is shown on the left side of Figure 18.2, where it is also made clear that a transition to state "A idle" can be made from every other state. For the duration of the actual call both receivers are off their hooks. If B terminates the call, the receiver of A continues to be off its hook, so there is a transition from "B off hook" to "A off hook". Since our real interest is in A alone, no "B idle" state is shown. After the "invalid number" or "all lines busy" message has been given, there is also a transition to state "A off hook".

However, what if A just keeps on staying in state "A off hook", or excessive time is taken over dialing, or A just keeps listening to B's busy signal or ringing tone? There should be a time-out facility. The state "time-out" is added in the augmented state transition diagram on the right side of Figure 18.2, and the four situations listed above result in a transition to this state, either directly or via state "A off hook".

Another type of process diagram is the data flow diagram. Let us look at a system that processes purchase orders. Figure 18.3 shows the structure of this system as a data flow diagram. The circles ("bubbles") represent processes or operations, and arrows represent data flows. Rectangular boxes represent external agents; those that supply inputs are called *sources*, and those that receive outputs from the system are *sinks*. Here,

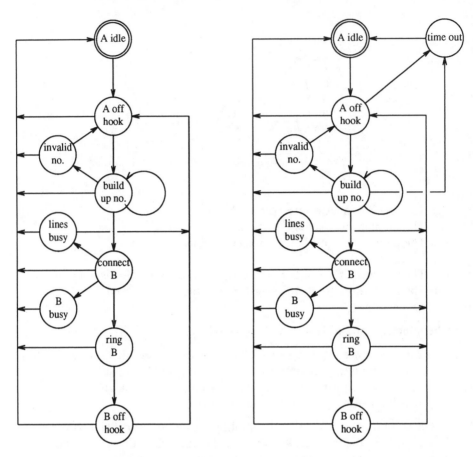

FIGURE 18.2. State transitions for telephone A.

CUSTOMER is both a source and a sink; FACTORY and WAREHOUSE
are sinks. A pair of parallel lines represents a data store. In Figure 18.3
there are three data stores: Customer file, Inventory file, and Order file.
Data file is a synonym of data store.

The main input to this system is a purchase order that moves from the
source/sink CUSTOMERS to the task CC (Check Credit). The order is
checked against the customer file and is either rejected or accepted,
depending on the customer's credit rating. In the case of a rejection, an
appropriate notice is sent to the customer. A valid order continues to the
task CI (Check Inventory). The order is checked against the inventory
file. If it can be filled, the order becomes part of the order file and is next
handed on to the task Ship. An order that cannot be filled causes a delay
notice to be sent to the customer, and the sink FACTORY then receives
notice of an inventory shortage that is to initiate inventory buildup.

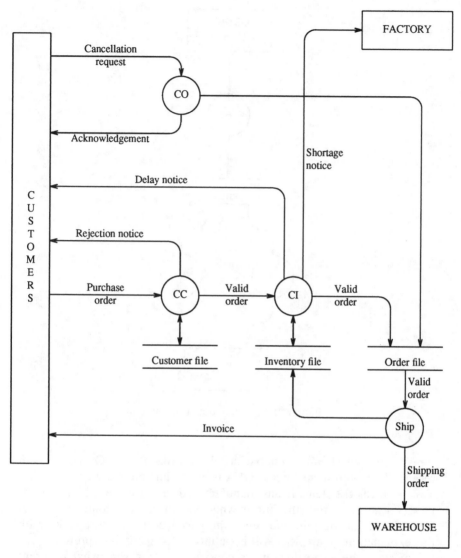

FIGURE 18.3. Data flow: processing of a purchase order (Version 1).

Task Ship adjusts the inventory file, issues a shipping order to sink WAREHOUSE, and invoices the customer. There is also provision for cancellation of orders, which is handled by the task CO (Cancel Order). We shall return to this diagram in Chapter 23.

However, data flow diagrams merely show that tasks interact, but they do not indicate the precise nature of the interactions. Let us consider a manufacturing process in which there are three tasks. Task A manufac-

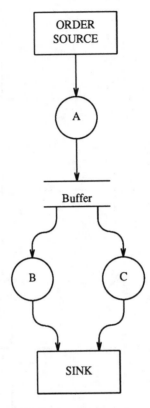

FIGURE 18.4. A manufacturing system.

tures items, which are then packaged by tasks B and C. The system
receives orders from a source, and A is busy while there are orders to fill.
Task A feeds the items it has manufactured into a buffer. Task B or C
picks up an item from the buffer whenever the task becomes idle, performs its packaging job, and sends the packaged item into a sink. With
this explanation Figure 18.4 will hopefully be correctly interpreted.

However, the same diagram is consistent with a somewhat different
interpretation of B and C; the original packaging task is split into two
activities: task B, which does the actual packaging of an item, and task C,
which produces a mailing label for the item. These are parallel activities
relating to the same item. Although a convention for drawing data flow
diagrams could be introduced that distinguishes between these two interpretations (under the second interpretation a single line originates from
the buffer, which then forks to go to B and C), misunderstandings will
still be likely, mainly because there is no established standard interpretation of data flow diagrams.

19
Control Flows in Terms
of Petri Nets

A process may have to interact with its environment, and the interaction can become very complicated. Also, all opportunities for parallel execution of parts of a process have to be indicated. Petri nets provide a visual representation of these aspects in an unambiguous way.

Petri nets are more complicated than data flow diagrams, but the diagrams have a universally accepted interpretation, so that there is less danger of misinterpretation. They are therefore extensively used to model the behavior of processes and to study interactions of components of processes and of processes themselves. A (place-transition) Petri net consists of a static process structure representation and a dynamically changing marking pattern that represents execution of the process. The structural components are places, transitions, and flow lines. Places are usually represented by circles and transitions by bars. A flow line may go from a place to a transition, or from a transition to a place, but never from place to place or transition to transition. All of the places from which there are flow lines to a transition form the *preset* of the transition; all of the places to which lines go from the transition form its *postset*. Presets and postsets of places are defined analogously. *Tokens* may be associated with places. Each assignment of tokens to places in a Petri net defines a *marking* of the net, but markings may change, thus introducing a dynamic element. An initial marking provides each place with zero or more tokens, and the net is then in its initial state. The net changes states by firings. A firing of a transition is enabled if each place in its preset holds at least one token. The result of the firing is twofold. First, for each place in the preset, a token is removed. Second, for each place in the postset, a token is added. Tokens may also be added during the running of a Petri net process as inputs.

Consider the situation shown on the left side of Figure 19.1. Here we have a transition with three "input" places that hold 3, 1, and 2 tokens, respectively, and two "output" places. The transition is enabled, i.e., it may fire. The effect of the firing is shown on the right side of Figure 19.1. Since the number of input places exceeds the number of output places,

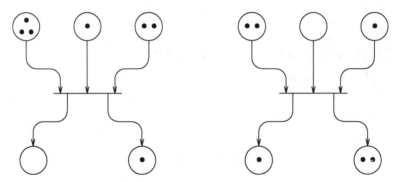

FIGURE 19.1. The firing of a transition.

the total number of tokens has decreased. There cannot be another firing because one of the input places no longer holds any tokens. Note that an enabled transition is not required to fire—it can stay forever in an enabled state without firing (but firing is enforced in *time* Petri nets, which will be discussed below).

Figure 19.2 shows a process in which two tasks are to have access to a particular resource, but never both at the same time. This is known as *mutual exclusion*. In Figure 19.2, let a token in P2 represent allocation of the resource to task A and a token in P4 allocation to task B. Under the marking shown in Figure 19.2, neither A nor B holds the resource, and both T1 and T3 are enabled to fire. Suppose that T1 fires. This removes tokens from P1 and P3 and places a token in P2. The resource belongs to task A for as long as this token remains in P2. During this time, transition T3 cannot fire, i.e., while there is a token in P2 there cannot be a token in P4, and vice versa. When task A surrenders the resource, T2 fires, the system is again in the state shown in Figure 19.2, and again T1 and T3 are both enabled.

Our next example introduces a bounded buffer. We consider a producer/consumer system in which the producer generates objects that are handed over to a consumer system. However, sometimes the producer

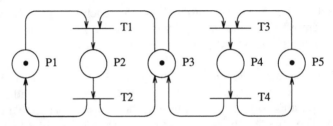

FIGURE 19.2. Petri net representation of mutual exclusion.

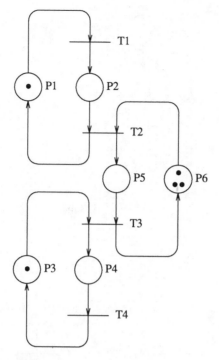

FIGURE 19.3. Petri net for a system with a bounded buffer.

may generate the objects faster than the consumer can deal with them, and a buffer is therefore interposed between the two systems. A common instance of such a system consists of a manufacturing process (producer), a warehouse (buffer), and a shipping process (consumer). Figure 19.3 illustrates this situation. Transition T1 sets the producer going, and P2 stands for the actual production of an object. Place P5 represents the buffer and the tokens at P6 bound its size. As is shown in Figure 19.3, the bound is 3. Thus, when T2 fires and an object goes into the buffer, P6 loses a token. The sum of the tokens in P5 and P6 always remains at 3. Hence, whenever P5 holds 3 tokens, the producer cannot deposit any additional objects into the buffer. Suppose that P5 holds 3 tokens and T3 fires. This transition initiates the consumer task P4, the token count at P5 is reduced, and the corresponding gain at P6 allows T2 to fire again. The tokens in P1 and P3 make sure that there is never more than one token at P2 and P4, respectively. The purpose of P6 here is similar to that of P5, say, in Figure 19.2—in Figure 19.2 the sum of the tokens in P4 and P5 is always 1; here, the sum of tokens in P5 and P6 may be greater than 1, but it must still be a constant.

Let us now represent the manufacturing system of Figure 18.4 by a Petri net; the result is Figure 19.4. The initial marking of the net would

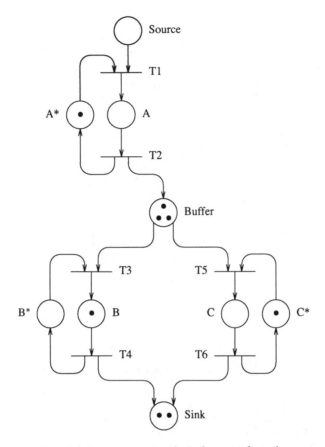

FIGURE 19.4. Petri net representation of a manufacturing system.

have consisted of one token each in places A*, B*, and C*. The system is started off by the arrival of an order, which is represented by placing one token into Source for each item being ordered. Since both Source and A* then contain tokens, T1 fires, depositing a token in A and depriving A* of its token. Place A represents the actual manufacturing process. During the manufacturing of an item, T1 cannot fire because A* contains no token. During this process the token in A remains there, but the end of the process is signaled by the firing of T2, which restores a token to A*, and T1 can fire again for as long as Source still holds tokens. The firing of T2 also adds a token to Buffer. As soon as this token is in place, either T3 or T5 can fire, which starts process B or C. As is shown in Figure 19.4, the system has advanced to a state in which no new items are to be manufactured (Source is empty), process B is active, and T5 is ready to fire, which would start process C as well. If no new orders are received, the system will become dormant when six items have ended up in Sink.

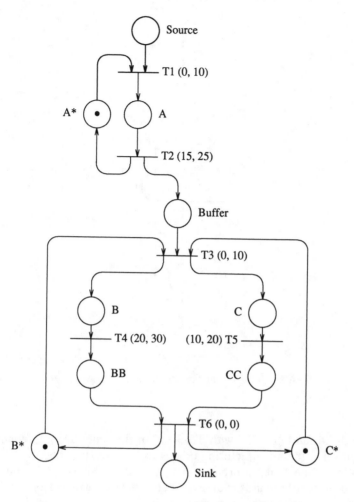

FIGURE 19.5. A variant of the manufacturing system.

The second version of the system, in which B packages and C produces labels, is shown in Figure 19.5 with its initial marking. Here, the firing of T3 starts both B and C. Let us interpret the pairs of numbers associated with the transition symbols. A serious problem with the net in Figure 19.4 is that it gives no indication of the time processes A, B, and C take—T2, say, could fire as soon as T1 has fired. This can be overcome by *time* Petri nets. In a time Petri net, each transition has two times associated with it, (t_1, t_2), and the transition must fire within the time interval $(e + t_1, e + t_2)$, where e is the time at which the transition becomes enabled (provided the firing of some other transition has not made it disenabled). In Figure 19.5, we have associated $(0, 10)$ with T1 and T3, $(15, 25)$ with T2, $(20,$

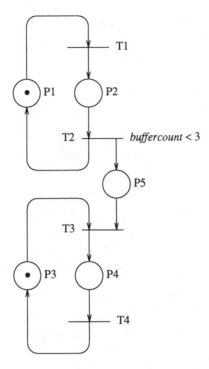

FIGURE 19.6. Variant of the bounded buffer system.

30) with T4, and (10, 20) with T5. If all of the times are in seconds, this indicates that the manufacturing time is 15 seconds, the time to package is 20 seconds, the time to produce a label is 10 seconds, and a period of slack of up to 10 seconds is allowed between two instances of a process.

Next consider the purpose of places BB and CC. Suppose that T4 and BB, and T5 and CC, were not there. Then we could assign (20, 30) to T6, but this would hide the fact that the times for processes B and C are different. The introduction of T4 and T5, with their respective interval assignments, emphasizes the difference. The assignment to T6 is (0, 0), so that T6 has to fire as soon as it has become enabled, i.e., as soon as T4 and T5 both have fired. Hence, the purpose of BB and CC is merely to pass through tokens from T4 to T6, and from T5 to T6.

The time Petri net is just one of the ways in which the pure Petri net has been extended. Another associates conditions with some of the transitions. A transition that has a condition associated with it may fire only if it is both enabled and the condition holds. This convention allows us to replace the bounded buffer net in Figure 19.3 with the simpler drawing shown in Figure 19.6. In the simpler variant a counter *buffercount* starts out with the value 0. Each time an item is added to the buffer by the firing of T2, the value of *buffercount* is to be increased by 1; each time an item is moved out of the buffer by the firing of T3, the value is to be decreased by 1; T2 can fire only if the value of *buffercount* is below 3.

We shall be dealing with situations in which a process starts on its own accord at a certain time, say every morning at 07:00. To allow for self-starting processes, we extend the "net with conditions" concept further: A transition that has a condition associated with it may exist without a preset; such a transition is enabled while the condition is true; if it fires, the result of the firing is to deposit a token into every place of its postset. This extension can be made to time Petri nets as well. A conditional transition with condition *Time* = 07:00 and time marking (0, 0) must fire as soon as the condition becomes true, i.e., at 07:00.

20
From ER Diagrams
to Information Modules

Modules should be identified with data types, where each data type consists of a set of entities and a collection of mappings. The description of an editorial office is converted into an ER diagram, and then into a data-type diagram. The latter defines a set of modules.

An example that we begin considering in this chapter, and will continue to develop in Chapters 21 and 25, relates to the editorial office of a scientific journal. An informal description of the office and the way it operates serves as the initial list of requirements for a software system that is to support the editorial process.

Authors submit papers to a journal, and the editorial office of the journal selects three referees for each paper. The referees are expected to submit their reports within 6 weeks of receiving a paper for review. If a referee has not responded at the end of this period, a reminder setting a deadline after a further 3 weeks is sent out. If the referee still does not respond, or a referee has at any time declined this refereeing task, replacement referees are sought. Before papers are sent to replacement referees, the potential referees are asked to guarantee that they will review the paper within 6 weeks, and, to be on the safe side, for every original referee who falls out, two replacements are picked. The editorial office makes a decision on a paper based on referees' reports after three reports are in, or when the reports of replacement referees become due, whichever comes first. A paper is then (i) accepted, (ii) rejected, (iii) required to be revised, or (iv) required to be rewritten. In the case where the paper is to be revised or rewritten, a cutoff date for submission of the new version is given, and, unless the editorial office grants an extension, papers resubmitted after the cutoff date are rejected. A paper may be required to be revised or rewritten more than once. Decisions on revised papers are made by the editorial office. However, if the revision has introduced much new material, the editorial office may decide to treat the paper as having been rewritten. A rewritten paper is sent to the referees of the original version, and they are to evaluate the new version within 6 weeks. After this time, the editorial office makes its decision. Again there are four possible outcomes. The editorial office communicates with referees and with the main author of each paper.

The first task is to determine what entity classes to define. This determination starts with the extraction of a list of nouns from the description of the office. The list is as follows:

accepted paper	original referee	rejected paper
author	paper	reminder
cutoff date	potential referee	replacement referee
editorial decision	referee	resubmission
editorial office	refereeing deadline	review
extension	refereeing task	revised paper
journal	referee's report	rewritten paper
new version of paper		

Some terms qualify a more inclusive term (*revised paper* qualifies *paper*), others denote attributes of more significant entities (*refereeing* deadline), and still others do not seem to be significant enough to warrant an entity class of their own (*extension*). Such analysis suggests that the truly significant terms are *editorial office*, *paper*, and *referee*.

However, the editorial office communicates with both referees and main authors, so that main authors need to have their addresses available. We therefore add an entity class of main authors. Further, since the need to possess addresses is shared by main authors, referees, and the editorial office, their entity types should be made subtypes of a single entity type. With regard to papers, the different versions of a paper are also important objects. Hence, an entity class for versions should be added. These entity classes appear as the main components in the ER diagram in Figure 20.1: *EdOffice, Paper, Referee, MainAuthor, Correspondent, Version*.

Additional diagramming conventions have been introduced in Figure 20.1. A triangle represents an "is-a" relation—X is-a Y tells that every entity in the entity class X also belongs to entity class Y; this means that it has all of the attributes of entities in class Y but may have additional attributes that entities in Y do not possess. For example, *Referee* is-a *Correspondent* tells that referees have all of the attributes of correspondents, e.g., an e-mail address and a fax number; in addition, referees have the attributes *PaperCount* and *BlackMarks*, which they do not share with other correspondents—the value of *PaperCount* is the number of papers a referee has reviewed or is in the process of reviewing in the current year, and *BlackMarks* indicates the number of times the referee has not completed an assignment. If X is-a Y, then X is called a subclass of Y (or a subclass of this is-a relation), and Y is called a superclass of X (or the superclass of this is-a). A bare triangle indicates that an entity in

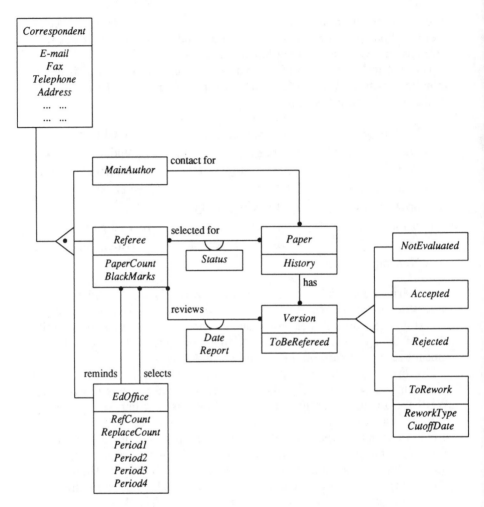

FIGURE 20.1. ER diagram for an editorial office.

the superclass of its is-a may belong to only one of its subclasses, e.g., a version of a paper may be in only one of the four subclasses of *Version*. A black circle in a triangle indicates that an entity in the superclass of its is-a can belong to more than one subclass, e.g., a referee can also be a main author. An entity in a superclass need not belong to any of its subclasses.

A box joined to a relationship line by a semicircle contains attributes of this relationship. In Figure 20.1 the relationship "selected for" has the attribute *Status*—a referee asked to review a paper has a particular status with respect to this paper (active referee, potential replacement referee, a referee who has declined the assignment, or a referee who did not complete the assignment). The actual review is carried out on a version of the paper (the original or a rewritten version), and *Date* gives the date on which this version was sent to the referee. Also, for completed assignments, there is the referee's report.

Additional attributes are as follows. For each paper, *History* is a record of what has been happening to it (e.g., date received, date evaluated, result of evaluation, date reworked version received, etc); for versions of the paper, *ToBeRefereed* tells whether or not this version requires referees' reports; for versions in the *ToRework* category, *ReworkType* indicates whether the paper was to be revised or rewritten, and *CutoffDate* gives the date by which the reworked version is to be resubmitted. The six attributes of *EdOffice* are in a special category. They are constants that relate to business rules under which the editorial office operates: *RefCount*, which is set at 3, tells how many referees are needed for a paper; *ReplaceCount*, set at 2, tells how many new referees are to be chosen when one of the original referees does not produce a report; the other four attributes have values of 42, 21, 42, and 42 days, respectively, and indicate when the reminder is to be sent out, how long after this replacement referees are to be chosen, how long after this the paper is to be evaluated, and when referee reports are due for a rewritten paper.

Rereading the requirements given at the beginning of the chapter will show that the ER diagram has correctly captured most of the requirements relating to the information base for the process. An exception is the requirement that only the original submission and rewritten papers are to be reviewed by referees, i.e., only the versions for which the attribute *ToBeRefereed* is true—the diagram gives the impression that every version is to have referees' reports. We shall now transform the ER diagram into a diagram of data types. The problem will be cleared up in this process.

Every data type is regarded as made up of a set and a collection of mappings (functions) from this set. Attributes are already functions, but we have to convert relations into functions. However, before doing so, we shall show that the number of data types can be made considerably less than ten, the number of entity classes in Figure 20.1. First, we eliminate *MainAuthor* by adding a function *MainAuthor* to the type Paper—the value of *MainAuthor(p)*, where *p* is a paper, is an element in the set of correspondents. As a general rule, every entity class without attributes is a candidate for elimination. Next, consider the subclasses of *Version*. Actually, acceptance and rejection relate more strongly to the paper than to a version of the paper. Therefore, we shall relate *NotEvaluated*, *Accepted*, and *Rejected* to *Paper*. Moreover, we shall not regard them as separate data types, but as subsets of the set of papers. Note also that if a paper is not in one of these subsets, then the editorial office has asked that it be reworked. We add a fourth subset for this category. For versions we shall have two subsets: one subset for versions that do not have to be refereed and the other for those that do. Referee reports relate to the latter alone. We end up with just five data types, which we list as follows with the names of their sets:

Correspondent—CORR
EdOffice—EDOFF (is-a *Correspondent*)
Referee—REF (is-a *Correspondent*)
Paper—PAP (subsets *NOTEV, ACC, REJ, REDO*)
Version—VER (subsets *RYES, RNO*)

In order to deal with the transformation of relations into functions, we need to introduce a few technicalities from Appendix A. A relation R from set X to set Y is a set of ordered pairs $<x, y>$, where x belongs to X and y to Y. The set of all possible such pairs is called the *Cartesian product* of X and Y, written $X \times Y$. Relation R is a subset of $X \times Y$.

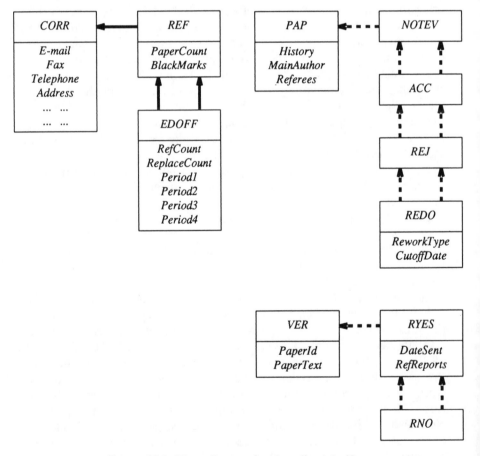

FIGURE 20.2. Type diagram for the editorial office.

Relation R is one-to-one if neither the first nor the second coordinates of this set of ordered pairs are duplicated; in a one-to-many relation duplicates will be found among the first coordinates alone; in a many-to-one relation, duplicates will be found among the second coordinates alone; in a many-to-many relation there can be duplicates in both coordinates.

Consider a relation from X to Y. If this relation is one-to-one, then it is already a function, either from X or from Y. If it is one-to-many, it can be regarded as a *set-valued* function from X to Y, or as an *element-valued* function from Y to X. Because the concept of an element-valued function is simpler than that of a set-valued function, preference may be given to the transformation of a one-to-many relation into a function from Y to X. The function resulting from a many-to-many relation necessarily will be set-valued. But should it be from X to Y, or from Y to X? If the choice is difficult, then it probably makes no difference, at least not during process specification. The same applies to attributes of relationships.

In carrying out the conversion of relationships into functions, we discover that two of our "relationships" are not really relationships, but identifiers of process steps—that the editorial office selects and reminds referees has little significance for the information base of the application. The data types are shown in Figure 20.2. Solid arrows indicate a subtype relationship, and all subtypes of the one type are joined by solid double arrows. Subset relationships are indicated by dashed arrows, and subsets of the same set are joined by dashed double arrows.

A type diagram gives an indication of the sets from which functions map, but it does not show the targets of the functions. Some of the targets can be quite complicated. Type diagrams should therefore be augmented with definitions of the functions. We do so for types *Paper* and *Version*:

TYPE *Paper*

History:	$PAP \rightarrow Text$–set
MainAuthor:	$PAP \rightarrow Correspondent$
Referees:	$PAP \rightarrow (Referee \times Status)$–set
ReworkType:	$REDO \rightarrow \{$"revise", "rewrite"$\}$
CutoffDate:	$REDO \rightarrow Date$

TYPE *Version*

PaperId:	$VER \rightarrow Paper$
PaperText:	$VER \rightarrow Text$
DateSent:	$RYES \rightarrow (Referee \times Date)$–set
RefReports:	$RYES \rightarrow (Referee \times Text \times Date)$–set

The mappings are from sets to types. The reasons for mapping to a type instead of to a set are rather technical, but may be of some interest. Suppose that an entity is removed from the set of the type, e.g., a person from set *CORR*. Then the element corresponding to this person has to be removed from every function that maps from *CORR* as well. This is quite easy because all of these functions belong to the same type. But we would also have to adjust functions that map to *CORR* in other types. This adjustment would not be as easy. Actually, we might want to keep a record of referees of old papers, as part of function *Referees*, even if these referees no longer belong to *CORR* (and hence cannot belong to *REF* either).

Some new types have been introduced. Types *Text* and *Date* are self-explanatory. The target of *ReworkType* is shown as {"revise", "rewrite"}, i.e., for a given paper p, the value of *ReworkType*(p) is either "revise" or "rewrite". Values that define type *Status* were listed earlier in this chapter. The target of *Referees* is written as (*Referee* × *Status*)–set. This means that for paper p the value of *Referees*(p) is a set of pairs, and each pair consists of a referee and his or her status. A similar interpretation applies to the targets of *DateSent* and *RefReports*.

21
From Flow Diagrams
to Process Modules

The data types of information modules define the information base of an organization. The addition of behavioral aspects superimposes a set of processes on this static scheme. The example of the editorial office is continued with the drawing of a Petri net that shows how the office processes a submitted paper.

In Chapter 20 we partitioned the set of papers submitted to the editorial office of a scientific journal into four subsets. We can think of the subsets as defining states of a paper—a paper changes state by moving from one subset into another. In Figure 21.1 the diagram on the left shows the state transitions of a submitted paper. The diagram on the right is a rudimentary data flow diagram (DFD) that shows how the editorial office interacts with the outside world. Although these orientation diagrams help to understand paper processing in very broad terms, there is not enough detail. Nearly all of the activities of the editorial office take place while a paper is in state *NOTEV*. These activities are not shown in Figure 21.1.

We need a more elaborate process diagram, and our choice for the representation of the paper evaluation process is the Petri net. Software developers accustomed to DFDs may prefer a DFD, but the Petri net has several advantages. First, transitions are enabled by conditions that can be precisely defined, so that we can get a clear understanding of the conditions under which the firing of a transition initiates a task—following the convention adopted in Chapter 19, places will represent tasks in the editorial process. We shall refer to the firing of a transition as a *transaction*, and tasks will be called *events*. Second, we make use of the convention that more than one flow line can go from a place to a transition, or from a transition to a place: if k flow lines go from transition T to place P, then the firing of T deposits k tokens in P; if k lines go from P to T, then T is not enabled unless P holds at least k tokens. Hence we can indicate that certain tasks have to be performed a given number of times, e.g., that the editorial office is to select three referees. A Petri net for the processing of papers by the editorial office is shown in Figure 21.2.

The Petri net in Figure 21.2 shows that the editorial office is involved in three major subprocesses, which are started when (a) the original version

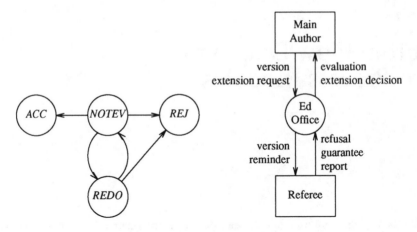

FIGURE 21.1. Orientation diagrams for the processing of a paper.

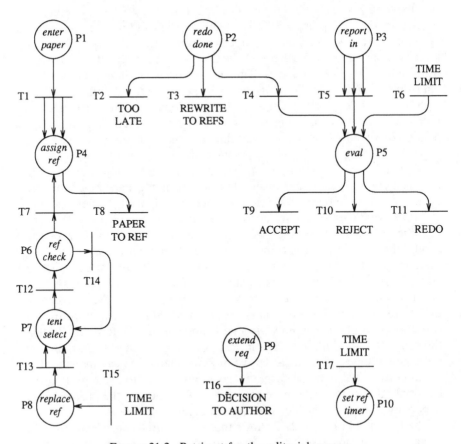

FIGURE 21.2. Petri net for the editorial process.

of a paper arrives at the office (P1), (b) a new version arrives (P2), or (c) three reviews of a version have arrived (P3). Other starting points relate to a request for the extension of the time limit for work on a new version (P9), and to actions to be taken when various time limits are exceeded (T6, T15, and T17). The Petri net gives a reasonably complete representation of the structure of the process. For example, when a referee for a paper has dropped out, which is indicated by a token in P8, the firing of T13 deposits two tokens in P7, and two referees are tentatively selected. Then, at P6, the willingness of each of the two referees is checked. If the referee is willing, T7 fires and, via P4, T8 fires, which results in the paper being sent to the referee; if not, T14 fires, indicating that another tentative selection is to be made. However, a lot of detail is still missing. For example, the net does not show that the subprocess starting at P3 can be initiated only if T8 or T3 has fired at some much earlier time, and that T11 must have fired before P2 can get a token. The precise nature of the time limits that cause T6, T15, and T17 to become enabled is also unclear. Even if it were possible to fit all of the details into the diagram, it would not be advisable to do so. The inclusion of annotations would make the diagram too "busy", and the essence of the diagram, which is to show the *structure* of the process, would become obscured. Instead, we develop a process dictionary that is keyed to the diagram but does not intrude into the diagram itself. The dictionary, which has an entry for every event and transaction, is also a link to the type diagram of Chapter 20 in that it records all sets and functions changed by an event. Since our Petri net contains 10 places and 17 transitions, the dictionary is to have 27 entries. We shall list only nine of them.

EVENT: P1 (*enter paper*)

Triggered by: Arrival of the first version of a paper at the editorial office

Action: Enter details regarding the paper in the information base; in particular, make the paper a member of *NOTEV* (and thus of *PAP*)

Information base changes:

(a) *PAP*
(b) *PAP. History*
(c) *PAP. MainAuthor*
(d) *VER. PaperId*
(e) *VER. PaperText*

Affects:

(a) T1, fired on completion of the action

TRANSACTION: T1

Enabled by: P1

Action: Trigger the event P4 (*assign ref*) by depositing 3 tokens in it

EVENT: P2 (*redo done*)

Triggered by: Arrival of revised or rewritten paper at the editorial office
Action: Determine whether to regard the paper as too late, revised, or rewritten
Information base changes:

(a) *PAP. History*

Affects:

(a) T2, fired if the time limit for making changes is exceeded
(b) T3, fired if the paper was rewritten
(c) T4, fired if the paper was revised

EVENT: P4 (*assign ref*)

Triggered by: T1 or T7
Action: Assign referee to a reviewing task
Information base changes:

(a) *PAP. History*
(b) *PAP. Referees*
(c) *REF. PaperCount*

Affects:

(a) T8, fired on completion of the action

EVENT: P5 (*eval*)

Triggered by: T4, T5, or T6
Action: Accept or reject a paper, or find it in need of further work by the authors
Information base changes:

(a) *PAP* (paper moved from one subset into another)
(b) *PAP. History*
(c) *REDO. ReworkType* (for papers to be redone)
(d) *REDO. CutoffDate* (for papers to be redone)

Affects:

(a) T9, fired on acceptance of paper
(b) T10, fired on rejection of paper
(c) T11, fired if paper is in need of further work

Note: For a refereed version of a paper, to prevent a firing of T5 to be follwed by the firing of T6, transaction T6 is to be conditional—it is to fire only if the paper under consideration is in subset *NOTEV*

TRANSACTION: T6

Enabled by: Time limit defined by *EDOFF.Period3* or *EDOFF.Period4*, and the condition that the paper under consideration is in subset *NOTEV*

Action: Trigger the event P5 (*eval*) by depositing a token in it

EVENT: P8 (*replace ref*)

Triggered by: T15, or when a referee assigned to a paper in P4 declines the assignment

Action: If triggered by T15, adjust *REF. BlackMarks*; otherwise, adjust *PAP. Referees* and *PAP. PaperCount*

Information base changes:

(a) *PAP. History*
(b) *PAP. Referees* (if referee declines)
(c) *REF. PaperCount* (if referee declines)
(d) *REF. BlackMarks* (if triggered by T15)

Affects:

(a) T13, fired on completion of the action

TRANSACTION: T8

Enabled by: P4 (*assign ref*)
Action: Send the paper to the referee assigned to it in P4

TRANSACTION: T15

Enabled by: Time limit defined by *EDOFF. Period2*
Action: Trigger event P8 by depositing a token in it

The 27 components of the Petri net in Figure 21.2, together with their connecting lines, define a process. We now have two options. One is to integrate the events and transactions with one of the five data type modules in Figure 20.2; the other is to implement the process as a separate module. The language we shall use in Chapter 25 to arrive at a formal specification of the editorial process favors the merger of the process definition into one of the data types. This resolves the problem of separate "ownership" of the process and the data that give primary support to the process. Both should be "owned" by the same manager (see, e.g., [Da93, p.88]). We therefore recommend that a process always be associated with some data type. Type *Paper* is the natural choice for the editorial process.

As a final remark, in some process definitions emphasis is put on the assignment of tasks to individual members of the process team. The team for the editorial office would be expected to contain an editor and a secretary, and different tasks would be allocated to each. This attitude is against the spirit of reengineering—the process teams of reengineered organzations work as teams, not as groups of individuals with preassigned duties. Of course, the evaluation of a paper based on referees' reports may require highly specialized knowledge, and only the editor has this knowledge. On the other hand, in many cases the decision can be made by the secretary, e.g., when all referees' reports on a paper recommend its rejection.

22
Validation of the Blueprint

The final form of the initial requirements document for a business process contains a data-type diagram, state transition diagrams, a process flow diagram, and a list of nonfunctional requirements. This document is examined by a carefully selected inspection team.

Before we discuss the validation of the initial requirements blueprint for a process, we must come to a clear understanding of what this "official" requirements blueprint is to contain. We suggest that a requirements document consist of the following three parts:

- Type I requirements of Chapter 17 and a type diagram, such as the one in Figure 20.2, together with relevant function definitions.
- Type II requirements of Chapter 17, which may be augmented with state transition diagrams, and a process diagram, such as the Petri net in Figure 21.2, together with a dictionary defining its components.
- Nonfunctional requirements, defined as Type III requirements in Chapter 17.

All subsequent process system development must be in strict accordance with this requirements statement. If it is discovered in later stages that any part of the system should be developed differently than is stated in the requirements, *the change first must be made in the requirements statement*, i.e., no deviation from requirements is to be tolerated. It is therefore essential to have tools to assist in the editing of the requirements document. Often the selection of a representation for the requirements is based on the availability of a particular tool. Sometimes this works out well, but system developers should not be forced to use a representation with which they are not comfortable.

In arriving at the official requirements document we may assemble a large collection of preliminary diagrams, such as Figures 20.1 and 21.1. What is to happen to all of this material after requirements gathering has been completed? Much can and should be discarded, but there should exist a full record of how the final requirements statements was arrived at. The best strategy is to keep a decision log throughout system development. Whenever a choice is made between alternatives, all of the alternatives should be listed and the motivation for the particular choice should be fully documented. If a diagram is part of this documentation, it should be preserved. Such logs are particularly useful when suggested changes are evaluated. A suggestion that looks very promising may have been considered during requirements gathering but was rejected for some very subtle reason. However, care must be taken because the reason for the initial rejection may have since disappeared.

Before the requirements document becomes truly "official", it has to be thoroughly validated to determine that the *expectations* of all parties concerned have been met. In general, validation is human- or machine-based. During requirements gathering human-based validation is the more important. However, if a prototype is constructed as part of requirements gathering, some machine-based testing can be carried out as well. The primary human-based approaches are walkthroughs and inspections, which can be applied to any software product, such as a requirements document, test plan, code, and software documentation. Both walkthroughs and inspections are performed by teams. Members of a team meet after having studied the software product beforehand. In an inspection, the software product is examined component by component with the aim of discovering errors or obscurities. In a walkthrough, a few previously prepared test case are "walked through" the product. In other words, a walkthrough is an inspection restricted to one particular mode of operation. We shall therefore talk here of inspections alone, with the understanding that any particular inspection may in fact be a walkthrough.

An inspection team consists of three to five members who fill as many of the following roles as possible:

- *Moderator*—The moderator calls the meeting and sees to it that all material is distributed to the members of the team beforehand. Neither the moderator nor any other member of the team should be a supervisor of the author of the product.
- *Presenter*—This member of the team presents the product at the meeting. Usually the presenter is the author, but there are three good reasons for choosing a presenter other than the author. First, the author may be blind to some types of errors and may transfer this blindness to other members of the team during the presentation. Second, the product may be too opaque to stand on its own, but this circumstance can be obscured by a dynamic presentation by the author. Third, if the presenter is not the author, then there are at least two persons with a very detailed knowledge of the product.
- *Author*—Must be present, at least to answer questions.
- *Secretary*—The secretary records all faults and places for improvement.

- *Language expert*—An expert on the language in which the product is expressed, which may be a graphical language such as that of ER diagrams or of Petri nets. In the case of documentation, the language expert may be an experienced technical writer.

- *Standards expert*—An expert whose role is to ensure that the product conforms to industry standards or company codes of practice.

- *Upstream representative*—The "upstream representative" belongs to the group that produced the document from which the product under consideration derives. In the inspection of a requirements document, the upstream representative represents users and is assumed to be familiar with the entire application domain. Thorough familiarity is expected of that part of the domain with which the requirements under consideration deal. The representative should be an actual user rather than an administrator.

- *Downstream representative*—The "downstream representative" will work from the product under examination. Thus, for the example of the editorial office, the downstream representative will be involved in converting the requirements as defined in Chapters 20 and 21 into the formal specification of Chapter 25.

The product to be inspected is distributed to the inspection team sufficiently in advance of the scheduled meeting to allow the members of the team to familiarize themselves with it. A checklist of faults to look for is also distributed. The period between distribution of this material and the meeting should not be longer than necessary. A long period has two adverse effects: first, development time is stretched out unnecessarily; and secon it may cause reduced familiarity with the product. Those who examined ﮐe distributed material at once will have lost some interest by the time of the meeting; those who did not, may not leave themselves enough time for a thorough study of the material.

The length of the meeting should be 90 minutes to 2 hours. A shorter period does not justify the effort of making all of the arrangements; the intense concentration that an inspection demands cannot be maintained for a longer period. This means that a complete requirements document may have to be inspected in parts over several sessions.

The purpose of an inspection is to improve a product, not to pass judgement on the author. It is therefore extremely important that all of the participants in an inspection have a positive attitude that is displayed through their manners. The smooth functioning of a session requires adherence to the following few basic rules:

- Do not come unprepared.
- Do not criticize the author. Note that the use of negative language is a criticism of the author. For example, one should ask "Could these process steps be simplified?" rather than "How can anybody be expected to understand this stuff?"

- Do not spend time on trivia, such as spelling errors or missing semicolons, or on games ("Bet you a dollar that you won't see what is wrong with the referee selection!")
- Do not try to fix faults on the spot, but general suggestions can be made. The language expert can make particularly valuable suggestions.
- Rule for the author: Do not apologize or explain.

The important tool for an inspection is a checklist for faults. The checklist can have several sections: principal section, domain-related section, and a level-specific section (e.g., specific for requirements inspection, or for the inspection of module interfaces), which can be partitioned into a general part and a language-specific part. A recent development is the partitioning of the checklist into components, which are assigned to individual team members. Then the primary responsibility for a member of the inspection team is to concentrate on looking for faults that relate to his or her component. Inspections derive their benefits from team dynamics, but this sharpening of focus for individual team members can enhance such benefits further.

The principal component relates to general principles, such as:

- *Completeness*: Has everything in the input from the upstream phase been considered?
- *Simplicity*: Can completeness be achieved with a simpler product?
- *Necessity*: Does this product go beyond what the input from the upstream phase requires?
- *Consistency*: Are there no conflicting parts?
- *Feasibility*: Is there a realistic appreciation of all constraints?
- *Robustness*: Can the system survive failures?
- *Extendibility*: Can new features be added without extensive reworking?

Some domain-related items are concerned with implementation constraints, e.g., limitations of available hardware or the need to make heavy use of software that already exists. The concern of others is the prospective user community: Is the terminology standard in the given application domain? Will prospective users be able to understand the formalisms? Are ease of learning and ease of use properly balanced?

The level-specific items are for the most part elaborations and adaptations of the principal component. For example, with regard to requirements, one would ask: Are the requirements complete? Has there been consultation with all prospective user groups? Is each requirement testable? Is it achievable? Is it necessary? Has maintainability of the requirements been considered? Is each requirement properly identified for ease of reference? Some level-specific items relate to the representation language. We shall list some level-specific items for the language SF in Chapter 24.

The result of the inspection is a list of corrections that have to be made. Inspection of the initial version of the diagrams for the editorial process of Chapters 20 and 21 revealed that *DateSent* had not been made an attribute of *RYES* in Figure 20.2, and that P9 and T16 had to be added in Figure 21.2. Also, the dictionary entry for T6 was found to be incomplete (it did not show that this transition could be enabled by EDOFF. *Period4*, and it had not been realized that T6 had to be a conditional transaction).

An important by-product of inspections is an improved checklist in that every new *type* of fault that is discovered is to be added to the checklist. With time, the checklists become valuable resources for an organization. If many corrections need to be made, or if the version under consideration contains some fundamental flaw, a new inspection of the corrected version may be needed.

V
Information-Control Systems

23
Specification of Business Processes

Desirable properties of a language for the specification of business processes are examined. The most important property is the independent specification of the structural aspects of the information base, its behavioral aspects, and the actual business processes.

The three central concerns of requirements analysis are the determination of requirements from a variety of sources, the mode of presentation of the requirements, and their validation. In Chapter 22 we showed how an initial requirements document for a process system, as defined at the start of the chapter, is to be validated under participation of at least one expected user of the system. This allows some faults to be removed, but Figures 20.2 and 21.2, even when augmented with function definitions and a process dictionary, are still not sufficiently detailed, and can be misinterpreted. We noted in Chapter 21 that the Petri net for the editorial office does not show that T8 or T3 must have fired before P3 can be initiated. The process dictionary does not show this constraint either—we have to deduce it from the initial description of the operation of the editorial office, as was given in the beginning of Chapter 20. It is unlikely that the relationship between T8, T3, and P3 will be misunderstood in the description, but, in general, since it is in English, there is room for misinterpretation. This suggests that, for a more thorough validation of requirements, the visual representations must be backed by a formal textual specification, preferably an executable specification.

Why then do we want to use diagrams? Although we now have looked at several different kinds of diagrams, we have not actually determined why diagrams should be used at all to express requirements. The following are a few reasons:

(a) Diagrams give a complete overview of all of the components or states of a system.
(b) Diagrams provide insight into relationships between the components or states of a system.

(c) Diagrams are an efficient means of communication between users and developers, or between developers.
(d) Inconsistent requirements are easier to detect in diagrams than in text.
(e) Effects of requirement changes are easier to trace in diagrams than in text.
(f) Diagrams allow easy switching between different levels of detail in system documentation.
(g) Diagrams assist in the efficient retrieval of system documentation in automated documentation maintenance systems.

In choosing diagrammatic representations and adopting conventions for the diagrams, it should also be kept in mind that diagrams have no intrinsic value. They acquire value only if they show aspects of real-life systems to which the process models under construction relate.

These observations lead us to formulate some general principles for the selection and use of diagrams:

• If the diagrams are used for user–developer communication, it must be ensured that the users fully understand all conventions in use. For this reason, complex conventions should be avoided.

• If the diagrams are used by a process development team for internal communication, a richer graphical language can be used. All members of the team must have a good grasp of all conventions. This is to avoid misunderstandings, or domination of the discussion by one or two people with a better understanding of the notation.

• Tools should be provided for easy editing of diagrams. Otherwise, there is a tendency to accept a well-made diagram even when it fails to be a well-made model of the real-life situations it is supposed to model.

• Keep in mind that different people have different preferences, particularly in choosing the level of annotation on a diagram.

We now turn to formal specifications. Formal specifications are a bridge between process participants and process system developers. A formal specification of a process must be an unambiguous statement of the expectations of process participants, but expressed in such a way that they can make sure that their expectations are in fact being met. It follows that the mode of presentation of a formal specification has to satisfy four criteria: requirements must be expressed unambiguously, they must be verifiable, they must be understandable by user representatives with little effort, and their form must allow a user representative to indicate clearly any changes that are to be made to the specifications. Simply put, specifications must be at the same time precise and readable, and this is difficult to achieve. We shall nevertheless attempt to achieve both goals with SF, which will be described in Chapter 24. This language will be found to satisfy the following ten properties of specification languages. The properties are consistent with the principles of specification and prototyping languages listed in [Ba79, Ro85, Be86, Lu91].

1. The language is to be totally unambiguous so that process developers have a precise understanding of what they have to develop. This means that the language must have sound theoretical foundations.

2. The language is to allow a reading knowledge to be acquired with little training. There is to be an economy of concepts.

3. The language is to allow the specification of a conceptual model of a process without having to define a detailed design or implementation model. It must allow a measure of nondeterminism in a process specification so that the decision of whether the implemented process is to have an essentially parallel or an essentially sequential mode can be postponed. However, it has been found that some intertwining of specification, design, and implementation of software is inevitable [Gu80, Sw82, Be90].

4. The language is to encourage development of a specification in the form of modules. Of the ten most serious sources of risk in software development, seven can be managed by incremental modular software development [Bo91]. Modularization based on data types is a natural choice.

5. The language is to require that the specification of a module consists of distinct parts that deal with the structural aspects of its information base, its behavioral aspects, and the actual business process. This contributes to the clarity of a specification and allows the specification of a module to be developed by several members of a reengineering team working in parallel.

6. The language is to enforce the principles of data abstraction—a data type is to consist of a set and of functions defined on this set. Moreover, the distinction between a data base and programs is to be deemphasized. We noted in Chapter 8 that a sunrise function could be implemented as a table or as a program. All that matters is that there is access to values of functions—at the specification stage the mechanisms by which the values are to be obtained is of no interest.

7. The language is to allow easy representation of integrity constraints on the information base of a module. To enforce accountability regarding the contents of the information base of a module, all changes to the information base are to be made exclusively by the owner of the module.

8. The language is to provide mechanisms for linking individual processing tasks into processes. Every process system is an information-control system embedded in some environment, ranging from mechanical devices, such as automobiles, to societies of people. The process part of a specification is to allow easy definition of interactions of a process system with its environment, including real-time interactions. It must be able to provide support for the automation of diverse applications, such as office activities, movement of goods, *total* self-service in stores (i.e., with fully automated checkouts), etc.

9. The language is to be supportive of an evolutionary development of specifications, i.e., it should allow easy modification and augmentation of an initially incomplete specification. This is particularly important for product development processes in which embedded systems and their hosts are developed in parallel, and an embedded system may have to accommodate radical changes to the host.

10. The language is to support reuse. For example, it should not require much effort to convert a system that processes hotel reservations into a system that handles rental car reservations.

Past efforts at the specification of software systems have rarely managed to combine properties 1 and 2 of our list, and where they have done so, their domains of applicability have been rather narrow. They certainly have not satisfied all ten requirements. In fact, there seems to be a polarization, with a multitude of diagramming conventions at one pole and sophisticated mathematical notations at the other. Let us look now at a few specification methodologies that have found some measure of acceptance in industry, particularly in Great Britain, and that go beyond inadequately interpreted diagramming techniques.

Jackson system development. A JSD specification makes use of diagrams, but the diagrams are not intended to do much more than help arrive at an intuitive understanding of a system. The actual specification resembles a program. The specification defines a distributed network of processes that communicate by message passing. However, the interpretation of the meaning of JSD constructs is left largely to the user's intuition, which makes it difficult to tell the precise nature of the message-passing mechanism. A serious flaw of JSD is its extreme process orientation, which leaves the data aspect underemphasized. First, this hinders modularization. Second, when a JSD system refers to a data base, the data base is regarded as being outside the system. Data base constraints and operations are therefore the concern of a data base administrator rather than the developer of a process system. In the 1970s, this was considered an advantage, but today we realize that data base constraints are rarely absolutes, i.e., that for the most part they are determined by the processes that make use of data. Indeed, as was already stated in Chapters 20 and 21, all data should belong to data types, and processes should be associated with data types, thus allowing the owner of a process to own the data associated with the process as well.

The statechart visual formalism. Statecharts are process diagrams similar to Figure 18.2, but with much more elaborate diagramming conventions that allow a process to be described in rigorous terms. Transitions carry labels. On the diagram the labels are represented in a shorthand notation, but a dictionary contains them in a fully expanded form, and the expansions are written in a formal language. Some process designers may feel happy working with diagrams supported by text, and for them Statecharts are probably the most appropriate notation. Others may feel happier working with text supported by diagrams. They may find the formalism we shall introduce in the next chapter more to their liking.

The specification language Z. A Z (pronounced "zed") specification consists of a declaration of the components of a data base, an expression in logic that defines valid states of the data base, and definitions of operations. Operations change data base states. Some background in discrete mathematics allows a reading knowledge of Z to be acquired fairly easily, but this does not mean that Z specifications are always easy to understand. The problem is that the state into which an operation brings the data base need not be a valid state, so that additional *implicit* operations may be needed to restore validity. Consequently, Z specifications are mathematically elegant, but are not easy to validate by potential system users who often lack the required mathematical sophistication. Moreover, Z lacks facilities for dealing with real-time and embedded systems. The emphasis that Z puts on states rather than types implies that there is no natural base for the modularization of large Z̈ pecifications.

Vienna development method (VDM). Originally developed for the precise definition of programming language constructs, VDM has become a widely used specification language. In VDM data are structured into records, and these records can serve as a base for modularization. However, just as with Z, there are no real-time facilities. We regard SF, which will be introduced in the next chapter, as a modernization and extension of VDM.

24
The Specification Language SF

The SF (Set-Function) language has been designed for the specification of information-control systems. An SF specification is derived from type, state transition, and data flow or Petri net diagrams. The SF language is shown to have a strong object orientation.

A specification of a process in the SF (Set-Function) language is called an SF segment, which corresponds to a data type. The segment has three parts: a schema that describes the information base of the process, events that change the information base and thus introduce behavioral aspects into the specification, and a control component, called the responder, which consists of transactions that allow events to be joined together into a process. The schema definition identifies the set of interest for the segment and defines functions that map from this set. For the most part, it is a type diagram (such as in Figure 20.2), together with its function definitions, but expressed in terms of the constructs of SF. Process building is by means of signals that are either "on" or "off", and that link events and transactions within and across segments. Events switch signals on; transactions switch them off. A signal may be a carrier of additional information that we want to send from one segment to another, or merely from one event to another. Hence, switching on a signal is in effect the sending of a message. Signals do not belong to data types, but all signals that originate in a segment have this segment for their home segment, and they are listed in a segment definition before the actual schema definition. Signals that are imported into the segment are also listed.

We shall use the library example from Chapter 17 to introduce the basic constructs of SF, but shall at times deviate from the rules of SF to avoid getting distracted by technical detail of little relevance in an introductory exposition. Readers not familiar with the notations should refer to Appendix A for a brief introduction. They should note that the use of mathematical notations in software specifications will definitely increase in the future.

The library example requires three segments—for titles, copies, and borrowers. The titles segment defines a miniprocess that introduces title data into the library catalog. The copies segment relates to the life process of a copy, from purchase to removal. The borrower segment has no process associated with it—it consists of little more than an information base. We shall not discuss it here, so that only the schemas for segments *Copies* and *Titles* will be listed.

SEGMENT   *Copies*;
  IMPORTEDSIGNAL   *TitleFixed(Copy, Title)*;
  SIGNALS   *CatalogCopy(Copy, Title)*;
              AddTitle(Copy, Title);   (* exported to segment *Titles* *)
              IncreaseCount(Borrower);   (* exported to segment *Borrowers* *)
              ReduceCount(Borrower);   (* exported to segment *Borrowers* *)
  TYPE   *Copy*;   SET *C* (SUBSETS: *AV, CO, BR, L, R*);
    FUNCTIONS   *BookId*:   *C → Title*;
                History: *C → (Borrower × Date)*–set;
  ENDTYPE;
SEGMENT   *Titles*;
  IMPORTEDSIGNAL   *AddTitle(Copy, Title)*;
  SIGNALS   *TitleFixed(Copy, Title)*; (* exported to segment *Copies* *)
  TYPE   *Title*;   SET *T*;
    SECONDARYTYPES   *Area; Author*;
    FUNCTIONS   *TitleText*:   *T → Text*;
                Authors: *T → Author*–set;
                Subjects: *T → Area*–set;
  ENDTYPE;

The set for data type *Copy* is *C*, and it is partitioned into subsets *AV, CO, BR, L,* and *R*, which correspond to the states shown in Figure 17.1. For each copy, function *BookId* tells to what title this copy belongs, and *History* gives its complete borrowing history. Four signals originate in this segment, and one is imported into it (from segment *Titles*). We shall explain their purposes later on. In the schema definition for *Titles*, the concept of a secondary type is introduced. Secondary types consist of entities with no attributes—there is no point in creating separate segments around them. In our example, they provide targets for the functions *Authors* and *Subjects*.

The specification of events consists of *preconditions* and *postconditions*. Preconditions determine under what circumstances an event may take place. They serve as a check on the feasibility of input values and embody consistency criteria for the information base of the segment. Postconditions are divided into *dataconditions* and *sigconditions*. Dataconditions indicate the changes that sets and maps undergo as consequences of an event taking place. Sigconditions send signals to transactions. An event is regarded as atomic, i.e., the objects with which the event deals are not accessible to other events until the event is done with them. Segment *Titles* has just one event. It adds title information to the library catalog:

EVENT   *EnterTitle*(*newcopy*: *Copy*, *book*: *Title*, *t*: *Text*, *A*: *Author*–set, *S*: *Area*–set);
    PRECONDITIONS   *book* ∉ *T*;
    DATACONDITIONS $T' = T \cup \{book\}$;
                              TitleText'(*book*) = *t*;
                                Authors'(*book*) = *A*;
                                Subjects'(*book*) = *S*;
    SIGCONDITIONS   (*TitleFixed*(*newcopy*, *book*))ON;
ENDEVENT;

Event *EnterTitle* has five arguments, and the heading lists the arguments together with their types. Two of the arguments are sets—a title can have more than one author, and it is almost certain to deal with more than one subject area. An event only takes place if its preconditions are satisfied. Here there is just one precondition, which is true if *book* has not already been used as a title identifier. The dataconditions now add *book* to set *T*, and the pairs *<book, t>*, *<book, A>*, and *<book, S>* to the three functions. The set and functions are changed as a result of the event, and the prime symbol denotes a changed quantity. Thus, the equation $T' = T \cup \{book\}$ tells us that T', the set after the event, is *T*, the set before the event, with *book* added to it. With the equation $fun'(x) = t$ there can be two cases. If function *fun* already contains some pair *<x, s>*, then *<x, t>* replaces this pair; if not, then pair *<x, t>* is simply added to the function. The event also raises signal *TitleFixed*, of which later.

Turning to segment *Copies*, we look first at Figure 17.1. Since the state transition diagram shows nine transitions, it appears that we need nine events, one for each transition. However, we also have to take care of the initial purchase of a copy, and this needs two events, which we list as *CheckCatalog* and *AddCopy* below. On the other hand, all three transitions into *R* can be handled by a single event. So there will be nine events after all. Let us list the events first, and then expand in full the three events marked with an asterisk:

AddCopy (*)	*MarkAsFound*
CheckCatalog (*)	*MarkAsLost*
CheckIn	*RemoveCopy*
CheckOut (*)	*ToRepair*
FromRepair	

Two events need explanation, *MarkAsLost* and *MarkAsFound*. Event *MarkAsLost* is initiated when library personnel or a borrower cannot find a copy that is in state *AV* and should be on the library shelves. If the copy has been merely misshelved, it will turn up again during a regular inventory check or even earlier. This is when event *MarkAsFound* is exercised. If, however, the inventory check does not turn up the copy, it has to be regarded as permanently lost, and the copy makes a transition from state L to state R—the event effecting this transition is *RemoveCopy*. Now the expansions:

EVENT   *AddCopy(newcopy: Copy, book: Title)*; (* initiated by a transaction *)
DATACONDITIONS $AV' = AV \cup \{newcopy\}$;
$\qquad\qquad\qquad\qquad BookId'(newcopy) = book$;
ENDEVENT;
EVENT   *CheckCatalog(newcopy: Copy, book: Title)*;
PRECONDITIONS $newcopy \notin C$;
SIGCONDITIONS $book \in T \rightarrow (CatalogCopy(newcopy, book))$ON;
$\qquad\qquad\qquad\quad book \notin T \rightarrow (AddTitle(newcopy, book))$ON;
ENDEVENT;
EVENT   *CheckOut(copy: Copy, borr: Borrower)*;
PRECONDITIONS $copy \in AV$;
$\qquad\qquad\qquad Borrower.CopiesOut(borr) < Borrower.Limit$;
DATACONDITIONS $AV' = AV - \{copy\}$;
$\qquad\qquad\qquad\qquad CO' = CO \cup \{copy\}$;
$\qquad\qquad\qquad\qquad History'(copy) = History(copy) \cup \{<borr,$
$\qquad\qquad\qquad\qquad DateNow>\}$;
SIGCONDITIONS $(IncreaseCount(borr))$ON;
ENDEVENT;

Again we see signals being switched on. In addition, a precondition of event *CheckOut* refers to the functions *CopiesOut* and *Limit* in the borrowers' segment—*Limit* is a constant that tells how many copies a borrower may hold at a time, and *CopiesOut* tells how many copies the borrower actually holds. Now, when a copy is checked out, the value of *CopiesOut* has to be increased, but only the owner of the borrowers' segment may change anything in the information base of that segment. Hence, *IncreaseCount* is switched on with the purpose of causing the adjustment of *CopiesOut* in the borrowers' segment. The *DateNow* that appears in the updating of *History* is a constant function whose value is the current date; most computer operating systems supply such a function.

Let us now look at what happens to signals. A signal is switched on by an event and is then picked up by a transaction in the same or another segment. A signal remains alive until it is explicitly turned off. Suppose that segment A wants segment B to perform some action. It makes the request by switching on a signal. This signal is *exported* by segment A and *imported* by segment B. Segment B may inform segment A of the completion of the action by an explicit second signal or merely by turning off the signal.

We now introduce two transactions belonging to *Copies* (*InternalOk* and *ExternalOk*) and one belonging to *Titles* (transaction *TitleToBeAdded*):

TRANSACTION   *InternalOk*;
  ON(*CatalogCopy*(*newcopy*, *book*))OFF: *AddCopy*(*newcopy*, *book*);
ENDTRANSACTION;
TRANSACTION   *ExternalOk*; (* *TitleFixed* is raised in segment *Titles* *)
  ON(*TitleFixed*(*newcopy*, *book*))OFF: *AddCopy*(*newcopy*, *book*);
ENDTRANSACTION;
TRANSACTION   *TitleToBeAdded*;
  ON(*AddTitle*(*newcopy*, *book*))OFF:
        PROMPT(*EnterTitle*(*newcopy*, *book*, _, _, _));
ENDTRANSACTION;

These transactions are part of the definition of the subprocess that adds a new copy to the library. The arrival of a new copy causes a librarian to initiate event *CheckCatalog*, for which the librarian has to supply a copy identifier (*newcopy*) and a title identifier (*book*). This event is a rare example of an event that does not change the information base of its segment. If *book* belongs to *T*, *CatalogCopy* is switched on, this signal is picked up by transaction *InternalOk*, and the transaction initiates event *AddCopy* on its own accord. If not, *AddTitle* is switched on and this signal is exported to *Titles*, where it is picked up by *TitleToBeAdded*. This transaction knows that event *EnterTitle* is to take place but cannot initiate it on its own. Hence it issues a prompt to a librarian who is to supply the three missing arguments for *EnterTitle*. As part of *EnterTitle*, the signal *TitleFixed* is switched on, which is picked up by *ExternalOk* in *Copies*, and *AddCopy* is initiated. We need two transactions to initiate *AddCopy* because the signals that enable them originate in different segments. The SF convention that requires that every signal have a home segment allows only its home segment to switch on the signal. On the other hand, several transactions in different segments may have the potential to switch off a signal, but only one transaction can actually do so in a given instance. This allows some nondeterminism.

Consider now how a transaction is initiated. This can be done in two ways. The first is by a signal; the transaction receives a signal, turns it off, and performs an action. In the examples given above, the action is either the automatic initiation of an event or a prompt to the process team to initiate an event. The transaction shown below introduces a third alternative, which is a reminder. Such a transaction can remind a process participant of anything at all.

The transaction shown below also introduces the second way of transaction initiation. In this mode, the transaction initiates itself at a given time. Here it reminds librarians every morning at 9:00 that they should check what progress has been made on the repairs of copies in subset *BR*.

The FORALL is an iterator—in our example it tells that the reminder is to be issued for every copy in subset BR:

TRANSACTION;
  @(09:00): FORALL(x): $x \in BR$: REMIND ("Check the progress on":
  x);
ENDTRANSACTION;

The separation of the action of sending out a message (i.e., switching on a signal as part of an event) from the definition of the ultimate effect of this message (in a transaction, which may reside in a different segment) has several attractive features. First, events can be defined independently of transactions, and all decisions regarding the precise effect of a message can be postponed. Second, because messages are not addressed, more than one transaction can pick up a message, which adds to the flexibility of the entire system. For example, the availability of a resource can be made known to several processes that may wish to use this resource without naming the processes. Third, all indications of the time dependence of the effect of a message belong to the definition of transactions, i.e., the specification of time-related aspects of the system is confined to the responder. Fourth, by confining all iterative actions to transactions, events are given a particularly simple structure.

Prompting or reminding transactions point out tasks that are candidates for automation. A prompting transaction knows that an event is to take place, but cannot supply all its arguments. If the supplying of the arguments is taken over by an expert system, the transaction can initiate the event on its own. If all of the activities of an organization are specified in SF, then prompting transactions indicate all of the opportunities for the introduction of expert systems, in each instance a cost-benefit analysis can be made, the opportunities can be ranked according to the results of the analysis, and expert systems can be developed incrementally in order of the ranking. If full automation is not called for, a decision support system can be made to assist the human decision maker in arriving at the appropriate inputs to the event to be initiated. Thus prompting events become the decision steps mentioned in Chapter 2. When full or partial automation is introduced by means of an expert system or a decision support system, the new process probably will be more complex than the approach it replaces. Reengineering does not always mean simplification— it means greatly increased effectiveness, but this may require a more complex process structure.

Reminders often relate to information that a process is to send into the outside world. This may consist of forms and data extracted from the information base. For example, with reference to transition T8 in Figure 21.2, the transition becomes an SF transaction and what is sent to a referee is actually a packet consisting of the text of the paper, refereeing guidelines, an evaluation sheet, a return envelope, etc. The SF language has facilities for defining such packets, and a "REMIND" can be replaced by a "MOVE" that has for its arguments the packet to be moved and the intended recipient of the packet. The preparation of the packet may be automated.

We shall now relate SF to object orientation. Origins of the object-oriented paradigm of software development are to be found in the programming language Simula, which was introduced in the 1960s; but it was not until the late 1980s that the business information systems community became interested in object orientation. Four features characterize the paradigm: data abstraction, encapsulation, inheritance, and message passing. The reason for its popularity is that these features facilitate modular development of software and allow fairly easy distribution of a large software system over several processing sites. In addition, software constructed according to the object-oriented paradigm is relatively easy to test and maintain. Moreover, easy maintenance implies easy reuse. We have already looked at data abstraction and encapsulation in Chapter 9, but will now expand on the discussion.

Data abstraction. Abstraction is the shutting out of irrelevancies. Turning again to the sunrise function that we looked at in Chapter 8, all we need to know is how to supply an argument, i.e., in what format we have to express the date for which we want the time of sunrise, and how to interpret the value that the function returns, i.e., whether it is given as a count of minutes from midnight or as an hours–minutes pair. Whether the value is calculated or looked up in a table is irrelevant. With data types we get the abstraction we want. A data type consists of objects and operations or functions associated with the objects. We have already looked at the data type of integers in Chapter 8. The objects of the data type considered here are the days of the year 2001, and the sunrise function is one of the functions of this type. In our SF example, one of the types is named *Title*, the set of objects of this type is *T*, and its operations are the three functions *TitleText*, *Authors*, and *Subjects*, as well as the event *EnterTitle*. Designing a process system around a set of data types introduces modularization in a natural way—a data type is a module.

Encapsulation. When a data type is encapsulated, the only way its components can be accessed is by means of its operations. Now, if the method of finding the sunrises were to be changed, such a change would not affect any program external to the type "days-of-the-year-2001". This is known as *data independence*, and it is very important for maintenance and testing. Suppose that we initially used an algorithm to compute the sunrises, but that this approach was found to be too slow. In changing over to a table, we would not have to change anything else in the system, and only the code that extracts a sunrise from the table would need to be tested. In terms of the SF type *Title*, encapsulation means that a value of one of the three functions can be obtained only by referencing this function by its name and supplying a title as the argument. The only way the functions can be changed is by means of the event *EnterTitle*.

Inheritance. The data types of a software system with object orientation are arranged in a hierarchy, and they inherit operations from other types higher up in the hierarchy. This is very important for data transformers, but not as important for the information components of a process system. In terms of the classification of the functions in Figure 8.1, the functions of data transformers are immutable. For example, we can set up a hierarchy in which the data type *Queue* of Chapter 9 is a subtype of a more general type *TwoEnded*. Type *TwoEnded* allows elements to be added to its top and bottom, and gives access to elements from both its top and bottom. Type *Queue* is a specialization that inherits from *TwoEnded* only a subset of these operations, namely the operations that add to its bottom and give access to its top. Operation *EnterTitle* of type *Title* is quite different: it changes the three functions of this type. Whenever we have mutable functions, only the "owner" of the module in which these functions reside should be permitted to make changes to the functions. If we relax this requirement, we surrender some of the advantages of data independence; if we do not, inheritance loses some of its punch. In SF, only module "owners" may change the data associated with a module. Inheritance facilities are provided to the full extent possible under this restriction.

Message passing. A paragraph in Chapter 9 explains that message passing between modules ensures a high degree of module autonomy, and this implies enhanced reuse potential of a module, a high degree of concurrency of execution, and reduced coupling between modules. This means that modules can be developed more or less independently of each other, that they can be distributed over several sites, and that they are relatively easy to test and maintain. Intermodule communication via message passing thus contributes most of the benefits that derive from object orientation. The signals of SF are messages, and this is one mechanism for allowing SF modules to work together. In addition, every function in one SF segment is accessible to other segments by means of a mechanism we call importation—for example, to evaluate the precondition of event *CheckOut*, the segment *Borrower* has to be consulted for the value of the constant function *Limit* and the value of *CopiesOut*. This can be regarded as message passing. For example, to access *CopiesOut*, the name of the function *CopiesOut* and the argument *borr* are sent to *Borrower*; segment *Borrower* sends back the value of *CopiesOut(borr)*. The message-passing concept is refined even further in that an event may initiate another event only by raising a signal that then causes a responder transaction to initiate the event.

Before an SF specification becomes implemented as a prototype or as a final process system, it has to be validated according to the inspection plan in Chapter 22. A checklist for the inspection is as follows:

Identifiers are well chosen
Subsets of the main set correspond to entity states
Arguments of events are used in the bodies of the events
Preconditions of events are realistic
Preconditions of events are sufficient
Event does modify all relevant functions
Internal events are triggered somewhere
Every signal is picked up somewhere
Sequencing of events agrees with user expectations
Arguments of signals are used by appropriate transactions
Failed prompted events are prompted again
Specifications are well annotated with comments

All of the items on the list should be understandable, except for "Failed prompted events are prompted again" and "Internal events are triggered somewhere." An internal event is an event that is supposed to be initiated by the system on its own, by means of a transaction—*AddCopy* is such an event in the library example. A prompted event is regarded as having failed if it is intentionally or unintentionally ignored by the process team that receives it. The signal that caused the prompt is, of course, switched off to prevent a continuous repetition of the prompt. But the transaction that issues a prompt can also initiate an event that switches the signal on again, say event *ResetSignal*, and SF has a delay feature that allows the initiation of *ResetSignal* to be delayed by some stated interval of time, say 4 hours. Thus the prompt is issued over and over again at intervals of 4 hours. To stop this cycle, the event that is initiated when the prompt is finally obeyed should set a parameter in the information base that causes a precondition of *ResetSignal* to become false.

The only way to remove ambiguity from specifications is to use a language based in mathematics. Necessarily, this is also the case with SF, but we have tried to make the mathematics not too forbidding. Thus, although all preconditions and dataconditions are assertions in logic, the notation is not obtrusive. The assertions use operations on sets, finite functions, and numerical and boolean data types. All such operations have well-understood mathematical definitions. Signals relate events and transactions: only an event can switch on a signal; only a transaction can switch it off. This follows the Petri net formalism in which places are linked with transitions, but no two places or two transitions may be linked directly. Manipulation of signals corresponds to the movement of tokens. The theory of Petri nets thus provides mathematical foundations for SF processes.

25
An SF Specification:
An Editorial Office

This specification derives from the diagrams in Chapters 20 and 21. As is usual in the specification of nontrivial systems, the diagrams change somewhat during the specification process.

We shall now use the diagrams in Chapters 20 and 21 to guide us in the development of an SF specification for the editorial office. Here we are dealing with a rather simple process that merely formalizes existing practices. Some parts of the system could be automated, such as referee selection, but the development of an expert system for this task would not be cost-effective. On the other hand, a decision support system for the standardization of referees' evaluations would be very valuable—some referees are much more likely to reject a paper than others. Introduction of advanced technology, such as electronic submission of papers, will not change the basic structure of the process.

Work on definitions of events nearly always suggests some reorganization of the data types. In our case, we found that the separate data types for papers and versions as shown in Figure 20.2 did not work out well. The decision for the separation had been suggested by the titles–copies separation in the library example, but the perceived analogy between the two cases is not really valid: whereas different copies of a title can exist simultaneously as independent objects, the versions of a paper represent a sequence of stages in the evolution of a single object. We therefore eliminate type *Version* and the list of functions of type *Paper* then becomes

$$
\begin{aligned}
\textit{MainAuthor:} \quad & \textit{PAP} \to \textit{Correspondent}; \\
\textit{CurrentVersion:} \quad & \textit{PAP} \to \textit{VersionId}; \\
\textit{PaperTexts:} \quad & \textit{PAP} \to (\textit{VersionId} \times \textit{Text} \times \textit{Date})\text{–set} \\
\textit{Referees:} \quad & \textit{PAP} \to (\textit{Referee} \times \textit{Status})\text{–set} \\
\textit{DateSent:} \quad & \textit{PAP} \to (\textit{VersionId} \times \textit{Referee} \times \textit{Date})\text{–set} \\
\textit{RefReports:} \quad & \textit{PAP} \to (\textit{VersionId} \times \textit{Referee} \times \textit{Text} \times \textit{Date})\text{–set} \\
\textit{ReworkType:} \quad & \textit{REDO} \to \{\text{"revise", "rewrite"}\} \\
\textit{CutoffDate:} \quad & \textit{REDO} \to \textit{Date}
\end{aligned}
$$

Type *VersionId* consists of version identifiers, which might be, for example, 1 for the original submission, 2 for the first reworked version, etc. The function *History* is dropped—all of the information this function should provide is now found in the other functions. With these changes the type configuration becomes as shown in Figure 25.1. Note that the "Information base changes" components in the dictionary entries in Chapter 21 will also be affected by the elimination of type *Version*. They must be appropriately amended to prevent inconsistencies between different representations of a system.

Since we now have four major data types, four segments will be needed. We shall not define their schemas but merely list the types and their sets. The type *Paper* is particularly important because it was decided to associate the editorial process with this type, but, since the targets of its functions have already been listed, the schema for even this type will not be written out in full. The four type declarations are

TYPE *Correspondent*; SET *CORR*;
TYPE *Referee* ISA *Correspondent*; SET *REF*;
TYPE *EdOffice* ISA *Correspondent*; SET *EDOFF*;
TYPE *Paper*; SET *PAP* (SUBSETS *NOTEV, ACC, REJ, REDO*);

We shall now give an SF specification of all events and transactions of the papers segment. However, before doing so, we note that in the writing of the specifications in SF we found that the Petri net in Figure 21.2 had to be slightly changed in a few places. The need for change arises all the time in software development. Often the diagrams and the

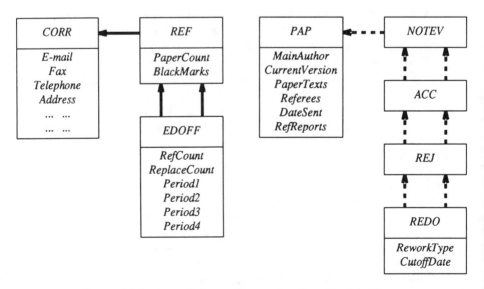

FIGURE 25.1. Amended type diagram for the editorial office.

formal specifications are developed in parallel, the development of one representation of the system providing the driving force for the development of the other. In our case we found that the following changes were needed:

(a) Instead of a single token enabling T1, and the firing of T1 depositing 3 tokens into P4, we now have just one line from T1 to P4. The process is started by depositing k tokens into P1, where $k = EdOffice. RefCount$, i.e., the number of referees that each paper should have. There is now greater flexibility because a change in the value of *RefCount* (in segment *EdOffice*) will not require the Petri net to be redrawn.

(b) Similarly, the three lines from P3 to T5 are replaced by a single line. Each time another referee's report comes in, a check is made whether the value of *RefCount* has been reached. If so, T5 is enabled, and, since it is implied that we are dealing with a time Petri net in which the time label on T5 is (0, 0), T5 fires at once.

(c) The two lines from T13 to P7 are replaced by a single line. The reason for the replacement is similar to that given under (a) above. This allows transition T14 to be eliminated. The line that in Figure 21.2 goes from P6 to P7 via T14 now goes via T13.

(d) After change (b), T4 and T5 have exactly the same purpose. We still need two transition symbols in the diagram, but the label on each can now be made T5. What this means is that there are still two transitions in the Petri net, but that they are represented by a single transaction in the corresponding SF specification.

(e) Transition T6 is split into T6A and T6B. Transition T6A is enabled when a time limit forces evaluation of the original version of a paper even though some referee's reports may still be outstanding; T6B is enabled when a rewritten version of a paper is to be evaluated.

A complete listing of the events and transactions that define the paper evaluation process now follows. We show the specification in full to demonstrate that the size of the specification of a nontrivial application can be fairly small. We have used SF because of our extensive experience with this language. Other languages could have been used, but, as we explained in Chapter 23, a specification language for business processes has to have certain properties that most specification languages lack. Note that SF is still a paper-and-pencil language, although it can be implemented fairly easily as a prototyping language. Most of the components of the specification will be preceded by explanations.

Event *EnterPaper* (P1 in Figure 21.2) is initiated by somebody in the editorial office on receiving a paper. This person supplies an identifier for the paper and a version identifier. A check is made that the identifier of the paper has not been used already. A triple is constructed that consists of the text of the paper, the version identifier, and the date the version is received (*DateNow*, supplied by the system). This triple enters the information base, as do other items as indicated by the dataconditions. The signal *SelectRef* is raised several times, the exact number being given by *EdOffice. RefCount*. The purpose of this signal is to initiate referee selection via transaction T1. The signal *EvalTrigger* is also raised, but it does not have an immediate effect—it is turned off by transaction T6A, which, after a considerable delay (42 + 21 + 42 days in our case), will issue a prompt asking that evaluation of the paper be undertaken.

EVENT *EnterPaper*(*pap*: *Paper, author*: *Correspondent, ver*:
VersionId, vertext: *Text*);
    PRECONDITIONS *pap* $\notin$ *PAP*;
    DATACONDITIONS *NOTEV'* = *NOTEV* $\cup$ {*pap*};
                    MainAuthor'(*pap*) = *author*;
                    CurrentVersion'(*pap*) = *ver*;
                    PaperTexts'(*pap*) = {<*ver, vertext*,
                      DateNow>};
                    Referees'(*pap*) = NULL;
                    DateSent'(*pap*) = NULL;
                    RefReports'(*pap*) = NULL;
    SIGCONDITIONS (*SelectRef*(*pap*))ON TIMES *EdOffice.*
                    RefCount;
                    (*EvalTrigger*(*pap*))ON;
    ENDEVENT;

The next event is initiated when a reworked version of a paper is received. A definition relates to textual substitution: If the definition has the form *a*: *b*, then *a* has been used in the event (or transaction) as an abbreviation for *b*. Here, *datetest* is an abbreviation for an expression relating the current date and the date by which the reworked version is to be received. The value of the expression is true or false. If it is true, the paper is rejected, i.e., it is moved from subset *REDO* to subset *REJ*, and signal *TooLate* is raised. Looking forward to event *Evaluation*, which would have preceded *RedoDone* in time, the result of the evaluation would have resulted in acceptance, rejection, or a demand that the paper be revised or rewritten, and the value of *ReworkType* for a paper in one of the two latter categories would have been set to "revise" or "rewrite"—these two labels constitute *RedoType*. A paper in category "rewrite" needs to be sent out to referees again; a paper in category "revise" is to be evaluated by the editorial office. However, the category assigned to the paper before it was reworked no longer may be appropriate—in particular, a "revise" paper may have been changed so extensively that another round of refereeing is required. Hence, the label *kind* is to be supplied by the editorial office. A paper regarded as having been revised is now to be evaluated. A paper considered rewritten is to be sent to referees, and signal *RewriteEvalTrigger* is raised. This signal is picked up by transaction T6B, and, after an appropriate delay, the editorial office is prompted to evaluate the rewritten paper.

EVENT *RedoDone*(*pap*: *Paper*, *ver*: *VersionId*, *vertext*: *Text*, *kind*: *RedoType*);

   DEFINITIONS *datetest*: $DateNow > CutoffDate(pap)$;
   PRECONDITIONS $pap \in REDO$;
  DATACONDITIONS $CurrentVersion'(pap) = ver$;
         $PaperTexts'(pap) = PaperTexts(pap) \cup \{<ver,$
          $vertext, DateNow>\}$;
         $REDO' = REDO - \{pap\}$;
         $datetest \rightarrow REJ' = REJ \cup \{pap\}$;
         $not(datetest) \rightarrow NOTEV' = NOTEV \cup \{pap\}$;
   SIGCONDITIONS $datetest \rightarrow (TooLate(pap))ON$;
         $not(datetest) \wedge kind =$ "rewrite" $\rightarrow$
          $(RewriteToRefs(pap))ON$;
         $not(datetest) \wedge kind =$ "rewrite" $\rightarrow$
          $(RewriteEvalTrigger(pap))ON$;
         $not(datetest) \wedge kind =$ "revise" $\rightarrow$
          $(EvaluatePap(pap))ON$;
ENDEVENT;

Event *ReportIn* is triggered by the arrival of a referee's report at the editorial office. A check is made that *ref* is indeed a referee of *pap*. Now, the value of *Referees*(*pap*) is a set of pairs of the form <referee, status>. Given a set of tuples S, $coord(k, S)$ is an SF system function that generates a set of the kth coordinates of all the tuples that make up S. Here it generates the set of all referees of *pap*. The value of the set-valued function *RefReports* is updated by adding to it a quadruple consisting of the version identifier, *ref*, *ref*'s report, and the current date. Evaluation of the original version can take place as soon as the required number of reports has been received; evaluation of a rewritten paper is triggered by transaction T6B.

EVENT *ReportIn*(*pap*: *Paper*, *ref*: *Referee*, *report*: *Text*);
   PRECONDITIONS $ref \in coord(1, Referees(pap))$;
  DATACONDITIONS $RefReports'(pap) = RefReports(pap) \cup$
         $\{<CurrentVersion(pap), ref, report,$
         $DateNow>\}$;
   SIGCONDITIONS $pap \notin REDO \wedge size(RefReports'(pap)) =$
         $EdOffice. RefCount \rightarrow$
         $(EvaluatePap(pap))ON$;
ENDEVENT;

The assignment of a referee to a paper in the next event is triggered by transaction T1 or transaction T7—transaction T1 issues a prompt, and the editorial office makes the selection; if T7 triggers the event, then a referee has already been selected (as part of event *TentativeRefSelection*). The pair <*ref*, "active"> is added to the value of *Referees* for *pap*. The label "active" belongs to the type *Status*—the other members of this type are "potref" (replacement referee has been selected but has not yet agreed to serve), "notwilling" (replacement referee does not agree to serve), "resigned" (original referee resigns), "notcompleted" (the original referee has not completed the assignment by the final due date). The values of *RefType* are "orig" and "replace", and the actual value supplied as argument *refkind* to the event tells how the value of *Referees*(*pap*) is to be updated. Actually, only one datacondition is necessary for this: if *refkind* = "orig", then there is no <*ref*, "potref"> in *Referees*(*pap*), and *diff* is equal to *Referees*(*pap*). Nevertheless, two dataconditions have been introduced. This is to emphasize the fact that event *AssignReferee* can be reached by two different paths. Signal *RaisePaperCount* goes to the referees segment, where 1 is added to the value of *PaperCount*(*ref*). If *refkind* of *ref* is "orig", then signal *RemindRef* is raised, to be picked up by T17. At T17, after an appropriate delay, if *ref* has not yet submitted a report and *ref* is still active (i.e., has not resigned), *ref* is reminded to submit a report and a cutoff procedure is primed—T17 initiates *SetRefTimer*, which raises *RefTimeLimit*; the latter is picked up by T15 and, after a proper delay, initiates an event that is to replace *ref* in case no report has been received from *ref*.

EVENT *AssignReferee*(*pap*: *Paper*, *ref*: *Referee*, *refkind*: *RefType*);

> DEFINITIONS   *diff*: (*Referees*(*pap*)—{<*ref*, "potref">});
> *curr*: *CurrentVersion*(*pap*);

> PRECONDITIONS   *pap* ∈ *PAP*; *ref* ∈ *REF*;

> DATACONDITIONS   *refkind* = "orig" →
> *Referees'*(*pap*) = *Referees*(*pap*) ∪ {<*ref*, "active">};
> *refkind* = "replace" →
> *Referees'*(*pap*) = *diff* ∪ {<*ref*, "active">};
> *DateSent'*(*pap*) = *DateSent*(*pap*) ∪ {<*curr*, *ref*, *DateNow*>};

> SIGCONDITIONS   (*RaisePapCount*(*ref*))ON;
> *refkind* = "orig" → (*PaperToRef*(*pap*, *ref*, *EdOffice*. *Period1*))ON;
> *refkind* = "orig" → (*RemindRef*(*pap*, *ref*))ON;
> *refkind* = "replace" → (*PaperToRef*(*pap*, *ref*, *EdOffice*. *Period3*))ON;

ENDEVENT;

Event *Evaluation* is triggered by T5, T6A, or T6B. The arguments *eval* and *duedate* are to be supplied by the editorial office—*EvalType*, to which the value of *eval* belongs, consists of the labels "accept", "revise", "rewrite", and "reject". In case the paper is to be revised or rewritten, the editorial office supplies a cutoff date by which it is to receive the reworked version of the paper. The date will depend on the amount of reworking needed.

EVENT *Evaluation(pap: Paper, eval: EvalType, duedate: Date)*;
      DEFINITIONS   *redo: eval* ∈ {"revise", "rewrite"};
DATACONDITIONS $NOTEV' = NOTEV - \{pap\}$;
                              eval = "accept" → $ACC' = ACC ∪ \{pap\}$;
                              eval = "reject" → $REJ' = REJ ∪ \{pap\}$;
                              redo → $REDO' = REDO ∪ \{pap\}$;
                              redo → *CutoffDate'(pap)* = *duedate*;
                              redo → *ReworkType'(pap)* = *eval*;
  SIGCONDITIONS   *eval* = "accept" → (*AcceptanceNotice(pap)*)ON;
                              eval = "reject" → (*RejectionNotice(pap)*)ON;
                              redo → (*RedoNotice(pap, eval, duedate)*)ON;
ENDEVENT;

The next three events deal with the replacement of a referee. Event *ReplaceRef* is initiated either by T15 when a referee has not sent in a report after having been reminded (21 days earlier in our case) or by the resignation of a referee. The two cases are distinguished by the argument *why*, which can take the value "notcompleted" or "resigned". Event *ReplaceRef* leads via T13 to event *TentativeRefSelection*, and the editorial office now suggests replacement referees. A precondition checks whether the referee being suggested is not already a referee of the paper. If not, the willingness of the referee to serve is determined via T12 at the event *RefereeCheck*—if *ref* is not willing, *ok* is false and the status of *ref* changes from "potref" to "notwilling"; otherwise, via T7, event *AssignReferee* is invoked automatically.

EVENT *RefereeCheck(pap: Paper, ref: Referee, ok: Boolean)*;
      DEFINITIONS   *diff*: (*Referees(pap)* − {<*ref*, "potref">});
    PRECONDITIONS   *pap* ∈ *PAP*; *ref* ∈ *REF*;
DATACONDITIONS   not(*ok*) → *Referees'(pap)* = *diff* ∪ {<*ref*, "notwilling">};
   SIGCONDITIONS   *ok* → (*DoAssignment(pap, ref)*)ON;
                              not(*ok*) → (*TentativeSelect(pap)*)ON;
ENDEVENT;

EVENT *TentativeRefSelection(pap: Paper, ref: Referee)*;
   PRECONDITIONS   *pap* ∈ *PAP*; *ref* ∈ *REF*;
                              ref ∉ *coord*(1, *Referees(pap)*);
DATACONDITIONS   *Referees'(pap)* = *Referees(pap)* ∪ {<*ref*, "potref">};
  SIGCONDITIONS   (*CheckWillingness(pap, ref)*)ON;
ENDEVENT;

EVENT *ReplaceRef*(*pap*: *Paper*, *ref*: *Referee*, *why*: *Status*);
    DEFINITIONS   *diff*: (*Referees*(*pap*) − {<*ref*, "active">});
                     cond: *why* = "notcompleted";
    PRECONDITIONS *pap* ∈ *PAP*; *ref* ∈ *REF*;
                     <*ref*, "active"> ∈ *Referees*(*pap*);
    DATACONDITIONS *Referees'*(*pap*) = *diff* ∪ {<*ref*, *why*>};
    SIGCONDITIONS *cond* → (*AddBlackMark*(*pap*, *ref*))ON;
                     (*LowerPapCount*(*ref*))ON;
                     (*TentativeSelect*(*pap*))ON TIMES *EdOffice*.
                     ReplaceCount;
ENDEVENT;

Event *ExtendRequest* is initiated by the editorial office whenever an extension of time is requested for the reworking of a paper. Denote this paper by *pap*. The argument *duedate* is supplied by the editorial office. This date is not to come before the current *CutoffDate*(*pap*). If it is the same as *CutoffDate*, then the request is denied. Transaction T16 is used to convey the decision to *MainAuthor*(*pap*).

EVENT *ExtendRequest*(*pap*: *Paper*, *duedate*: *Date*);
    DEFINITIONS   *iftruethennogo*: *duedate* = *CutoffDate*(*pap*);
    PRECONDITIONS *pap* ∈ *REDO*;
                     duedate ≥ *CuoffDate*(*pap*);
    DATACONDITIONS *CutoffDate'*(*pap*) = *duedate*;
    SIGCONDITIONS (*ConveyDecision*(*pap*, *iftruethennogo*))ON;
ENDEVENT;

Events that do not change the information base very rarely arise in SF—*SetRefTimer* is an example of such an event.

    EVENT *SetRefTimer*(*pap*: *Paper*, *ref*: *Referee*);
       SIGCONDITIONS (*RefTimeLimit*(*pap*, *ref*))ON;
    ENDEVENT;

The purpose of most of the transactions to follow has already been explained in our discussion of the events. A construct that still needs an explanation is the

$$coord \ (2, \ \{x | x \in PaperTexts(pap) \wedge x = \\ <CurrentVersion(pap), \_\_, \_\_>\}) \qquad (25.1)$$

of T3 and similar expressions. The expression within the braces {. . .} is used to extract from the set of triples *PaperTexts*(*pap*) just those triples that have *CurrentVersion*(*pap*) for their first coordinates. Then the second coordinates are extracted from these triples, and the set of these coordinates is the value of Equation (25.1). However, only one triple in *PaperTexts*(*pap*) has *CurrentVersion*(*pap*) for its first coordinate, so that the set contains a single element and *coord* extracts its second coordinate, the text of the current version of the paper. The interpretation of

$<\_\_, ref, \_\_, \_\_> \notin RefReports(pap)$

is similar. Every element of *RefReports(pap)* is examined. If no element is found that has *ref* for its second coordinate, then the expression is true; otherwise, it is false.

TRANSACTION T1;
  ON(*SelectRef(pap)*)OFF: PROMPT (*AssignReferee(pap, __, "orig")*);
ENDTRANSACTION;

TRANSACTION T2;
  ON(*TooLate(pap)*)OFF: REMIND("Send too late notification": *pap,
    MainAuthor(pap)*);
ENDTRANSACTION;

TRANSACTION T3;
  DEFINITIONS *text*: *coord* (2, $\{x \mid x \in PaperTexts(pap) \land x =$
    $<CurrentVersion(pap), \_\_, \_\_>\}$);
  refset: *coord*(2, *RefReports(pap)*);
  ON(*RewriteToRefs(pap)*)OFF: FORALL (x): $x \in refset$:
    REMIND("Send rewrite to referee": *pap, x, text, EdOffice.
    Period*4);
ENDTRANSACTION;

TRANSACTION T5;
  ON(*EvaluatePap(pap)*)OFF: PROMPT (*Evaluation(pap, __, __)*);
ENDTRANSACTION;

TRANSACTION T6A;
  DEFINITIONS *delaytime*: *EdOffice. Period*1 + *EdOffice. Period*2 +
    *EdOffice. Period*3;
  ON(*EvalTrigger(pap)*)OFF: DELAY(*delaytime*):
    $pap \in NOTEV \rightarrow$ PROMPT (*Evaluation(pap, __, __)*);
ENDTRANSACTION;
TRANSACTION T6B;
  ON(*RewriteEvalTrigger(pap)*)OFF: DELAY(*EdOffice. Period*4):
    $pap \in NOTEV \rightarrow$ PROMPT(*Evaluation(pap, __, __)*);
ENDTRANSACTION;

TRANSACTION T7;
  ON(*DoAssignment(pap, ref)*)OFF: *AssignReferee(pap, ref,*
    "replace");
ENDTRANSACTION;

TRANSACTION T8;
  DEFINITIONS *text*: *coord* (2, $\{x \mid x \in PaperTexts(pap) \land x =$
    $<CurrentVersion(pap), \_\_, \_\_>\}$);
  ON(*PaperToRef(pap, ref, time)*)OFF:
    REMIND ("Send paper to referee": *pap, text, ref, time*);
ENDTRANSACTION;

TRANSACTION T9;
  DEFINITIONS *reports*: *coord*(3, {*x* | *x* ∈ *RefReports*(*pap*) ∧ *x* =
    <*CurrentVersion*(*pap*), —, —, —>});
  ON(*AcceptanceNotice*(*pap*))OFF :
    REMIND("Send acceptance notice": *MainAuthor*(*pap*), *reports*);
ENDTRANSACTION;

TRANSACTION T10;
  DEFINITIONS *reports*: *coord*(3, {*x* | *x* ∈ *RefReports*(*pap*) ∧ *x* =
    <*CurrentVersion*(*pap*), —, —, —>});
  ON(*RejectionNotice*(*pap*))OFF:
    REMIND("Send rejection notice}": *MainAuthor*(*pap*), *reports*);
ENDTRANSACTION;

TRANSACTION T11;
  DEFINITIONS *reports*: *coord*(3, {*x* | *x* ∈ *RefReports*(*pap*) ∧ *x* =
    <*CurrentVersion*(*pap*), —, —, —>});
  ON(*RedoNotice*(*pap*, *eval*, *duedate*))OFF:
    REMIND("Send redo notice": *MainAuthor*(*pap*), *reports*, *eval*,
    duedate);
ENDTRANSACTION;

TRANSACTION T12;
  ON(*CheckWillingness*(*pap*, *ref*))OFF: PROMPT(*RefereeCheck*(*pap*,
    ref, —));
ENDTRANSACTION;

TRANSACTION T13;
  ON(*TentativeSelect*(*pap*))OFF: PROMPT
      (*TentativeRefSelection*(*pap*, —));
ENDTRANSACTION;

TRANSACTION T15;
  ON(*RefTimeLimit*(*pap*, *ref*))OFF: DELAY (*EdOffice. Period2*):
    <—, *ref*—, —> ∉ *RefReports*(*pap*) → *ReplaceRef*(*pap*, *ref*,
    "notcompleted");
ENDTRANSACTION;

TRANSACTION T16;
  ON(*ConveyDecision*(*pap*, *iftruethennogo*))OFF:
    iftruethennogo → REMIND("Send denied notice":
    MainAuthor(*pap*));
    not(*iftruethennogo*) → REMIND("Send granted notice":
    MainAuthor(*pap*), *CutoffDate*(*pap*));
ENDTRANSACTION;

TRANSACTION T17;
  ON(*RemindRef*(*pap*, *ref*))OFF:

DELAY (*EdOffice. Period*1):
   <*ref*, "active"> ∈ *Referees*(*pap*) ∧ *ref* ∉ *coord*(2,
      RefReports(*pap*))
   → REMIND ("No report yet": *pap*, *ref*);
DELAY (*EdOffice. Period*1):
   <*ref*, "active"> ∈ *Referees*(*pap*) ∧ *ref* ∉ *coord*(2,
      RefReports(*pap*))
    → *SetRefTimer*(*pap*, *ref*);
ENDTRANSACTION;

26
A Case Study: Order Processing

Order processing is a very important business activity. This example illustrates the transition from an existing to a reengineered process.

Thoughtful application of statistical quality-control techniques has given the Titanic Manufacturing Company an enviable reputation for product quality. However, sales have been stagnant and profits are on a downward slide. There have been customer complaints, and they relate for the most part to the processing of customer orders. Titanic takes customer complaints very seriously and continuously tries to improve its way of doing business. A sample of complaints, and management reaction to the complaints, follows:

(A) After placing an order, the customer typically has to wait ten days for a response, which may take the form of a delay notice, i.e., an indication that the order cannot be filled at once because inventory is low. Solution: The customer receives an acknowledgement of an order as soon as the order is received by Titanic, and streamlining of handovers of the order and of the order processing tasks reduces the processing time to seven days.

(B) Customers complain that the expected delivery date on a delay notice may underestimate actual delivery by as much as three weeks. Solution: After calculating the expected delivery date, add 21 days to this date.

(C) Customers often find invoices inconsistent with shipments. This was diagnosed as primarily due to partial filling of an order because of inventory shortages but invoicing for the entire order. Solution: No attempt is made to fill orders partially; a delay notice goes out for the entire order.

If this were not enough, internal problems have also surfaced. Several of these problems with attempted solutions are

(D) Inconsistencies have been found between the inventory data base and actual inventory. In some cases, invoices had been sent to customers for orders that could not be filled although the data base indicated adequate stock levels. The inconsistencies were traced to delays in updates of the data base and to pilfering. Solution: Increased security at the warehouse, and adjustment of the inventory data base at the time the order moves on to the warehouse rather than at the time of shipment of the goods.

(E) On receiving a delay notice the customer may cancel an order. However, sometimes inventory has already been built up for filling this order. In the case of a large order, this raises inventory-carrying costs unnecessarily. Part of the problem is that on the average it takes three days to track down the original order corresponding to a cancellation. Solution: Before an attempt is made to build up inventory in case of a shortage, the customer is contacted to determine the likelihood of order cancellation.

(F) The company has seen a steady growth in the ratio of bad debts to sales, which has affected profits and hence the market value of the company. Solution: The credit department has been ordered to tighten credit checks.

Unfortunately, the solutions as implemented have improved neither sales nor productivity. Instead, sales have begun to drop, and profits are now dropping at an alarming rate. Serious morale problems have arisen, particularly in the sales department. Sales personnel are complaining that they are wasting time exploring prospects—almost invariably the credit department turns down an order from a new customer. At this point, the CEO calls in the Chief Operating Officer, and they jointly decide that radical reengineering of order fulfillment has to be undertaken. The COO is a great believer in process charts, and on his office wall there is a data flow diagram for order processing. This was shown in Figure 18.3, and this diagram is to become the starting point for reengineering.

The reengineering of order fulfillment is to be undertaken in several stages. The purpose of the first stage is to change the process structure so that it looks as shown in Figure 26.1. At a quick glance the new data flow diagram does not seem to differ much from Figure 18.3, but the differences are significant:

(a) The data stores have been eliminated. Instead of bubbles having local data stores attached to them, a global information base is assumed, which is to be accessible to all.

(b) On receiving an order, now the first task is to enter the order into the information base. This is the purpose of bubble RO (short for Register Order) in Figure 26.1.

(c) Some of the solid lines in Figure 18.3 have been replaced by dashed lines in Figure 26.1. Our convention is that solid lines represent communication of the process world with the world outside it; dashed lines represent internal communication by means of signals.

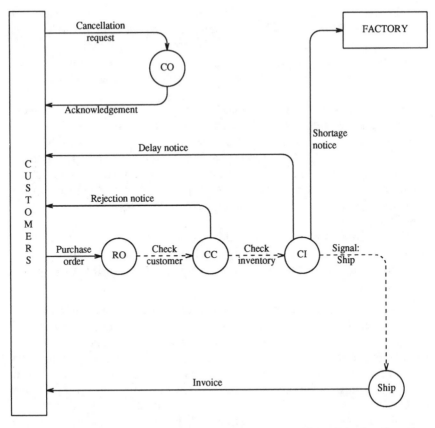

FIGURE 26.1. Data flow: processing of a purchase order (Version 2).

(d) The WAREHOUSE box has been eliminated. The bubble Ship now relates to the assembling and shipping of orders, and with the preparation of invoices to accompany the orders. This change requires that the task represented by Ship be executed at the warehouse, and that the warehouse have full access to the information base of the process.

The data flow diagram suggests that there should be three segments, *Orders*, *Customers*, and *Inventory*. Bubbles RO and CO relate to *Orders*, CC to *Customers*, and CI and Ship to *Inventory*. We could now try to write SF specifications for the three segments, but that would be premature. We see that Figure 26.1 provides an adequate level of guidance for the time being, but that we lack proper requirements for the steps of the process. The three main problems to be solved are customer credit checks, inventory maintenance, and partial shipments.

An audit of the operation of the credit department discloses that credit checks had been made by the manager of the department by himself, that this had sometimes taken a whole week, that there was a standstill whenever the credit manager was away, that the credit manager had just left the company, and that nobody else knows how he had arrived at his credit ratings. A decision is made that this aspect of the process is to be totally overhauled. The determination of credit ratings is to be outsourced. A credit company is to rate all established customers twice a year, and the ratings are to be held in the customer information base. Before sales personnel approach a prospective customer, a credit rating of the prospect is to be obtained from the credit company. Orders from customers with poor credit ratings are not to be turned down, but such orders are to be prepaid.

In general, outsourcing is to be approached with caution to prevent a company from being overdependent on one supplier. Particularly dangerous is the situation in which defense contractors in country A become dependent on suppliers in country B, and B, although it may have the same policy goals as A at the moment, need not have the same goals in the future. However, a credit company is a service company, and outsourcing of services is less likely to lead to undue dependence.

Since partial shipments relate to inventory, partial shipments and inventory maintenance are both inventory control problems. An order is now to be treated as follows. Items from inventory required to fill the order are reserved for the order in bubble CI, and assembling of the order begins. If there is a discrepancy between the information base and the actual inventory such that the order cannot be filled, the order is to be treated as a partial shipment order, to be satisfied to the extent that the actual inventory permits it. In such a case, a correction is to be made to the inventory data in the information base, and the items required for the partial filling of the order are to be reserved for this order. Still at CI, a process team member contacts the customer company and determines how the customer wants to proceed. The customer is given an estimated delivery date, which should be as accurate as possible. This is also done when no part of the order can be refilled.

We have seven cases: (1) the entire order can be filled; (2) none of the order can be filled, and the customer cancels; (3) none of the order can be filled, and the customer upholds the order; (4) partial shipment is possible, but the customer cancels; (5) partial shipment is possible, the customer accepts partial shipment but cancels the rest of the order; (6) partial shipment is possible, the customer accepts partial shipment and upholds the order for the items outstanding; and (7) partial shipment is possible, but the customer elects to wait until the order can be filled in full. In addition, there is case (8): the customer cancels the order for reasons unrelated to inventory shortages. Now let us consider the cases in turn.

1. The order is assembled, appropriate adjustments are made to inventory values in the information base, and the order is shipped accompanied by the appropriate invoice.

2. The order is marked as canceled in the information base and the reason for the cancellation is noted.
3. An appropriate shortage notice is sent to the factory and the client is formally notified of an expected delivery date.
4. Same as for (2). In addition, the reserved items are released back to general inventory.
5. This is a combination of (1) and (4).
6. This is a combination of (1) and (3).
7. This is essentially (3).
8. Depending on when the cancellation is made, we have a variant of either case (2) or case (4). It is best to treat this case as a separate subprocess, and we shall do so.

These different possibilities show that node CI of Figure 26.1 represents a rather complex process, but the identification of the various cases allows us now to construct a Petri net for this process quite rapidly. Figure 26.2 shows the internal structure of CI, and how CI interacts with Ship.

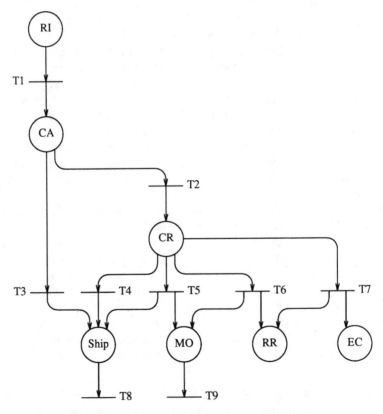

FIGURE 26.2. Petri net: filling of a purchase order.

An explanation of the place names and transition labels in Figure 26.2 is as follows:

RI: Reserve inventory for the order
CA: Compare inventory data with actual inventory (correct the information base if needed)
CR: Obtain customer response in case of shortage
Ship: Prepare order for shipping
MO: Prepare manufacturing order to be sent to factory
RR: Release reserved inventory
EC: Enter cancellation in the information base
T1:   Prompt—Check the inventory
T2:   Prompt—Contact the customer for instructions
T3:   Ship the entire order
T4:   Ship partial order
T5:   Ship partial order; Prompt—Issue manufacturing order
T6:   Prompt—Issue manufacturing order; release inventory
T7:   Release inventory; enter cancellation
T8:   Remind—Send out the shipment
T9:   Remind—Send manufacturing order to factory

Let us now relate case (8) to the process in Figure 26.2. The cancellation request is received at bubble CO in Figure 26.1. The cancellation request now initiates three actions: (i) an acknowledgement is sent to the customer; (ii) the cancellation is entered into the information base; and (iii) inventory that has been reserved for this order is released. The last two actions are precisely the actions that T7 in Figure 26.2 causes to happen. So, the code that implements T7, RR, and RC in Figure 26.2 also can become part of the implementation of subprocess CO. A special case arises if task RI in Figure 26.2 has not yet been performed on the order to be canceled. Then no inventory has been reserved, i.e., there is no inventory to release, but task RR can still be performed, with the amount of inventory to be released equal to zero.

The process as now defined is still problematic in one respect. Suppose that an order is received from customer Q, that the credit check reveals that orders from Q are to be prepaid, that Q resubmits the order accompanied by payment, and that only now is the inventory discovered to be too low to satisfy the order. This is the way the case is treated according to our process diagrams, but is it the right way? We leave it to the reader to define other courses of action, and to determine the advantages and disadvantages of each approach.

The most complex component of the Petri net in Figure 26.2 is the place (event) MO. Here a determination has to be made how big a manufacturing order is to go to the factory, and what the expected delivery date of the backorder will be. The method for arriving at these data will necessarily vary from company to company. What matters is that an order now can be processed in several hours, as long as there is an information system that provides adequate support.

Such an information system can be set up in several ways. One is to locate an information system consisting of the three segments *Orders*, *Customers*, and *Inventory* at the warehouse, and to move the process team to this location. The information system does not have to be located on one machine. It can be distributed over several PCs or workstations, and these machines do not even have to be joined by a network. As long as they are in close physical proximity, members of the process team can move from machine to machine as needed.

Another option is to assemble the process team at a single location, but not at the warehouse. The team can then communicate with the warehouse by fax or voice telephone. Under this approach, there are more opportunities for misunderstandings and for the introduction of erroneous data into the information system. The ideal solution is to have the process team and the warehouse joined in a network. Physical proximity is then of little concern, unless the process team is expected to carry out visual checks of the actual inventory.

This analysis shows that in the initial reengineering phase great gains can be achieved with minimal investment in technology. The initial phase should serve to effect a smooth changeover from a departmental structure to a process team structure. The next stage relates manufacturing to order fulfillment, but we should actually consider how three major processes affect each other. They are sales, which generates purchase orders, fulfillment of purchase orders, and manufacturing, which is driven by purchase orders. In this second reengineering stage, these three processes should be integrated by means of giving the respective process teams access to a common composite information base.

At this point technology does become important. As sales personnel pursue a sale, they update an information base that relates to prospective orders. By consulting this information base, and inventory information, manufacturing runs can be planned to increase inventory of those items for which there is the greatest likelihood of future demand. This suggests equipping sales personnel with laptop computers and linking manufacturing with the rest of the organization into a wide area network (WAN). This is particularly important when manufacturing is distributed over several sites, which may be located in more than one country.

The warehouse became an integral part of the order fulfillment process in the very first stage of the reengineering of this process. If the company has just one warehouse, well and good. If it has several, we would have carved out a sales region centered on one warehouse and limited our initial process implementation to this sales region. Many companies find it advantageous to maintain several warehouses. Generally, this lowers transportation costs and provides a company with a measure of local identity. However, inventory control is more complicated—not only is inventory to be kept at the most effective level, but the right level is to be maintained at the right place and the right time for this place. In these circumstances, economical considerations make it more or less imperative that order fulfillment be supported with a WAN.

The interesting part is that this does not change the process diagram (Figure 26.2). Each sales order is shunted to the processing team responsible for the sales region in which the order originates, and this team starts to process the order at place RI. The only change is in the interpretation of MO and T9. Now, if an order cannot be filled by the local warehouse, an attempt is made to use inventory held at the other warehouses. Thus, if order processing team A discovers by consulting a company-wide inventory information system that the parts of the order it cannot fill could be filled by order processing team B, it asks B to check that the physical inventory to do so is actually there and, if it is, to fill the rest of the order.

In the third phase, the information system of the supplier interacts directly with the information systems of its customers. The best known example of such an interaction has been established between Wal-Mart and Procter & Gamble. In essence, P&G checks inventory levels at Wal-Mart warehouses. By tracking patterns of inventory levels, P&G is able to tell at which Wal-Mart warehouses stocks need to be replenished. It then goes ahead and ships the goods. The benefits from this arrangement, which derive from the expertise P&G has developed with regard to inventory control, are shared by both parties: Wal-Mart benefits by having its inventory-carrying costs reduced, and P&G benefits by a reduction in the probability that its products will not be available on Wal-Mart shelves. In the context of order processing, the information base of Titanic Manufacturing could interact directly with the information base of the credit company that is to supply the credit ratings for Titanic's customers.

Let us now see how the order fulfillment process relates to the property that, according to the Preface, defines our approach—a process definition is independent of organizational structure. When we look at Figure 26.1, it does not really matter who performs the various tasks, as long as the process personnel fully understands the entire process and sees itself as a team. If the passing of signals is fast, it does not matter all that much whether the person who looks up a customer's credit rating still sits in a credit department or officially belongs to an order processing team. Also, it does not matter whether this person just looks up credit ratings or also walks into a warehouse and counts stock items. Ultimately, in the interests of customer relations and team efficiency, it will help to have each member of the process team responsible for dealing with all orders from a given set of customers. At this point the change from departmental to process team structure must already have taken place, but this change would not have affected the process diagrams.

VI
Implementation of Reengineering

27
The Reengineering Process

The 16-step reengineering plan in Chapter 4 is reexamined with a software engineering attitude. The five chapters that then follow deal with the most important aspects of the reengineering process.

Reengineering is innovative radical change rather than improvement of what already exists. Some processes cannot be improved at all, particularly in the service sector. An example of such a process has been singled out by the economist William Baumol (reported in [Bw93b]): Just as in 1792, the year of Mozart's death, so today a Mozart string quartet requires four players, four string instruments, and a certain length of playing time. Obviously the playing process itself cannot be improved. So let us look at the dissemination process. In 1792, the quartet was performed in an Archduke's or an Archbishop's palace to a select group of 50 guests. Today it is likely to be played in a concert hall to an audience of 500. This is improvement in dissemination. But radical innovation looks beyond live audiences—an unlimited number of people can listen to the quartet on tape or disc. This illustrates two key aspects of reengineering: the existence of enabling technology and imaginative application of the technology. But this is not enough. Not only must the technology exist and be applicable, it also must be accepted by the players and the listeners. Much of the effort spent on reengineering goes into breaking down resistance. Keeping this in mind, let us reexamine the 16 reengineering steps in Chapter 4.

1. *Management support.* Top management, perhaps even the board of directors, must be made aware of possible resistance to a reengineering effort, the risks arising from such resistance, and the results of cost-benefit analysis performed on the reengineering plan. Top management must be convinced that the reengineering personnel are competent and will carry out their task with minimal disruption in the operation of the organization.

2. *Manager selection.* In Chapter 4, the CIO was suggested as the best choice for the operational manager of the reengineering process. We have

now seen that the process view that characterizes a reengineered enterprise can be captured in process specifications, and that the development of such specifications is a skilled task for specialists. The reasons for our initial suggestion have thus been strengthened further.

3. *Reengineering teams.* The reengineering teams must be selected not on the basis of their technical competence and learning ability alone; they must also be innovative. Unfortunately, it is difficult to spot this quality in an employee. In many organizations, innovative ideas have been discouraged. An enterprise that has established an organizational structure for processing employee suggestions is now in a happy situation— it can turn to its information base of suggestions and pick out employees with an innovative bent. The ideal member of a reengineering team is technically competent, innovative, and eager to learn.

4. *Initial education.* The educational goal as stated in Chapter 4 for this step has to be broadened. Everybody in an organization must come to understand the nature of reengineering, but members of reengineering teams must also be instructed in methodology. They must become competent in the use of three classes of diagrams—schema diagrams (ER diagrams, or data-type diagrams), state transition diagrams for individual entities (such as Figure 17.1), and process diagrams (data flow diagrams, system state transition diagrams, or Petri nets). The use of a specification language such as SF for an intermediate representation between diagrams and the final implementation is not strictly necessary, but we have found that the use of a formal specification language is quite effective in preventing the introduction of faults, and, if faults have slipped in, often they can be more easily discovered in a specification than in code. If a specification language is to be used, the educational program has to build up competence in the use of the language. If a formal specification language is not used, then the diagrams, together with their component dictionaries, are regarded as the specification.

5. *Process identification.* See step 6.

6. *Process specification.* Although process identification and process specification usually are regarded as separate steps that are taken one after the other, sometimes it helps to consider them as intermixed in a single amalgamated step. We saw in Chapter 25 that the initial Petri net for the editorial office had to be modified during the specification phase. Similarly, the initial assignment of the activities of an organization to processes may have to be modified once specification of the processes begins.

7. *Implementation alternatives.* It needs to be remembered that any specification, be it expressed as diagrams or text, should leave the implementer with some choice. We have seen that SF specifications tend to leave it open whether a function value is to be obtained by interaction with a sensor, looking up a table, or having a function subprogram compute it.

8. *Cost-benefit analysis*. Cost-benefit analysis that relates to step 7 is cost-benefit analysis "in-the-small". The cost differences are small, and so are the differences in benefits. However, a trade-off may have to be considered between reliability and performance. Hardware can be made arbitrarily reliable by redundancy—the failure of a component has a negligible effect on the entire system because a reserve component takes over the functions of the failed component. Hardware failures are for the most part due to defects in the material, and the failure of one instance of a component is independent of the failures experienced by other instances of the component. Software failures, on the other hand, are due to design errors, and often the same error can affect every instance of a software component, even though the components may have been developed by different people, i.e., redundancy can only partially improve the reliability of a software system. On the other hand, software is faster than hardware. Therefore, performance can be improved by shifting the software–hardware boundary so that more tasks are allocated to software; reliability may be improved by moving the boundary in the other direction. The precise boundary is determined by cost-benefit analysis "in-the-small". Of course, if the design error is so fundamental that it relates to the entire system, shifting the boundary has no effect. Cost-benefit analysis "in-the-large" should determine which processes are to be reengineered first— obviously, they are the processes that lead to the greatest improvement at the lowest cost, but unfortunately an "improvement" rarely can be measured in quantitative terms. Nevertheless, an approximate ranking of reengineering tasks is possible and should be undertaken, but this is step 10.

9. *Infrastructure definition*. This is such an important topic that all of Chapter 30 is dedicated to it.

10. *Setting of priorities*. This is another important topic that requires a separate chapter—Chapter 28 deals with priorities. A special aspect of this topic is the adaptation of existing software to the needs of the reengineered organization. Legacy software is discussed in Chapter 29.

11. *Second education phase*. By now there has to be a clear under-standing of the duties of each process team. Although these duties were not explicitly spelled out in Chapters 25 and 26, the full specification would have made the duties quite clear. Turning to the Petri net in Figure 21.2, and coordinating the diagram with the textual specification, we see that the process team has to look after every event in the paper processing segment except P8 (*ReplaceRef*) and P10 (*SetRefTimer*). The latter are the only two events that are initiated by a transaction on its own. An operations manual is now to be produced for each process, the process team is to come to an understanding of all of the activities that the manual assigns to them, and they should go through hands-on simulation sessions to gain practical experience with their roles in the operation of the process. Expert systems have been developed for tutoring human

participants in processes, and such systems could be developed for the processes under consideration. Of particular importance are systems that simulate disaster scenarios in safety-critical applications of information-control systems. The second educational phase must prepare process teams for full participation in the operation of their processes, make it clear that further incremental improvement of a process is primarily the responsibility of the process team, and that management expects processes to be improved. Process education could be split into two parts. The first part of a process education course would get the process team ready to take on the process. In a second part, the team would have gathered some experience, would be ready to suggest how the first part of the course could be improved, and could consider their future responsibilities as process improvers with confidence.

12. *Pilot implementation*. The modes under which a pilot implementation of a process can take place were discussed in some detail under the corresponding heading in Chapter 4. In extending the discussion we note first that no major investment in infrastructure should be undertaken during pilot implementation. A large investment in information technology is justified only if an organization has a corporate culture and well trained personnel to make proper use of the information technology. A purchasing plan has to be drawn up carefully. The organization should start with hardware and software resources just sufficient to support the pilot implementation and then add to these resources incrementally, in step with the master plan for reengineering the organization. In the early stages of reengineering it would be very dangerous to try to introduce two aspects of reengineering simultaneously, e.g., to base a pilot implementation on imperfectly understood wide area network technology. Pilot processes should be confined to local settings.

13. *Reengineering reexamined*. This is the step in which top management has to be shown that the initial steps of the reengineering effort have been successful. If at this point the reengineering teams do not succeed in fully convincing top management of the benefits of reengineering, the future of reengineering in this organization is very bleak, as is the future of the members of the reengineering teams. This is one aspect that keeps people from volunteering for the reengineering teams. The irony in this is that lack of success often can be traced to lack of effective management support. Without moral support and adequate resources, there can be no reengineering. Reengineering is no miracle cure. As with every other business activity, benefits do cost, and success must be measured in terms of a cost-benefit analysis. Again the problem is that benefits rarely can be expressed in quantitative terms. When it comes to qualitative improvements, supporters of reengineering will see them, opponents will not. Therefore, to ensure that the reexamination of reengineering does result in approval of continuation of the reengineering

process, management is to be educated on the benefits of reengineering throughout the process.

14. *Completion of implementation.* After the reengineering process has survived step 13, it may seem that the reengineering teams can take a relaxing break and then tie up some few remaining loose ends. Actually, step 14 will probably take several years. Although the initial reengineering teams now have some experience in looking at the activities of an organization as a collection of processes, people not so enthusiastic about reengineering still need to be won over, and made effective personnel of reengineering teams and process teams. At this stage, much thought has to be given to a smooth integration of existing software, the processes arising from reengineering, and the infrastructure that is to support all information and control needs as well as all collaborative work.

15. *Continuing automation.* One of our reasons for choosing SF as the specification language for processes was the support it gives to continuing automation. Once all of the major processes of an organization have been defined in SF, prompting and reminding transactions indicate every opportunity for automation, as was noted in Chapter 24. It remains to examine each such opportunity and determine where actual automation would be cost-effective.

16. *Automatic linkages.* In Chapter 24 we noted that, when a REMIND is replaced by a MOVE, the process sends information into its environment. This is a primitive way for two organizations to exchange information. The linkage of networks is much more effective in that it allows one organization to access the information system of another organization directly. Consider a situation in which company Y is a supplier for company X. Under a conventional arrangement, an inventory tracking program would determine the time when X should send an order to Y. Under a cooperative arrangement made possible by automatic linkage, X would have access not only to its own inventory information base, but to that of the supplier as well, and Y could consult the inventories of all of the companies it supplies. Then Y would have very precise information for deciding when to build up its inventory by means of a manufacturing run, and X would be certain to be supplied precisely when it needs to replenish its inventory.

Finally, it has to be fully understood that our 16–step process relates primarily to just the technical aspects of the reengineering effort. We can have the best technology and the best enterprise model in place, and they will be totally useless unless they are employed creatively to improve the organization. Today's solutions will not fit tomorrow's problems. Therefore, the enterprise model has to be highly flexible to respond to changes in the environment rapidly and effectively. Recall that the goal we set for ourselves in Chapter 2 was to arrive at a decision-making mode of operation for organizations. A reengineered organization passes its real-life test when all of its processes are so flexible and so well understood that the organization can, for example, match any innovative marketing initiative of its competition within a few days. This can be achieved only if there is broad acceptance of the reengineering effort throughout the organization. What matters in the end is not technology and methods, but acceptance of the technology and methods by people.

28
Determination of Priorities

The actual reengineering of an organization starts with the definition of the organization in terms of processes, and specification of the processes. The costs, risks, and benefits associated with different processes and their implementation variants determine reengineering priorities. Of particular concern is the process that converts research and development findings into products for the market.

An important concern of reengineering is the order in which reengineered processes are to be made part of an organization; but before a decision can be made on the order of their implementation, processes have to be identified, specified, and analyzed with respect to costs and risks. The definition of a process tells *what* tasks belong to the process and the order in which the tasks are to be carried out, but it does not tell *how* to carry out the tasks, i.e., who is to be responsible for which task.

When asked to identify their major processes, companies come up with very different answers [Da93, p. 29]. The differences stem primarily from a tendency of companies to identify processes too closely with their products. By stepping back, so that our vision is no longer focused on a product line, we can identify a limited number of core processes that are found in some form or another in most organizations. Reexamination of these processes should receive top priority. They fall into two categories: operations and management. The core processes in the operations category are marketing and sales, order fulfillment, manufacturing, and customer service. We consider only one process to be a true management process. This process is strategic planning. The other activities that are usually regarded as management processes are actually services that support our five major processes. These services are information and communication, and the management of human resources, finances, and facilities. We put the development of new products in a totally separate category—as was noted in Chapter 13, R&D can be regarded as a separate organization at some distance from the rest of the company. In looking at the form the core processes and support services take, we shall be particularly concerned with nonmanufacturing organizations. For this we have selected a bank, a newspaper, a charitable foundation, and a university.

Marketing and sales. The purpose of this process is to attract new customers, seek repeat orders from established customers, and gather information for R&D. Banks want to attract deposits and also lend money, a newspaper hopes to increase its number of subscribers and its advertising revenues, a charitable foundation tries to find new donors, and a university tries to recruit new students and also looks for donors. In addition, sales personnel should gather information on what improvements customers would like to see in the products or services supplied by their organization, and should always be looking at ways their customers' satisfaction could be improved by a new product or service. This applies also to internally provided services. The information systems of my bank could be greatly improved if a representative from Information Systems were to observe operations in my branch office for a day or two—for example, the last time I needed a foreign bank draft made out, the process took 33 minutes, about 30 minutes more than it would have taken if a printer had been used in place of a typewriter; another time, I had to watch the amazement of a group of businessmen from Asia when they could not arrange a transfer of funds from Switzerland to the Pittsburgh bank because there were no fax facilities at the branch office.

Order fulfillment. We examined this process at some length in Chapter 26. A bank processes a loan application very much as is shown in Figure 26.1—the application is entered into the information base, the credit worthiness of the applicant is determined, the bank checks that it has the money to lend, and the loan is made. The same goes for advertisers in newspapers, except that "Check Inventory" will be different; there is no "inventory", but a feature story or news item may have to be cut to free up space for the advertisement. The charitable foundation receives requests for funds—the evaluation of a request is very similar to the processing of a loan application, except that under "Check Customer" the organization checks for need rather than credit worthiness. In the university context, student registration is a kind of order fulfillment. A student submits a registration form, the "Check Customer" is now a determination that the student is in good financial standing and that prerequisites are satisfied for the selected courses, and "Check Inventory" determines that the courses are still open.

Manufacturing. Nonmanufacturing enterprises do not manufacture products in the conventional sense, but newspapers have to be printed and distributed, which is a kind of manufacturing. So is the provision of courses by a university. On the other hand, the production of various documents by a bank or a university (statements and transcripts, respectively) is customer service rather than manufacturing.

Customer service. Banks are highly dependent on customer satisfaction, particularly the satisfaction of depositors when interest rates are low. But, as banks have moved various operations to different sites (the credit card department of my Pittsburgh bank is in Delaware, and the mortgage department is in Colorado), the mechanisms for dealing with customer problems have not kept pace with the moves. The newspaper should have a process for responding rapidly when a subscriber has not received the morning paper—the time between the complaint call and delivery of the paper should not exceed 15 minutes, and such times have been achieved [Ta93, p. 106]. A charitable foundation is unlikely to receive complaints from recipients of its funds, but donors have been known to complain about how donated funds have been distributed. Most universities are very large organizations, and a lot of mishaps can arise. Therefore, universities need properly defined systems for dealing with student complaints, and most universities do have such systems for most categories of complaints. In the analysis of customer services it has to be kept in mind that the customer base of an organization can vary greatly from organization to organization. First, an organization may cater to a business market, to a consumer market, or to both. At one extreme is a parts manufacturer supplying automakers; at the other is a small retail shop that sells on a cash-only basis. Second, the size of the customer base varies. The manufacturer of auto parts may have a single customer; the subscribers to a magazine may number in the millions.

Strategic planning. The effectiveness of this process determines the survival potential of an organization. Strategic planning should be concerned with opening new markets, deciding on new products, decreasing development times for the new products, balancing market share against profits, and this list can be easily extended. Thus, determination of reengineering priorities is also part of strategic planning. Let us consider how market share and profits relate to decreased development time. First, the company that is first in bringing a product to market has an immediate competitive advantage. Second, greater consumer concern with price for perceived value has changed pricing policies by companies. Instead of totaling costs and adding on a profit margin, nowadays a company decides on a price and then determines an exact specification for the product and the manufacturing process that allows the company to hold to this price and still make a profit. Under this fixed price approach, if a company takes too long to introduce its new product, the profit margin is in danger of disappearing.

Support services. The services with which an organization supports its major processes are in two categories: (a) resources, which consist of personnel, finance, and facilities; and (b) an information and communication infrastructure. Every organization has to provide such support, but in a small charitable foundation the support services will not be as important as in a large university. Here we shall not consider (a), except to note again that a reengineering effort does at some stage require a thorough change in personnel structures, although this can be delayed until well after the new process structures have been defined. Also, the aim of instruction in the use of available resources is to make personnel actually use the resources. Returning again to my bank, a while back all of the tellers were given little machines for counting banknotes, but I have yet to see a teller use one of the machines. The type (b) services are particularly important for a newspaper. For example, a reporter can compose a story on a laptop in the field and transmit it ready for press. We shall discuss type (b) services at some length in Chapter 30.

Research and development. The newspaper must experiment with new layouts, new printing inks, and the proper use of color. It could also determine the effectiveness of different locations of an advertisement. Just as many books on computing are now sold with an attached disk containing program code, so Sunday papers may some day come with a video supplement. A bank has to analyze the effect of offering new services. I have always wondered why checks have to be endorsed on the back. The bank R&D section could investigate the effect of all marking going just on the face of a check. The charitable foundation can determine giving patterns of its donors over the course of a year, and make its appeals at the most effective times. Universities are extremely conservative organizations, and very little effort is made to improve curricula—a student at any liberal arts college is likely to be taught how Rome got its water 2000 years ago, but the student is very unlikely to be taught how water is supplied to a modern city. If students are to learn how to cope with today's world, they should first understand how this world functions.

Software costs and risks were briefly discussed in Chapter 12. There, under risks, we considered the consequences of software not being delivered on time and within budget, and of software failures. To this we now add risks of a broader significance. Many companies that have undertaken reengineering have had to cope with employee resistance at all levels of the work force. Where there is no actual resistance, failure to educate personnel properly for the changeover can still lead to personnel dissatisfaction, to costly mistakes in dealing with customers, and ultimately to general disenchantment with reengineering. To summarize, there are five kinds of risks:

- risks due to employee resistance to reengineering;
- risks due to inadequate preparation for reengineering;
- risks due to schedule overruns in the development of process software;
- risks due to cost overruns in the development of process software;
- risks due to process software failure.

To minimize these risks, the reengineering schedule has to be very carefully planned, and the worst mistake is to try to attempt too much too quickly.

Reengineering has three aspects: definition of the business activities of an organization as processes, implementation of the processes in a way that improves the effectiveness of the organization, and introduction of new technology to support the achievement of even higher effectiveness goals, and this is the sequence in which the three aspects should be considered. As has already been said before, process specification tells what is to be done, and the "what" part of a process is to be thoroughly understood by all participants in the process before an attempt is made to improve the "how" part, i.e., the way the process is implemented. Note again that most of the processes considered under reengineering already exist in some form in the organization. The task of reengineering is to make the structure of each process explicit, and then to use this explicit specification as a guide for an implementation that makes the process more effective. Initially, the process implementation is to be based entirely on information technology that already exists. Process implementers must be thoroughly knowledgeable in the use of this technology. If they are not, training related to the technology has to precede process implementation.

The worst situation arises when users depend on stand-alone PCs or workstations, and the information base is distributed over these machines. In order to interact with the entire information base, the user has to move from computer to computer, and may be confronted with different user interfaces at the different computers. When the computers are linked by a LAN or WAN, the interaction of the user with the system is not really different from interaction with a mainframe from a terminal. Therefore, in the stage in which the information technology is changed, going from a mainframe architecture to a client-server architecture may be easier than going from stand-alone workstations to network-based client-server computing.

Let us assume that all of the major processes of an organization have been defined. Now the order in which they are to be given a reengineered implementation has to be determined. Of course, the processes that are most critical for the operation of an organization should be considered first. The difficulty lies in the definition of "critical"—is this to be determined by the level of interaction between customers and the process, or by the ease with which personnel can adapt to the new form of the process, or by the cost reduction the reengineering is to bring about? Management will have to weigh these factors carefully. The criticality of the processes for a particular organization will be determined by the conditions affecting the organization, i.e., by the most pressing problems experienced by the organization.

Of special concern in setting priorities is R&D, and the process that converts R&D findings into marketable products. American companies have had serious problems with this process. The "Made in Japan" label on many products should read "Invented in USA; made in Japan." Closer to home, much of the user-friendly interface technology that started the PC revolution was developed by the Xerox PARC research facility. However, Xerox failed to exploit the technology, and its chief beneficiaries became Apple and Microsoft. Corporations simply cannot afford to waste research budgets. It is therefore imperative that problems to be solved and suggestions for new products to be developed are passed to R&D efficiently, and that R&D takes a two-prong approach to improving the standing of its corporate parent. Day-to-day competitiveness is to be improved by solving immediate problems; development of new products is to preserve the health of the corporation in years to come. This requires that R&D closely monitors all processes of the corporation, and that corporate management has the vision to recognize R&D inventions with a marketing potential. We should not spell out R&D: then it can be interpreted not only as the conventional Research & Development, but also as Recognition & Dissemination, with both interpretations equally important.

Once the decision to manufacture a product has been made, the time to market becomes most important. Competition has to be forestalled, and the R&D expenditures relating to the product recovered in the shortest possible time. Of American manufacturing companies, 95% realize this, but up to 1993 only 12% had managed to reduce the time to market [Cw93].

29
Legacy Software

The existing software systems of an organization represent a major investment. Moreover, they are reasonably reliable. This legacy software is to be integrated into the process systems of the reengineered organization, but only if the software does not impose heavy constraints on how the reengineering teams are to proceed.

One of the major problems associated with radical business reengineering is what to do with the software that has accumulated over the years but does not display the process orientation characteristic of a reengineered business. The legacy software cannot just be discarded. It embodies essential information, represents a large investment, and has become quite reliable over the years. As an illustration, in the early 1980s, the ITT corporation had a software library of 65 million DLC, with a replacement cost in excess of 2 billion dollars [Jo91, p. 25].

We have to consider how legacy software is to be transformed so that it fits into a software base for the reengineered organization. The transformation of the legacy software may be viewed as a three-stage process. First, a software support system for each of the reengineered processes is defined, and its components are classified on the basis of whether their purpose is to (a) support the internal operation of the organization, or (b) communicate with the outside world. The result is a set of events and a set of transactions. Second, existing software is analyzed on the same basis. Third, the existing software is mapped to the new software structure. Various decision support systems (DSSs) have been proposed and developed for the different stages of software development. These DSSs are called *apprentices*. An apprentice should also be considered for the mapping of legacy software to an improved form.

To bring our discussion to a concrete level, let us look again at order processing. Our task is to convert the process in Figure 18.3 into the process in Figures 26.1 and 26.2 in a way that preserves the existing software base of the process to the greatest possible extent. Let us start with a listing of the software requirements of the reengineered process. Recall from Chapter 17 that requirements define the structure of the information base that a system is to provide, when and how the information base may be changed, and what operational constraints the system has to satisfy.

(a) Internal operation. The information base of the reengineered process has to contain data relating to purchase orders, customers, and inventory. We assume that constraints on changes in the information base are expressed in terms of preconditions on events (in the SF sense). One event relates to the entering of a purchase order into the information base and another to the canceling of an order (RO and CO in Figure 26.1—RO is straightforward, and in Chapter 26 we discussed the relation of CO to the Petri net in Figure 26.2 in some detail). The checking of the credit rating of a customer is only slightly more complicated. The credit ratings are all in the information base and are consulted as part of CC. The result of this determines whether fulfillment of the customer's order is to be continued. The credit rating component of the customer information base is updated whenever a prospective customer is added to the information base and when the credit company supplies full ratings once every 6 months. Other information, such as addresses and fax numbers, may also have to be changed. The internal structure of CI is defined in Figure 26.2.

We shall not define the information base—by now it should be reasonably clear what information is needed to support order fulfillment. Let us count the number of events required. To begin with, there are RO, CC, and Ship, which are not expanded further. Figure 26.2 shows that CI is refined into a process consisting of six events. In addition, events are needed to update the inventory when the warehouse receives a shipment from the factory, to update a credit rating, and to update other information relating to a customer. Bubble CO becomes an event that causes events RR and EC in Figure 26.2 to take place, but we already have counted these two events. Thus, the order fulfillment process is defined by 13 events. To summarize, the thirteen events are RO, CC, RI, CA, CR, Ship, MO, RR, EC, CO, and the three updating events.

(b) External communication. The interactions of the order fulfillment process with the outside world belong to two categories, inputs received from the environment of the process system and outputs sent into the environment. The inputs initiate events and supply the events with arguments. Thus, a purchase order initiates event RO and supplies RO with the details of the order that are to be entered into the information base. For our purposes here it is irrelevant whether the order comes from a sales representative or directly from a customer, and whether the mode of transmission is conventional mail, phone, fax, e-mail, or even direct computer–computer communication initiated by a trigger in the information base of the customer. The events initiated by input received from customers are RO, CO, CR, and the three updating events.

Information moves also in the other direction: The process system sends information to customers and to the factory. An important piece of such information is the "Rejection notice" in Figure 26.1. In the re-engineered process the order is not rejected, but the customer is asked to prepay for the order. Nothing further happens to this order, and our process diagrams suggest that if the customer now sends in a prepaid order, this is treated as a new order. The "Delay notice" in Figure 26.1 corresponds to a prompt issued by T2 in Figure 26.2 and the "Shortage notice" to a reminder issued by T9. The "Acknowledgement" and "Invoice", originate at CO and Ship, need no explanation.

Turning now to Figure 18.3, we note that the three files in this data flow diagram relate to customers, orders, and inventory. As we shall now show, the existing software consists of little more than these files.

(a) *Internal operation.* The internal tasks are all manual: a purchase order moves from desk to desk, and something is done with it at each desk. The credit manager in Chapter 26 derived credit ratings by consulting a customer file, apparently starting from scratch whenever a new order arrived, but, as was pointed out, nobody knows how the credit manager did it. The inventory file is consulted in another department. There does exist a program that determines how large an order to send to the factory when there are shortages and another that estimates how long it will take before a backorder can be processed.

(b) *External communication.* Under the existing process structure as shown in Figure 18.3, a purchase order that gets through the process without becoming invalidated would have triggered initiation of all three of the tasks CC, CI, and Ship. A cancellation triggers CO. All of the messages or forms that are sent to customers are shown in exactly the same way in Figures 18.3 and 26.1.

Now, in the third stage of the preservation of legacy software, the existing software is to become part of the new process system. With regard to external communication, the software that printed invoices and cancellation acknowledgements (if there was such software) can be used as is. The same goes for the shortage notice, now called a manufacturing order; but every attempt is to be made to move all communication between units of the same company away from paper and into electronics as soon as possible, and, when this happens, the manufacturing order becomes a signal. The "Rejection notice" needs to be reformulated, and the "Delay notice" is replaced by interactive communication between the process team and the customer.

The information base supporting internal operations must be pre-served—for many companies, their information bases have become their most valuable resources. However, the three "files" that make up our information base may follow different data modeling conventions, and users may have to interact with them across different interfaces. The linking up of such information bases is an ongoing research topic.

Difficulties arise when the interface to the existing information base is not provided by a data base management system, but is dispersed through thousands of lines of Cobol code. Then the first step is to identify the components of the information base, and to partition the Cobol code into statements that refer to the information base and statements that do not. This is not as hard as it may seem because the information base has to be persistent, and persistent data, as well as all references to such data, can be identified by an appropriate "apprentice". The next step is to gather up the components of the information base and to give some structure to the information base. A statement of the information needs of a reengineered process should be available by now, and this statement is to provide guidance for the structuring of the information base.

Apart from the information base, there is very little to preserve. The main purpose for the reengineering of order fulfillment was to move from manual operations to a process in which a software system performs some tasks on its own and reminds or prompts the process team when it cannot perform a task by itself. No such software system exists in the old setting. We noted earlier that the old system contains programs to determine how large an order to send to the factory, and to estimate how long the processing of a backorder will take. These are very useful pieces of software to preserve, provided their code can be separated out from the code surrounding them, and that the methods implemented by the code are based on sound theory or practical experience. In our case, this is unlikely. One of the problems listed in Chapter 26 was gross underestimation of the time for filling backorders.

Protection of existing investments is not always the best policy. There have been many complaints that investment in information technology has not paid off. Where it has not, the fault is with the software, or, to be more precise, the processes implemented by the software. A clean break from antiquated code written in an antiquated style and defining antiquated processes is often the only way to make information technology pay. One of the most pernicious myths is that software costs are unreasonably high. They are unreasonably high only when an imperfectly understood process system is implemented at breakneck speed, only to be changed over and over again as some understanding of the process is gained. If a process is properly defined at the very start, as order fulfillment is by Figures 26.1 and 26.2, then coding is fast and the code is generally reliable.

Often an attempt is made to salvage old programs by reverse engineering. The purpose of reverse engineering is to determine the design underlying the code. After this, forward engineering uses the design to arrive at a new implementation that is better structured, or modifies the design if changes are required. The complete process, reverse and forward engineering, is called *software reengineering*. Software reengineering can contribute to business reengineering, but, since the purpose of the latter is to bring about a major reorganization of the entire process structure of an enterprise, the contribution will be fairly modest.

Processes for which extremely high reliability is needed fall into a special category. If there already exists software of ultrahigh reliability, then it is more or less essential to continue to use such software where safety is critical. An example is given in [Mu87, p. 205]. The example relates to a computer operating system used to support software for a safety-critical application. With 5000 such operating systems having been installed, and each having been run for 24 hours a day for three and a half years, analysis of failures observed over this time suggested that only 0.9 failures could be expected in the next 1000 years of operation of one such operating system. Of course, this being a statistical estimate, there is always a small probability that a higher number of failures could occur in the next 1000 years, say 3.0. Such low values are reassuring, particularly when we keep in mind that if the operating system fails, this does not necessarily have to put the safety-critical process into an unsafe state.

The year 2000 presents a special problem with legacy software. Memory used to be very costly, so the convention was adopted to store the year 1985 as just 85, and the year 1900 as 00. This means that on January 1, 2000, our software will not know whether we are in fact in the year 2000, or back in 1900. Conversions to remove the problem must be started now.

30
The Communication Infrastructure

Most reengineered organizations depend on local area and wide area networks for communication. An imaginative use of these facilities can raise significantly the effectiveness of an organization.

Recently I sent an e-mail message from Pittsburgh to Stockholm with the name of the addressee misspelled. The response from the Stockholm host telling me that it did not know anyone by that name was instantaneous. It was so much faster than the responses I get from our local file server that I did not believe the message had originated in Stockholm. I kept misinterpreting the message in every conceivable way, and only after an hour or so did I finally check the way I had spelled my Stockholm friend's name, something the message told me to do, and something I would have done immediately had not the speed of the Stockholm message disoriented me. The moral of the story is that adjustment to new modes of communication takes some time.

Adjustment to new ways of doing business also takes time. Technology actually can help perpetuate outdated business practices while giving an appearance of modernity. Workflow combined with imaging technology allows the same old purchase order to be shunted, as an electronic lifelike image, between the same old tired desks. I do not object to imaging. When I travel, I would wish to be shown on a screen where exactly my airplane seat will be located, what my hotel room will look like, and what the view will be like on the drive from the airport to the hotel. I do not object to workflow methods either. Since both workflow and SF define processes as structures of events, workflow is a good way of implementing SF processes. What I find ironic is the use of imaging and workflow as a means of postponing true reengineering of an organization and then calling this halfhearted measure reengineering. The moral of this is that modern technology alone does not make reengineering.

A Paul Bocuse can cook up a memorable meal with a few simple ingredients and a single saucepan, but he will do even better with choice produce and a well-equipped kitchen. Reengineered business processes are first and foremost the result of creative thought; but at some stage they do need technological support, and this support is provided by information systems and communication systems. The more closely these two systems are integrated, the better support they provide. The enabling technology for the integration arose in the switch from host-based to network-based computing. Under host-based computing, the host, a mainframe computer, interacts with a bunch of PCs and "dumb" terminals. In such a setting, a PC can be used in two modes. Under one mode it is an independent stand-alone computer; under the other it drops in status to become a dumb terminal of the host. Now, if the PC can work on its own at one moment and be communicating with the mainframe the next moment, why not let it work on its own for the most part and communicate with the mainframe only as needed, and set this up in such a way that the user is not aware of the switch from one mode to the other? Why not let it communicate not just with the mainframe, but with other PCs as well? All that is needed is technology to tie all of the machines together, and networking is this enabling technology.

Networks did not spring into existence suddenly. Technology usually develops from one or two research investigations carried out by a few enthusiasts. Such investigations do not always result in commercial products, but some do, and network technology is one of them. Without going into a detailed history, let us just note that networks were operational as early as the 1960s. One of the earliest networks was a WAN, the ARPANET (developed for the Advanced Research Projects Agency of the US Department of Defense in 1969), and its primary purpose was to allow somebody at point X to execute a program on a specialized computer located at some other point Y. Today such uses of a network would be rare. This goes to show that the really significant applications of a new technology are often unanticipated.

Most of the uses of networking developed over the following 20 years, and as each new use was discovered the popularity of networks grew. Let us list a few of the uses of local area networks. First, a LAN can combine equipment from different manufacturers, ending the dependence of Information Systems on a single vendor. Second, in many organizations a mainframe computer is not really necessary. A collection of PCs communicating over a network can provide the same computing power as a mainframe but at a greatly reduced cost. Third, an interconnected network of PCs or workstations is more robust than a system that depends entirely on the health of a central mainframe. If some communication links or PCs are out of service, the system as a whole can continue to function. Fourth, the user community in a LAN environment can be expected to achieve a higher level of computer literacy. In particular, once personnel have become accustomed to electronic mail, this fast and informal means of communication leads to the very rapid resolution of many business problems. Of course, in a particular organization the initial decision to introduce a LAN would probably be motivated by only one or two of these factors. The benefits of LANs are now widely recognized in some countries—in 1993 businesses in the United States had 41.7 PCs per 100 workers, and 55.7% of these PCs were connected into LANs; by contrast, in Japan the number of PCs per 100 workers was only 9.9, and only 13.4% of these were connected into LANs [Ny93].

Let us look at what distinguishes a WAN from a LAN. The big difference is that a LAN uses an internal communication structure and a WAN uses an outside carrier to see to the transmission of information; but this, taken by itself, is of little concern for network users. What does matter to me as a user is how long it takes to send a file of information from my office at the University of Pittsburgh to a colleague across the hallway, and how long it takes to send the same file to a colleague in Stockholm. This is determined by the bandwidth of the network, and a WAN is likely to have a narrower bandwidth than a LAN. Thus, the transmission rate on a typical LAN is 10 Mbps (Mbps = million bits per second, where one character of text normally needs eight bits for its representation). The transmission rate of WANs has improved from around one-thousandth to about one-tenth of this. To make these rates understandable, the transmission of the manuscript of this book across the hallway would have been accomplished in about one-half of a second, while transmission to Stockholm might have taken 5 seconds. Such a WAN transmission rate is not yet high enough to allow a team of engineers who are dispersed over several locations to modify a complex technical drawing cooperatively in real time, but availability of economically feasible transmission rates that will allow such an interaction is just a question of time. In addition, improved data compression techniques are reducing the amount of data that is to be transmitted. We shall not go into the technicalities of networking here—appropriate references are listed in Appendix B.

What then does a WAN provide? Its two most important uses are e-mail and the transfer of data files, such as manuscripts of papers submitted to a conference. Let us consider the submission of papers in some detail. As program chairman of a conference I was receiving many submissions of papers during December 1993 and January 1994. The papers still arrived as hard copy, but 96% of the submitters, who represented 21 countries, included their Internet e-mail addresses so that I could immediately acknowledge receipt of their papers. One paper was actually sent electronically from Norway as a formatted file. Since I have access to a printer that recognizes the formatting convention used for the paper, I could reproduce a high-quality hard copy of the paper locally in Pittsburgh, diagrams and all. Access to Internet by 96% of our submitters was made possible by the rapid growth of Internet: in October 1988 there were just 56,000 hosts; by October 1990, the number was 313,000; by October 1992, the number of hosts had risen to 1,136,000 [Ma93, p. 136].

Moreover, some of the hosts are truly gigantic—CompuServe alone had 1,300,000 subscribers in 1993 [Bw94].

However, we are not all-electronic yet. After the submissions had arrived, the papers had to be sent to referees, who also lived in many countries. Copies of the papers were placed in envelopes, four or five to an envelope, addresses of referees were written out on the envelopes, the envelopes were reinforced with tape and stamped "Air Mail" or "First Class Mail", and the papers were on their way—to arrive at their destinations 5 or 10 or 15 days later. We are already in a position to process the submissions entirely electronically: a paper is sent electronically to the program chairman; the program chairman prints out the paper and by looking through it decides on three referees; the electronic form of the paper is sent to these referees; the referees print out the paper, evaluate it, and send back their findings electronically; these evaluations are used to decide whether to accept the paper; the decision is conveyed electronically to the author. The whole process need not have taken longer than a few days instead of the 6 to 8 weeks it still tends to take. What holds us back is mainly force of habit.

For our second example let us consider the reservation system of a hotel chain. In the United States a reservation is usually made by calling an 800-number. However, when a reservation is made this way, there can be no bargaining. Travelers are therefore increasingly calling hotels directly—the aim is to negotiate a more advantageous room rate. Our task is to find the appropriate structure for the information base of the reservation system. Under one variant, the information base is centrally located. Let us call it CIB. Under a second variant, it is distributed over the computers of individual hotels. We shall call each local information base a LIB. In either case, a WAN is needed. We want to discuss which of the two variants is preferable under the criteria of amount of network traffic and effect of equipment failures.

Suppose we opt for the CIB. Then every reservation made locally has to be entered into the CIB. Moreover, whenever the hotel staff needs information about their own hotel, they have to access the CIB, which generates much traffic. Problems will arise in case of network disruption or failure of a local computer, but they are not too serious—hotel personnel can obtain information from the centralized reservation office by telephone. But operations more or less collapse if the CIB becomes unavailable, which may well happen if the centralized office is located in one of the earthquake zones of California.

With LIBs the amount of network traffic is significantly reduced—there is no need for a hotel to consult the reservation office, and the latter consults a LIB only when a reservation is actually requested. The advantage is even greater with regard to equipment failure. Suppose the local computer fails. It should not be difficult to design a mode of operation that allows a smooth transition to manual room allocation—maintaining hard-copy backup reservation data for a single hotel is not at all difficult.

Networks support a class of software that has become known as *groupware*. The purpose of groupware is to facilitate the work of teams, and it is therefore an important enabling technology for reengineering and for the execution of reengineered business processes. Groupware is particularly important for supporting JAD workshops and the Delphi method (see Chapter 15).

A groupware product is a computer-based system that supports the collaboration of a group of people engaged in a common task. Very often the common task is to arrive at a decision. For example, when a decision needs to be reached about whether or not to go ahead with a project, groupware-supported Delphi can provide a quantitative cost-benefit estimate on which to base the decision. Some groupware systems are therefore called *group decision support systems* (GDSSs), but GDSSs are not exactly a subclass of DSSs. With a DSS, the emphasis is on the methods for getting the information on which to base a decision, e.g., regression analysis and time-series analysis; with a GDSS, the emphasis is on how a group of people is to achieve effective interaction for reaching a collective decision.

The most common groupware product is e-mail, and the most common groupware problem is how to deal with an e-mail overload. The overload arises when e-mail is used thoughtlessly—broadcast too widely and with no identification of the message content. I do not mind receiving a message advertising the graduate students' Halloween party—actually, I welcome it; what I do mind is receiving copies of 73 responses to this message, all without a content identifier that would allow me to filter out these 73 messages. In e-mail, messages about different topics from different sources are all mixed together so that the "engaged in a common task" part of the definition of groupware is not fully satisfied.

The "common task" objective is met by electronic bulletin boards, which are intended for the exchange of messages on a single topic by a fixed group of participants. Only the level of sophistication of the equipment limits what can be posted on a bulletin board, but participants are not to alter each other's contributions—they may merely comment on previously posted matter. A higher level of group interaction is obtained when a participant may introduce alterations in existing contributions. This can reduce clutter on the bulletin board, but the system must save all versions of a contribution so that the history of changes can be traced and, if needed, a contribution restored to one of its earlier versions.

E-mail and bulletin boards operate asynchronously, that is, a response from a recipient of a communication, if it is expected at all, is not expected at once. With a synchronous bulletin board, a group interface allows several participants to share a screen window. This window appears on the screens of all their workstations, and they may all make alterations to the displayed information in full view of the other participants.

The synchronous bulletin board can be used with dispersed work-stations, or it can be used in an electronic meeting room. The most common purpose of an electronic meeting room is to house a GDSS. The equipment of a typical such facility includes a battery of workstations plugged into a LAN, and large electronic and conventional display surfaces. Magnetic whiteboards are particularly convenient because they can be used for writing, for overhead projection, and for setting up easily changed process diagrams by means of magnetic icons that can be moved around the board. Research on GDSSs continues. The initial GDSS research at the PlexCenter Planning and Design Support Laboratory at the University of Arizona was based on a facility with eight workstations, but the research was expanded to a large-group meeting room with 24 workstations. Only recently have companies become converted to e-mail, and this in a hesitant fashion. There is even less readiness for groupware—in looking through a few books on the application of computer networks I did not find much on groupware that went beyond the use of group calendars for the scheduling of meetings. This, however, is a technology of greatest importance for defining the processes of a reengineered business.

31
User Interfaces

Most of the software systems that support business processes interact with human participants in these processes. Although it is difficult to express user-friendliness in quantitative terms, benchmarking allows the quality of a user interface to be measured. Experimental data exist on the effectiveness of different modes of user–system communication.

When I sit down at a workstation, I want to face a system that is useful, usable, and user-friendly. Although these terms sometimes are used interchangeably, they refer to different aspects of the human perception of computer-based systems. A system is *useful* if it performs a task that needs to be done, but which humans do not like to do, do not do effectively or efficiently, or do not have the time to do. The system is *usable* if it is available when the task needs to be done, is reliable in the execution of the task, and performs the task to the users' satisfaction. The system is *user-friendly* if users have easy access to it. Since ease of access contributes to user satisfaction, user-friendliness can be regarded as a component of usability.

Whether or not a system is useful can in principle be determined by cost-benefit analysis, but it is difficult to express some of the benefits in quantitative terms. For example, given that a reengineered process system has taken over tasks that personnel did not like to do themselves, and that personnel turnover has gone down since the system was implemented, can we tell how much of the reduction is due to the reengineered system?

Usability depends on reliability and maintainability. A system is to be reliable in terms of functional and nonfunctional requirements, but, if it does fail, fault detection and fault removal should be rapid—which will be the case for a system with a high maintainability rating. One way of measuring usability is by subjective scoring. Users are given forms and are required to rate on a scale of 1 to 5, say, their degree of satisfaction with the system in general and with particular aspects of the system.

When we narrow our concern to the act of interaction of a user with a system, which occurs across a user interface, objective criteria can be used as well. They relate to learning time and operational use. Let us consider a benchmark for evaluating user interfaces in terms of the following three components:

1. *The learning effort*. It has been found that an effective learning strategy is to present the material in small segments, with each presentation followed by a test relating to the segment presented. The system developers have to define the segments, determine an appropriate learning period for each segment of the material, and decide on what the test is to measure. It is customary to measure the time to perform a given task, and to count the errors made by the subject.

2. *Operational use*. On the day after the learning session, the subjects are to perform a benchmark task that is to range over the entire functionality of the software system, hopefully in proportion to the expected use of each function.

3. *Retention*. One week after the learning session, the subjects are to perform the same task they performed 6 days earlier.

Usability requirements should specify the learning period and levels to be attained in the three kinds of tests, or just the operational use and retention tests. For example, the requirements may state that in a test with 10 users and a training time of 3 hours, (a) the average total time for the segment tests is to be 20 minutes, with the average total number of errors not to exceed 2; (b) the average total time for the benchmark test is to be 20 minutes after one day and 30 minutes after seven days, and the average error rate for these tests is not to exceed 1.4 and 1.6, respectively. But much care has to be exercised in setting up the testing process. We would have hardly any problems if the purpose of the tests were to compare, say, two commercially available software products. Then the users would be randomly partitioned into two groups and the group averages compared. Any advantage some users might have by having had prior exposure to this or a similar system would hopefully be averaged out. When the comparison is not between two sets of test results, but between test results and a requirement, the composition of the user group must be carefully specified.

The primary purpose of usability tests is to improve the user interface. Problems with usability should induce interface changes, or, if the defect is so fundamental that the system behind the interface has to be changed, to change system requirements. This is in keeping with one of the key principles of design for usability as formulated by John Gould and his colleagues [Go85, Go91], namely, that software design should be iterative. We now look at these key principles.

Iterative design. In Figure 11.3, we showed prototype-based iterative development of software systems. This is our preferred model for the software development process, partly because it explicitly recognizes that changes will be made to requirements. Developers should not be afraid to allow changes, but the introduction of changes has to be painless, and this requires a good set of tools. The incorporation of changes in a design, and the checking of the effect of such changes on other parts of the design as well as on help systems, user manuals, and other ancillary parts should be monitored by software tools. But keep in mind that tools do not design systems; people do.

Early focus on users. The most important feature of prototype-based process system development is user participation in the testing of the prototype. This is to be full user participation rather than the monitoring of the testing process by a representative of management. In selecting user representatives it is important to consider the diversity of users and try to find a representative sample. A problem that often arises is that management cannot be easily persuaded to provide access to users. The importance of user participation is to be pointed out to management as a well-presented cost-benefit argument in which the cost of user participation time is weighed against the cost of making changes to the system after its release, and the consequences of user resistance to an improperly constructed system also are to be pointed out.

Continual testing of user behavior. In testing user interaction with a prototype system the developers should not sit back and passively wait for users' comments. There has to be explicit monitoring of user behavior, which may include the tracking of eye movements, recording of all of a user's actions, and timing of benchmark tasks. The system developer should use the behavior data as a guide for system modification—some of the modifications will be purely at the implementation level while others will belong to the changes that in Figure 11.3 affect the requirements document. For example, the requirements document may require that a particular set of data is to appear on the screen all at the same time, but behavioral studies may show that users find this volume of data overwhelming.

Integrated design. Gould uses this term to refer to the parallel evolution of all aspects of usability, such as user interface, system documentation, training plan, and help system. Integrated design in this sense is sometimes called *concurrent software engineering*. Some concurrency is essential. For example, if the user of a prototype makes an error that puts the system in an unexpected state, the user would appreciate a help system that assists in undoing the error, i.e., backtracking to the state in which the error was made. On the other hand, spending much effort on documenting a system that continues to change can become an extravagance.

The concurrent software engineering that is fostered by prototype-based system development relates not just to usability, but to other properties as well. The phased life-cycle model follows an orderly progression from requirements gathering through specification, architectural design, and detailed design to implementation. In Chapter 11 we advocated early modularization, which is another term for architectural design. The model in Figure 11.3 assumes early modularization, and under this model detailed design and implementation are integrated with specification and architectural design.

While prototyping promotes integration, there is at the same time a trend toward specialization, with content being separated from style and each put in the care of different experts. Content consists of functionality requirements that relate to users' needs. Style requirements relate to the selection of interface devices, methods by which users communicate with the system, and layouts. Under ITS (Interactive Transaction System) [Wi90], an IBM applications development system, content is defined by domain experts. Domain experts also provide some guidance to style experts. Style experts select software implementations of methods of user–system communication from a library or have software for new interaction modes created by style programmers.

A process system in operation is a set of modules that communicate across interfaces. The users of the system can also be regarded as modules that communicate with the software modules across human–computer interfaces. Whereas software modules are, at least in principle, predictable, the behavior of users is unpredictable. Tests on interfaces between software modules can be defined by looking at the specifications of interfacing modules. There are no specifications of the users, which means that the only way to test the appropriateness of human–computer interfaces is to observe users in action. However, there has to be a user interface with which to begin the observations, and some initial requirements for this interface have to be defined. Data extracted by Rosson, Maass, and Kellogg [Ro88] from interviews conducted with designers of 22 successfully completed projects suggest the following as the more important principles of user interface design:

Use analogies or metaphors;
Match user expectations;
Create a novice–expert path;
Follow standards;
Minimize input movements;
Use menus or prompts;
Be careful in choice of terminology.

Let us discuss these principles; we shall not necessarily keep to the order in which they are listed. The use of analogies or metaphors has become widespread, particularly as pictorial icons. Instead of typing that file *Temp.Chap31* is to be deleted, one uses a mouse to move an iconic representation of *Temp.Chap31* on the screen into the representation of a waste basket. This has several advantages. First, humans locate the icon representing file *Temp.Chap31* faster than the name of the file in a linear list. Second, it is an extreme act of user-unfriendliness to let a user delete a file without allowing this action to be annulled, as is the case with some file systems. Under the iconic paradigm, the user sees what is in the waste basket and has an opportunity to recover a deleted file until the very end of the interaction session. In general, iconic displays make it easier to show which actions are reversible. Third, icons have an immediate cognitive impact on the user.

But much care should be exercised in the choice of icons and other representations. A few years ago, I had to work with two file management systems nearly every day. On one, files were renamed using an *rn* command. If you tried *rn* on the other, you got screen after screen of information about *read news*. So you looked at all the consonants in *rename* and tried *rm*. But in this system *rm* stands for *remove*, and this irretrievably wipes out the file (the correct command is *mv*, for *move*). This experience teaches two things. One, commands should be standardized. Two, symbols that are assumed to be self-explanatory are not interpreted the same way by all people or all systems. However, once a *standard* symbol has been used a few times, its interpretation will have been assimilated by most users. The problem of choice, remembering when to use which interpretation, is therefore more serious. This problem arises primarily with interface design for transfer of information *from user to machine*. It is:

> The issuing of commands, which is how users let machines know what they want the machines to do. A special case are the commands by which users define information that they want to look at. Another aspect of input relates to data that are to be used to update the information base of a system.

Information is transferred the other way as well, *from machine to user*, and then the concern is:

> Presentation of information. This relates to the way the information is structured when it is presented on a screen or as hard copy. Here the criterion of good interface design is understandability, which is a prerequisite for the rapid assimilation of the information by the user.

In both kinds of information transfer, efficiency is based on clarity. Clarity is achieved when proper attention is paid to the design of each individual symbol in a display, and to the design of the layout of an entire screen. There is loss of clarity when there is too much on the screen, which may be due to a poor representation being used. But often there is too much on the screen because the system itself is unnecessarily complex. Clarity suffers when too many features have to be considered. A cover story in *Business Week* in 1991 dealt with frustrations caused by household electronics devices that are overloaded with functions hardly anyone uses [Bw91]. With regard to user interfaces, a real puzzle is why for many years nobody thought of projecting the instructions for operating a VCR on the screen of the television set to which the VCR is hooked up. In prototyping, it is particularly important that instructions to users be given in a straightforward manner—prototype users cannot invest much time in learning about features that will not necessarily be implemented in the final system. The initial version of the user manual should therefore be presented to users as much as possible on the screen as steps to follow.

The most radical solution to the problem of too many features is to trim the system by throwing out many of the features. Reengineering is just the right time for this. But sometimes versatility is seen as an essential feature of a system. Then an attempt should be made to eliminate its drawbacks, and this can be done by the related techniques of customization and the use of levels of emphasis. Under customization, the user is allowed a limited selection from a large choice of features. Just as in buying an automobile the buyer can decide on blue color, air conditioning, power steering, and tinted windows, so in interacting with a process system a user can select just those interface features the user needs; then all of the other features become unavailable to this user. Also, just as the automobile can be repainted at a later date, the user can have the selection altered (hopefully with much less trouble than the repainting job). Under levels of emphasis the features in which the user is most interested are given special emphasis. All of the other features are still available, but at a low emphasis level, which means that special effort is needed to access them.

Clarity is helped by proper use of available technologies. For example, the most convenient access to a computer-supported directory of shops in a shopping mall is by a touch screen. By touching the name of a shop on the screen, or of the merchandise in which the shop specializes, a user causes the system to display directions for getting to the shop. But it is very easy to let the technology dominate. For example, nothing would be gained by replacing every circle in Figure 18.1 by a three-dimensional object resembling a checker piece. It should also be kept in mind that clearer displays can often be obtained in black and white than in color, particularly when an interface designer has no training in the proper use of color. Henri Matisse, who understood color better than most other artists, possibly better than any other artist in this century, would not let his students touch color before they had thoroughly understood shape.

This does not mean that three-dimensional checker pieces or color displays are always to be avoided. For example, when the display shows how a model relates to reality, the objects from the real world could be shown in three dimensions and the corresponding model objects in two dimensions. The display for an airline reservation system can make good use of color: the dominant color for the representation can be gray, with free seats shown in green, say, and free seats adjacent to window exits shown in red. But the use of color is to be approached with much care:

although color can enhance both textual and pictorial information, thus improving understanding and human response times, the use of too many colors, the use of clashing colors, and the misuse of receding colors can increase rather than reduce confusion.

The matching of user expectations is often neglected. In going from an existing software system to a new system, users hardly ever state as explicit requirements features of the existing system with which they are satisfied, assuming that the new system will have these features in any case. Interface designers should therefore keep the existing human–computer interface intact unless they are explicitly asked to make changes. Moreover, there should be stylistic uniformity across interfaces to all process systems with which a user is expected to interact.

Novices put quite different demands on a system than experts. Novices have to be led through a task step by step, but, as they acquire expertise, they begin to find the novice–system interaction mode tedious. Suppose a fast-food company redesigns its order-taking process so that all employees, even accountants from corporate headquarters, can take orders when needed. This is a laudable aim, as long as the help the system gives an accountant is not given to the experienced staff. Otherwise, the experts will be slowed down, with the result that their time will be used inefficiently, and customers will have to wait in queues a long time. Eventually some customers will just walk away, and business will be lost. For most applications it is therefore essential to develop a novice–expert path that starts out long for the novice but gets shortened with increased experience.

32
Maintainability and Reusability

Maintenance of a process is corrective, adaptive, perfective, or preventive. Maintenance is facilitated if the need for future maintenance is anticipated at the time the process is designed. Software maintenance is sometimes considered as little different from software reuse. A special case of reuse is the adaptation of a product for international markets.

The costs of maintaining a software system ultimately overtake the costs of the initial development of the system, even when corrected for inflation. Some estimates put maintenance costs at 60% of the total expenditure for a system. Maintenance is of four types—corrective, adaptive, perfective, and preventive. The four types are said to account for 21%, 25%, 50%, and 4%, respectively, of the maintenance budget [Li80]. Corrective maintenance removes faults, adaptive maintenance relates to the modification of software in response to changes in the processing environment or the application domain, perfective maintenance adds new features and improves existing parts of the system, and preventive maintenance changes the structure of a software system to make maintenance easier to undertake in the future. Note that when a process is being reengineered the concern is not actual maintenance, but the *maintainability* of the process system that is being developed—more specifically, it is the search for a way of measuring maintainability. Unfortunately, no satisfactory quantitative measure of maintainability has yet been found.

In terms of Figure 11.3, the need for corrective maintenance is caused by the imperfect transformation of software requirements into an operational system or by requirements having been misunderstood. In the first case, maintenance is fault removal, which is closely related to reliability: reliability theory gives an estimate of how often faults will arise while maintainability relates to the time that will have to be spent removing the faults. In the second case, if requirements have been misunderstood, they should be reformulated, and then we actually have a situation closer to adaptive than to corrective maintenance.

Adaptive maintenance has two causes, platform changes and changes in the processes supported by the platform. Platform change is the introduction of a new network, replacement of the computer on which a process is run, or of its operating system, or of an interface device, and initial design should make sure that software changes caused by a platform change would be minimal and confined to a few submodules. This again points out the need for well-thought-out partitioning of the system into modules. Process changes first have to be recognized in requirements, and the process system then is to be changed to correspond to the new requirements. As was noted above, this is also what happens when requirements have been misunderstood. If adaptive maintenance is to respond to process changes, then it is more difficult to limit all changes to just a few modules, but a particular process change should not affect more than a few submodules. Of course, this does not refer to the initial reengineering of a process, when all changes are major, but to later changes to the reengineered process.

Perfective maintenance can be interpreted as the development of a new software system in which parts of the old system are being reused [Ba90], which means that reusability and perfective maintainability are really the same thing. Ideally, the addition of new parts should not necessitate any changes to the existing system. Proper modularization is again essential for the achievement of this ideal. Perfective maintenance sometimes can lead to a large increase in the size of a process system.

Preventive maintenance is essentially a repackaging of a system into modules in such a way that future changes to the system will require minimal effort. Maintainability should measure how well a system has been partitioned into modules, i.e., the complexity of the product, but this is not all that easy to discuss. To begin with, the interpretation of complexity is itself complex. Grady and Caswell [Gr87] identify four types of complexity:

- *Inherent complexity*, which is a feature of the problem the system solves and is the type of complexity that concerns us most;
- *Unnecessary complexity*, which arises from the choice of a design that is inappropriate for the problem being solved;
- *Psychological complexity*, which arises from a mismatch between the problem and the programming language, as well as between different representations of the software, such as design and code;
- *Communication complexity*, which relates to the structure of the interpersonal network within which the software development team communicates and the volume of communication relating to the problem— this, though an important concern in the management of maintenance, has little effect on maintainability itself.

Except for communication complexity, all of these types can affect maintainability. Nothing can be done about inherent complexity. Unnecessary complexity results in more code than needed, and in code that is difficult to understand. Design inspections can reduce this type of complexity by detecting inappropriate designs. Instances of psychological complexity can be due to limited experience of developers or to the imposition of company standards that are too rigid.

Inherent complexity depends on the type of software. In Chapter 8 we referred to organic, semidetached, and embedded software. Intuition tells us that embedded software will be more complex than organic software, but this is not enough. We need a quantitative measure. An appropriate measure of the effort that will have to be expended on corrective maintenance of a system is its total complexity, which we should be able to measure reasonably well. Let us call this metric the *observable complexity*. We could then use the ratio of inherent to observable complexity as a maintainability metric—this parameter has to lie between 0 and 1, with a larger value indicating better maintainability. But, although observable complexity is in principle measurable, inherent complexity is another matter. With our present state of knowledge it seems to be a very difficult problem. Therefore, we are not able to measure maintainability, at least not at this time. Instead, we have to be satisfied with the measurement of observable complexity, which is difficult enough. This discussion of the distinction between maintainability and maintenance is no idle academic exercise. A low maintainability value would point out the need for preventive maintenance; a high observable complexity merely indicates that maintenance will be difficult, and this could be due totally to inherent complexity.

It appears that there is no single number that can capture all the factors that contribute to observable complexity, and that the best measure is probably some combination of the following, with the exact mix of these components determined by prior experience with similar software systems:

size of modules;
cyclomatic number;
adequate internal documentation;
traceability with respect to the upstream source document;
consistent style for the entire system;
size of module interfaces.

The consistent style requirement relates to the use of revealing mnemonics for identifiers, and the use of the same naming conventions in all modules. The upstream source document is the input used to produce the current representation of the system, e.g., process requirements in the case of process system design. The cyclomatic number derives from the representation of a program as a control flow diagram. Where control diverges, diverging lines are drawn from this point; where control merges, lines come together. For a well-structured program the diagram can be drawn so that the lines never cross, and the diagram is to be so drawn. Figure 32.1 shows a control flow diagram. The cyclomatic number, also called McCabe's metric, is the number of enclosed areas in the diagram plus one more for the area that encloses the entire diagram. These areas are numbered 1 through 6 in Figure 32.1.

The advocacy of a composite complexity measure has an empirical basis. Gremillion [Gr84] has found the number of lines of code in a program a more reliable predictor of the number of program repair requests than more sophisticated software metrics. Lind and Vairavan [Li89] used 390 modules (of total size 40 KDLC), selected at random from a 400-KDLC real-time medical imaging system that had gone through five releases, to study various software metrics. They found that the number of code changes in a module was most strongly related to the number of comments in that module, the total lines of code and comments, total number of characters, number of code characters, number of code lines, and the cyclomatic number, in order of decreasing strength. Here the most interesting finding is the strongest dependence on the number of comments—it appears that programmers get a good understanding of the complexity of a module as they develop it, and that the number of comments is an indication of this understanding. Although the comment count has a fairly high correlation with the count of code lines (0.72), the correlation is sufficiently low to support the hypothesis that the comment count is an independent measure of complexity. Gill and Kemerer [Gi91] studied seven maintenance projects on systems ranging in size from 2.0 to 7.1 KDLC. The changes could be relatively small (adding 0.3 KDLC to a system of size 6.1 KDLC) or extensive (2.1 KDLC added to a system of initial size 3.4 KDLC). They found the best predictor of

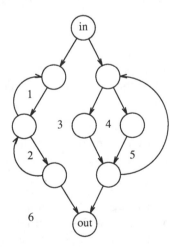

FIGURE 32.1. A program control graph.

maintenance productivity to be a complexity *density* measure, i.e., the cyclomatic number normalized by division by system size.

What general technique for measuring maintainability can be derived from these experiments? The high correlation between complexity and number of comments observed by Lind and Vairavan suggests that software developers can recognize modules of high complexity, and that most of their documentation effort is expended on such modules. What we do not know, but should find out, is whether the recognition comes before or after design and coding. If experienced software developers can estimate maintainability already from requirements, then a panel of experts could use, say, the Delphi technique to determine a reasonable maintainability requirement for a software product. This would be related to inherent complexity. Then, although we cannot measure inherent complexity, we can reduce the difference between observed and inherent complexity. Design for maintainability would attempt precisely this. As part of acceptance testing a group of experts would determine whether the maintainability objective is being met. If observable complexity could be measured, and if this were within the required complexity value, then the inherent complexity requirement would be satisfied. For measuring observed complexity, techniques can be adapted from those used to introduce objectivity in the judging of sports such as figure skating or gymnastics. A numerical scale similar to those used for these sports can be developed, but a drawback of the whole approach is its fairly high cost.

Despite appearances, the count of lines of code is not inconsistent with the preference expressed for function points in Chapter 12. A program for a particular task may be 600 lines long or 900 lines long, but function points will be the same for both programs. We expect, however, that the longer program will not be as well designed and hence will be more difficult to maintain. Could we not use some metric based on lines of code to measure observed complexity, and function points to measure inherent complexity? Not easily, because function points do not deal with the internal structure of a program well enough, not even when augmented with a count of algorithms. It seems though that an investigation of the relationship between a measure of observable complexity and a measure that extends the notion of function points is the most promising approach to the development of a metric for maintainability.

For the present we have to find empirical methods that will reduce the difference between observed and inherent complexity. The simplest is to impose an upper limit on the size of modules. In Chapter 20 we recommended that modules be identified with data types and processes. Any reasonable size limit is automatically satisfied by data-type modules in which each operation is implemented as a submodule. Also, if the implementation of a process consists primarily of sequences of calls to the operations of data types, a size limit on process modules should be easy to meet. If not, subprocesses with a single entry and single exit should be extracted as separate submodules.

A different approach is to use a benchmark maintenance task. An external consultant devises a maintenance task before software development starts. The task is not revealed to the software developers until the system has been implemented. Several maintenance teams then carry out the maintenance activity, and the system is found to have acceptable maintainability if the least maintenance time does not exceed a limit set by the consultant.

An example of such a task relates to a system that controls a bank of elevators. There are two modules, the elevator module and a dispatcher module. One of the functions of the elevator module is *agenda*, which is set-valued and consists of all the floors the elevator is to visit. When a person inside the elevator presses a floor button, this floor is added to the agenda. When a person arrives at the bank of elevators and presses an up or down button, this is registered by the dispatcher. The dispatcher selects the elevator that is to visit this floor and adds the floor to the agenda of the elevator by means of a signal. Now a change is proposed. Because there have been communication breaks between the dispatcher and the elevators, people had been waiting for elevators that never came. The new strategy: when an up or a down button is pressed, the floor is added directly to the agenda of every elevator; when an elevator visits this floor, the floor is taken off the agendas of the other elevators. Even with a dispatcher–elevator communication break we have a fail-safe situation—elevators will stop at some floors unnecessarily, but nobody will be forgotten. The required changes to an SF specification of the elevator module were made in less than an hour.

Next we turn to portability. Portability has two aspects: adaptation of a system to a new processing environment (new operating system or new hardware) and adaptation of the system to a new social environment (new class of users). Most programs or software systems have a much longer life than the hardware on which they were first implemented or the support software that provided the program–hardware interface for this implementation. Let us consider a typical software system. For the sake of simplicity, we assume that it is all written in a single programming language. The first concern is the recompilation of the software. Fortunately, programming languages are standardized, and some languages that have gone through several language definitions have retained backward compatibility—a Fortran program written in February 1957, the month in which IBM released its first Fortran, will be accepted by today's Fortran compilers.

The compiled application system uses memory and there is interaction with various input/output devices, but the operating system takes care of all this. Hardly ever is there a need for the user to interact directly with the hardware. This setting is illustrated in Figure 32.2. Here the hardware

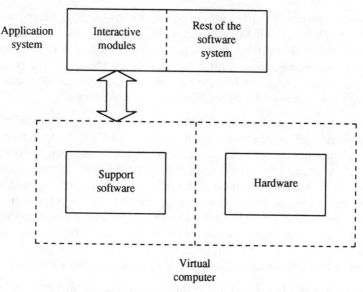

FIGURE 32.2. Total system architecture (much simplified).

and the support software, where the latter consists of an operating system, a data base management system, compilers, etc., constitutes a *virtual* machine in which the support software acts as a buffer between the hardware and the outside world. The application system is partitioned between modules that interact with the virtual machine and modules that do not. So, if the hardware platform is changed, only the support software needs to be changed, and hopefully not much of it. If the support software is changed, then only the interactive modules of the application system will be affected.

In Chapter 31 it was pointed out that a process system can be regarded as being composed of software modules and human process operators or users. So far we have looked at the effect on the user of changes in the software system. The other aspect of portability relates to the ability of different classes of users to get the same benefits from the system. We shall consider a number of situations that can arise.

• The user talks on a telephone and uses the system at the same time. This situation arises when customers of a company make phone enquiries, order goods, make hotel or airline reservations, etc.

• A handicapped person uses the system. The handicap may be impaired vision or hearing, inability to use both hands, etc. In each case, the user–computer interface needs to be adapted in a different way.

• The system conventions are inconsistent with the general educational level of the user, or the user's experience with the system. One example of such inconsistency is to require mathematically unsophisticated users to interpret or construct formal logical expressions. Another example is the use of unfamiliar terminology, such as a reference to McCabe's metric without an explanation of what it is. This can be particularly annoying in a help system—designers of help systems should realize that users often turn to help systems for explanation of unfamiliar terms.

International use of software has become an important special case of portability of an application system to a new cultural environment. This kind of portability becomes a problem for multinational corporations when they attempt to introduce a reengineered process throughout the corporation. Although English is the primary language of communication at top management levels in such corporations, the process teams may not be able to use English. Our concern is that the process support software be consistent with the educational background of users in general terms and, specifically, their readiness to interact with computers and the particular process system. The following special concerns can arise:

• The length of text may change in translation, requiring reformatting of the areas set aside for the text. Also, fewer characters are needed in Chinese than in English, Greek, or Arabic to express the same message, but Chinese characters are both wider and higher. Moreover, because there are about 6000 complex ideographic characters in "basic" Chinese, Japanese, and Korean, and as many as 30,000 characters in traditional Chinese, the single-byte character format used for Latin or Greek character sets is inadequate.

• In some cultures, reading is from left to right and in others right to left. This means that provision should be made to flip a screen image through 180° about the N–S axis.

• Representation of dates varies within English-speaking countries, as do time indications (12-hour versus 24-hour clock). In many cultures, the numbering of years does not derive from the Christian tradition. In communication between offices in different countries, it has to be realized that they may lie in different time zones—timestamps should therefore indicate both local time and GMT.

• In using Pic, a typesetting system for diagrams, to define the diagrams in this book all distances were expressed in inches; in most countries of the world, the metric system is the norm.

• Icons have to be adapted to the culture. Since most icons do not have strong cultural roots, this is not a critical concern—most icons need to be learned in any case, irrespective of the society in which they are being used. Therefore, even though a knife-and-fork icon is used on highway signs in California to indicate that there is a restaurant at the next exit, and a pair-of-chopsticks icon serves the same purpose in Taiwan, adapting to the local icon in either place should not require excessive adjustment—adjusting to the food probably will be more

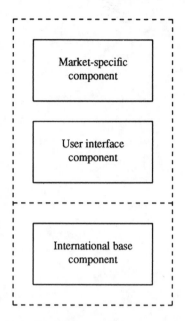

FIGURE 32.3. Digital's international product model.

difficult. Keep in mind that most Americans traveling for the first time to Europe are at a loss to interpret most of the internationally accepted icons at European airports but will understand them reasonably well the next time.

• Some icons may have different connotations in different cultures. If a particular icon is likely to cause dissatisfaction on cultural or religious grounds, this icon should be changed. Examples are icons that strongly resemble religious symbols.

Digital Equipment Corporation has developed an international software product model with three components, as shown in Figure 32.3. The international base component does not change when the product is adapted for a different country, but the user interface and market-specific components have to be adapted to local conditions. The market-specific component takes into account usage differences that may exist between populations that speak the same language, as in Brazil and Portugal.

Appendices

A
Basic Mathematical Notations

This appendix introduces some basic notations of set theory and logic. Its main purpose is to help in the reading of SF specifications.

To define a concept is to describe the concept in terms of concepts that we already understand. The first few basic concepts of set theory cannot be defined because, to begin with, there are no concepts to use in their definitions. The undefined concepts are *set* and *membership*. Informally, a set consists of entities (or members, or elements) that have some common property and that can be distinguished one from another. Sets are usually represented by capital letters, e.g., A, B, Q, X. A particular set is defined by listing all of its members within a pair of braces, as in $\{1, 2, 3, 4, 5, 6\}$, or by a defining expression, as in

$$\{x|x \text{ is an integer and } 1 \leq x \leq 6\}.$$

Listing an entity twice has no significance: $\{1, 2, 2, 3\}$ and $\{1, 2, 3, 3\}$ represent the same set; the members of this set are 1, 2, and 3. Membership is indicated with the symbol $\in$; so $x \in Q$ states that x is a member of the set Q. Similarly, $y \notin R$ states that y is not a member of set R.

Set algebra provides operations that can be used to combine sets in different ways. The three most commonly used operations are *union* (represented by the operator $\cup$), *intersection* (operator $\cap$), and *difference* (operator $-$). In terms of defining expressions we have

$$A \cup B = \{x|x \in A \text{ or } x \in B\}, \tag{A.1}$$

$$A \cap B = \{x|x \in A \text{ and } x \in B\}, \tag{A.2}$$

$$A - B = \{x|x \in A \text{ and } x \notin B\}. \tag{A.3}$$

In words, an element belongs to the union of two sets if it belongs to either of the sets or to both sets. An element belongs to the intersection of two sets if it belongs to both sets. The set difference $A - B$ consists of those elements of A that are not in B, i.e., it is the set A from which every element that it shares with B has been removed. Obviously, $A - B \neq B - A$.

It is possible to have a set with no elements—this is the *empty set* or the *null set*, and we shall denote it by the symbol NULL. Two sets are *disjoint* if they have no element in common, i.e., if their intersection is the null set. A collection of sets $A_1, A_2, \ldots, A_k$ is a *partition* of a set A if every element of A is to be found in one and only one A_i belonging to the collection, i.e., a partition splits up a set into a collection of disjoint subsets.

The membership concept, which relates an element with a set, can be extended to two sets, and we get the *subset* relation: set A is a subset of set B if every element of A occurs also in B, written as $A \subseteq B$.

The members of a set do not have to be simple elements. They can be various aggregates of data, e.g., we can have a set of sets, or a set of tuples. An *n-tuple* is an ordered sequence of n elements. For example, $<$o, r, d, e, r$>$ is a 5-tuple in which each element comes from the set of the 26 letters of the English lowercase alphabet L. For low values of n, tuples have special names; thus, a 2-tuple is a *pair* (often called an *ordered pair*), a 3-tuple is a *triple*, a 4-tuple a *quadruple*, and a 5-tuple a *quintuple*. The elements of a tuple are called *coordinates*. Consider $<w, x, y, z>$. The first coordinate of this quadruple is w, the second is x, and the fourth is z.

A simple example of a set of pairs is a set in which each element consists of a positive integer and its square. We write this infinite set as

$$S = \{<1, 1>, <2, 4>, <3, 9>, <4, 16>, \ldots \}. \qquad (A.4)$$

Let us denote the set of positive integers by N. Then the set of *all* possible pairs $<x, y>$ of positive integers is denoted by $N \times N$. Such aggregates of tuples are called Cartesian products. The set of pairs S in Equation (A.4) is a subset of the Cartesian product $N \times N$. The tuple $<$o, r, d, e, r$>$ belongs to $L \times L \times L \times L \times L$.

A set of pairs defines a *binary relation*. Let P be the set of people in a country and M the set of periodicals that are published in this country. Define the relation

$$R = \{<a, b>|a \in P \text{ and } b \in M \text{ and } a \text{ subscribes to } b\}. \qquad (A.5)$$

Relation R is a subset of the Cartesian product $P \times M$.

A binary relation is is 1–1 (read "one to one") if it contains no two first coordinates that are the same and no second coordinates that are the same. Set S of Equation (A.4) is a 1–1 relation. A binary relation is N–1 ("many to one") if its second coordinates can be duplicated. An example is a relation that links people and their ages: Joe and Mary can both be 36, but Joe cannot be both 36 and 76—we have $<$Joe, 36$>$ and $<$Mary, 36$>$ in the relation. A binary relation is N–N or N–M ("many to many") if both its first and second coordinates can be duplicated. Relation R in Equation (A.5) is such a relation.

When all of the first coordinates of a relation are distinct, then this relation is a *function*, i.e., 1–1 and N–1 relations are functions. Thus, the

S in Equation (A.4) is a function, but the R in Equation (A.5) is not because a person will appear as a first coordinate as many times as there are periodicals to which this person subscribes. But each coordinate of a tuple can itself be a tuple, a set, or even a set of tuples. Hence, the relation R can be changed into a set-valued function consisting of pairs $<a, b>$ such that a still belongs to P, but b is now a subset of M consisting of all the periodicals to which a subscribes.

A function is said to map from one set to another, and functions have names. To show what the mapping looks like for the S in Equation (A.4), we write

$$S: N \to N.$$

Function S maps from set N to set N. Similarly, for Equation (A.5) we write, with R now a function,

$$R: P \to M-\text{set},$$

where the set to which R maps consists itself of sets, namely, of all possible subsets of set M. The value of $R(p)$ is the set of all magazines to which p subscribes.

An analysis in Chapter 17 of a specification given in English shows that natural language tends to be ambiguous. Even in our definition (A.1) of set union, the "or" could be interpreted in two different ways, either allowing or not allowing an element to be a member of the union of the two sets when it belongs to both sets. A substitution of logic for natural language often improves matters. Mathematical logic deals with statements for which it can be established by general agreement whether they are true or false. Such statements are called *propositions*. Some examples of propositions are

"There are 38 people in this room"
"2 + 2 = 4"
"2 + 2 = 692"

The statement "Is it raining?" is not a proposition, nor is the statement "Please get me two opera tickets for Wednesday night." The question of whether these statements are true or false does not arise.

There are, of course, statements for which we find it difficult to arrive at general agreement regarding their truth or falsity, at least without knowing the context. The following are a few examples:

- "The elevator is at floor 6." Do we consider it to be still at floor 6 when it has just started on its movement toward floor 5 or floor 7?
- "This system is user-friendly." I may think it is, but not everybody needs to share my opinion.
- "It is raining." Here we should indicate a location.

These statements are still propositions, because once the appropriate context has been established, their truth or falsity can be determined.

More importantly, logic is not concerned with the determination of the truth or falsity of individual propositions. Instead, one concern of logic is the way the truth value of a composite proposition can be derived from the truth values of its constituents. For example,

"There are 38 people in this room or $2 + 2 = 4$"

is false *only* if both of its components are false. On the other hand,

"There are 38 people in this room and $2 + 2 = 4$"

is true *only* if both of its components are true. We use the symbol $\vee$ for "or", and the symbol $\wedge$ for "and". We shall also denote our two propositions by symbols—

p: There are 38 people in this room
q: $2 + 2 = 4$

Then the composite propositions are written $p \vee q$ and $p \wedge q$. They are called *disjunction* and *conjunction*, respectively. We shall use the symbol "not" to indicate truth negation: if p is true, then not(p) is false; and if p is false, then not(p) is true. We can now write a general statement about p that is *always* true: $p \vee$ not(p). On the other hand, $p \wedge$ not(p) is *always* false. Propositions that are always true are called *tautologies*; propositions that are always false are called *contradictions*. Symbols such as "not", $\vee$, and $\wedge$ are called *logical connectives*.

Now consider the statement

"If a theater has 600 seats or more, then a fireman is in attendance."

This composite proposition is called an *implication*, and it is made up of the propositions

"A theater has 600 seats or more" (p)
"A fireman is in attendance" (q)

Symbolically, our composite proposition is represented by $p \rightarrow q$, where p is called the *antecedent* and q the *consequent* of the implication. The implication $p \rightarrow q$ is false *only* if p is true but q is false. The following possibilities can arise:

The theater has less than 600 seats
No fireman is in attendance
   The theater has less than 600 seats
   A fireman is in attendance
The theater has 600 or more seats
No fireman is in attendance
   The theater has 600 or more seats
   A fireman is in attendance

When a theater has less than 600 seats, a fireman need not be there, but there is nothing wrong with having a fireman there. However, when a theater has 600 or more seats, then a fireman must be there. Consequently, only the third combination contradicts the implication statement. This suggests that when we encounter $p \rightarrow q$ in a specification, only the situations in which p is true are of interest, and then we have to ensure that q is also true. Two additional examples of implications are

"If the current account balance is negative, the borrower is a bad risk"
"If the temperature is at $-10°$, then precipitation is in the form of snow"

Two propositions are *equivalent* when they always have the same truth value. We shall use the symbol $\equiv$ for equivalence, as in $p \equiv q$. Equivalence is expressed using the phrase "if and only if" (sometimes shortened to iff):

"The boiling point of water is 100°C if and only if the pressure is 760 mm"

Equivalence can be defined in terms of implication:

$$(p \equiv q) \equiv (p \rightarrow q \wedge q \rightarrow p)$$

Our interest is primarily in conjunction, disjunction, and implication, and we summarize their properties by means of a truth table:

p	q	$p \wedge q$	$p \vee q$	$p \rightarrow q$
T	T	T	T	T
T	F	F	T	F
F	T	F	T	T
F	F	F	F	T

Sometimes we want to introduce a variable into a proposition:

"i is a prime"
"Array X is sorted in ascending order"

Since these propositions will be true for some values of the variable and false for other values, they can be interpreted as functions that return the value T or F, e.g., $prime(2) = T$, $prime(6) = F$, $upsorted([1, 3, 8]) = T$, $upsorted([3, 7, 2]) = F$, $upsorted([8, 3, 1]) = F$. Such functions are called *predicates*.

When we defined the set operations, we were using what we now know to be predicates. Predicates were also used to define sets. Let us look at an additional example. The set of all primes between 10 and 20 can be enumerated, $\{11, 13, 17, 19\}$, but if we wanted to define the set of all primes between 10 and 100, then a more concise specification of the set is

$$\{x|prime(x) \land 10 \le x \le 100\},$$

where the notation $\{x|P(x)\}$ stands for the set of all those elements x for which the predicate $P(x)$ is true. The $\{x|P(x)\}$ is interpreted as follows: For all x in a particular universe (here the set of natural numbers), test that the predicate is true. If it is, include x in the set; if it is not, do not include x in the set. In our instance, the predicate $P(x)$ is "$prime(x) \land 10 \le x \le 100$." Note that $prime(x)$ and $10 \le x \le 100$ by themselves are also predicates. The set membership symbol $\in$ also names a predicate. For example, given $S = \{4, 9, 12\}$, $9 \in S$ is true, but $15 \in S$ is false, i.e., $15 \notin S$ holds.

Suppose we wanted to be more precise about what we mean by saying that array A is sorted in ascending order. Denote the array by $A[1..5]$. Then the more precise statement would be

$$A[1] \le A[2] \land A[2] \le A[3] \land A[3] \le A[4] \land A[4] \le A[5],$$

but we want a more compact way of expressing this. A more compact way is provided by *quantification*. If we want to say that predicate $P(i)$ is true for *all* i in set S, we express this as

$$\forall i : i \in S : P(i);$$

and if we want to say that $P(i)$ is true for *some* i in S, we write

$$\exists i : i \in S : P(i)$$

where $\forall$ is the *universal* quantification symbol and $\exists$ is the *existential* quantification symbol. The quantified expressions are themselves predicates that could be true or false. The predicate $P(i)$ for the ascending order property is $A[i] \le A[i + 1]$, and the compact definition of *upsorted* with respect to array $A[1..n]$ becomes $\forall i : 1 \le i < n : A[i] \le A[i + 1]$. The expression $\forall i : 10 \le i \le 20 : prime(i)$ is false, but the expression $\exists i : 10 \le i \le 20 : prime(i)$ is true. These two expressions can be expanded as, respectively,

$$prime(10) \land prime(11) \land \ldots \land prime(20),$$
$$prime(10) \lor prime(11) \lor \ldots \lor prime(20).$$

B
A Reading Guide

The reading guide refers mainly to books in which some of the topics raised in the text are discussed in detail. For the most part, the organization of the reading guide follows the order in which these topics are dealt with in the text.

In this survey of the literature relevant to business reengineering I have not attempted to be exhaustive. Neither do I anywhere in the references pay much attention to who did what first. The reference section is intended merely to lead the reader to more detailed coverage of a topic or a different viewpoint from that expressed in this book, or to attribute some of the material used in the book. In this reading guide emphasis is on books, but references are also given to articles that have appeared in conference proceedings or journals. The intention is to allow the reader to get a state-of-the-art view of some particularly important topics. In addition to strictly technical literature, I regularly go through seven periodicals: *Business Week* and *Fortune* for new developments in the business world; *Computerworld* for trends in the information systems area; *Communications of the ACM* and the IEEE publications *Computer*, *IEEE Software*, and *IEEE Expert* for more in-depth treatment of software trends. Anybody who builds software systems to support business processes will find something of use in all of these publications.

As is only appropriate, we start with general texts on business reengineering. Toffler's *Powershift* [To90] and Drucker's *Post-Capitalist Society* [Dr93] concentrate on social aspects, the major changes in social structures that have made business reengineering necessary. The most compact and also the most enthusiastic book on reengineering is Hammer and Champy's *Reengineering the Corporation* [Ha93]. In a later work, Champy [Ch95] is more cautious. So is Davenport in his *Process Innovation* [Da93]—he points out that reengineering is risky and that legacy software imposes serious constraints. He seems to imply that, because of high risks, preemptive reengineering should not be undertaken. Davenport makes much use of Harvard Business School case studies. Whereas most books on business innovation emphasize what is happening in the

United States, Peters' *Liberation Management* [Pe92] ranges all over the world. This 830-page book is a plea for disorganization as a means of bringing about radical process innovation. Even if one disagrees with some of Peters' more extreme views, the book is full of stimulating ideas. An international flavor can also be found in *Business Process Reengineering* by Johansson et al. [Jo93]—some of their examples relate to Britain. One very interesting approach they take is to consider reengineering as having three aims, which, in order of ambition, start with cost reduction and go on to achievement of parity with competition, ultimately aspiring to competitive dominance. In the latter case, they say that a company has achieved a "BreakPoint." Tapscott and Caston in their *Paradigm Shift* [Ta93] concentrate on information technology as the enabling agent for reengineering. A valuable feature of this book is the clear explanation it provides of some of the buzzwords, such as object-oriented software development, open systems in support of network-based computing, and client-server computing. To determine how ready your organization is for reengineering, try the quiz in [Fo94a].

In Chapter 1 we refer to nonstandard processes that are to deal with crisis situations. Planning for such situations is discussed in [My93]. On fuzzy decision theory, which was mentioned in Chapter 4, see [Ka92a]. In [Be90c] I have attempted to classify various types of uncertainty and to survey the methods that have been developed to deal with the uncertainties. We also noted in Chapter 4 that the continuous improvement of reengineered processes is the responsibility of the process teams. The number of books on continuous improvement is overwhelming—I have found [Bo91b] very interesting reading. The success of business reengineering depends largely on how well the teams function, both the reengineering teams and the teams that operate the reengineered processes. Three books that will help understand teams are [Ha90, Ka93, Le93]. The October 1993 issue of the *Communications of the ACM* contains a number of articles on software development teams—[Wa93] is a particularly relevant study of how a team of ten members actually went about the development of a software product. It is very important to coordinate the efforts of all of the participants in a large project—[Kr95] is a study of the factors that contribute to successful coordination. An outline of how four companies are making the transfer from a hierarchical to a horizontal organization is given in [Fo95]. Joint Application Development is described in [Au91, Wo95], and a comparative evaluation of JAD and Participatory Design can be found in [Ca93].

Turning now to software engineering, a good introduction is provided by any one of [Fa85, Pf87, Pr87, Ma90, Gh91, Bl92, So92, Co94]—I hesitate to rank them; however, the emphasis given to Petri nets in [Gh91] makes this book my favorite. In teaching I have found my class notes to be best complemented by [Fa85]. This text is very strong on how the various documents that relate to a software project should be structured. This advice transfers readily to the documentation that is to define business reengineering projects. Developers of business information systems may appreciate the business orientation of [Co94]. This book has a chapter on the reengineering and planning of enterprises. A modern approach to the development of software for business processes is taken in [Sc94a]. The engineering principles listed in Chapter 7 were first discussed in [Be92]. New CASE (Computer Assisted Software Engineering) tools are being developed all the time—Capers Jones [Jo94] estimates that in 1993 the number of commercially available CASE tools was 8500. Hence, any survey of existing tools would be overwhelming, and it would soon be out of date. However, general principles on how to evaluate CASE products do not go out of date—[Qe89] remains a good survey of such principles. In most software engineering texts, nonfunctional software quality attributes are discussed too briefly. The most thorough treatment of the more important nonfunctional requirements is to be found in [Sm90] (performance) and the rather technical [Mu87] (reliability). Reliability determination in the Cleanroom context is described in [Dy92]; a brief introduction will be found in [Mi87].

We noted in Chapter 4 that an information systems department that is to provide effective software support for business reengineering must have reached Level 2 of the software process maturity model developed by the Software Engineering Institute. A thorough discussion of the five levels of the model may be found in [Hu89]. Some aspects of the original model have been found wanting [Bo91a]; a modified model is briefly outlined in [Pa93] and is defined in detail in various SEI reports. The experience of companies that have advanced to the higher levels of the SEI model is documented in [Hu91, Hu91a]. In order to reach the higher levels, a company must keep records of its experiences in software development as quantitative data. Otherwise, it is in no position to make reliable cost and risk estimates. The classic on software cost estimation is [Bo81]; on risk estimation see [Ch89, Ch90, Jo94] and a collection of articles edited by Boehm [Bo89]—an overview of risk management is given by [Bo91]. To what extent the models introduced in these references are portable is discussed in Chapter 15 of [Ab91]. Software measurements in more general terms are covered in [Co86a, Gr87, Jo91, Gr92, Pu92]; [Jo91] is an excellent source of information on the function-points methodology, particularly on how function points relate to software productivity. The measurements are to provide guidance on how to improve the software development process so that the development time and the number of faults in the software are both reduced.

The business analysis techniques listed in Chapter 13 are briefly surveyed in [Da82]; [Ro79] introduced the CSF methodology. The broad area of requirements determination is explored in a thorough manner and a lively style in [Ga89]; determination of software requirements is discussed in [Da90] and the more compact [Ma88]. In Chapter 13 we briefly noted that a problem, which has been suspected to be a software problem, may turn out to be something entirely different. The whimsical [Ga82] will help differentiate between a perceived problem and the real problem.

Diagramming techniques are surveyed in [Ma85], and additional sources of information are [Bi85] and [Da90]. Entity-Relationship diagrams were introduced by Chen in 1976 [Ch76]. If you want to see a really large ER diagram, consult the insert that comes with [Sc92]—the size of the diagram is 59 × 88 cm, and, unless I miscounted, it contains 219 boxes and diamonds. There are numerous conventions for drawing data flow diagrams—for two such conventions see [De78, Ga79]. An introduction to Petri nets is to be found in [Pe77]; for book-length surveys see [Pe81, Re85]. Examples of the use of time Petri nets are given in [Be91].

Validation by means of technical inspections is surveyed in [Fr81, Ho90]; [Br93] contains references to more recent work in this area. Some advice on how to improve inspections, based on inspection data gathered over several years and relating to more than 6000 inspection sessions, can be found in [We93]. Metrics that allow code inspections to be improved are discussed in [Ba94a].

An introduction to JSD is given by [Ca86]; [Ca89] is an extensive exposition of the methodology. Statecharts are discussed in [Ha88, Ha90]; they form part of the OMT approach to software development described in [Ru91]. There are now many books on Z—I found [Po91] the easiest to read; [In92] combines an introduction to discrete mathematics with Z; on VDM see [Co86, Jo86]. The SF language was introduced in [Be86]; [Be90a] defines the language; several examples of SF specifications can be found in [Be90b]. The SF language has a strong object orientation—the literature on object orientation is vast; I particularly like the comprehensive and thoughtful overview in [Be93] (it is well stocked with references for further reading). Formal methods for the specification of most processes will become standard at some time in the future; for me, the only question is when. This prediction is based on discussions and examples of the use of formal methods in [Ha90b, Ke90, Ge94].

In Chapter 26 we make the point that product quality alone does not guarantee the success of a company. Quality efforts have to be all-pervasive, but the cost of each quality improvement must be carefully balanced against the benefits in increased market share, improved employee morale, reduced rework costs, etc. For experiences of some companies that have made quality pay, see [Bw94a].

Reengineering of order processing at Corning Glass is described in [Cw94]. The interconnection of different information systems is not without its problems; some of the problems are discussed in [An93] and [Sh90] and [Wi92] are also relevant. At various places in the book we have mentioned decision support systems and expert systems. For a recent introduction to decision support systems see [Al92]. The principles of expert systems are explained in very clear terms in the still-current

[Wa86]; for recent trends see [Da93a], which is a collection of papers. Case studies of how businesses use decision support systems and expert systems sometimes appear in *IEEE Expert*. For example, [St94] describes a system at the Canadian telecommunications company AGT that permits customer service representatives to do some marketing; [Co94a] outlines a system that the 3M Company uses to schedule service personnel; in [Si94] artificial intelligence and data base techniques are combined in the processing of service orders; [Sc94] describes Salto, a system that is used at several airports to allocate aircraft to tarmac stands. In Chapter 29 we suggested that an expert system functioning as an "apprentice" could assist in preserving legacy software—various apprentices are described in [Ri90]. Very little has been written on legacy software as such, but work on software reengineering has some relevance—[Ar93] is a collection of papers that deal with software reengineering; [Be95] is a more recent survey. A very brief list of suggestions on how to transfer a legacy system to a new environment is to be found in [Cw94c]. The impact that 24 recent technological developments, which include electronic note pads, fuzzy logic, and diamond thin-films, could have on organizations of various kinds is explored in [Bu93].

Many books have recently appeared on networking—I have found [Sc92a, Ma93, Ba94], which complement each other, very useful. On the change to network-based systems, see [Gu92]. Note, though, that mainframe computers are by no means dead—on opposing viewpoints on this see [Cw94a]. Networking specifically in the context of business reengineering is surveyed in [Ja94]. Groupware is surveyed in [Ma92, Op92]. In [Ve95] a distinction is made between taskware, teamware, and groupware, where taskware is concerned with the essence of an application, and groupware with implementation concerns. A short introduction is to be found in [Fo93]; [El91] is a survey and experience paper with an extensive bibliography; some of the negative effects of e-mail are examined in [Ma94]. An implementation of network-based Delphi is described in [Ke93a]. For a good general survey of user interfaces see [Hu90]; a more detailed survey of screen displays, including a serious discussion on the use of color, can be found in [Ba92]. The benchmark for evaluating user interfaces derives from [De90]. In Chapter 32 we refer to maintainability and reusability—[Bi89] is a collection of papers that address themselves to various aspects of reusability; [La92] deals with maintenance in a succinct but informative manner. International use of software is discussed in [Di91, Ta92, Ka92].

References

A change from convention in this reference section is the replacement of the place of publication for books, which makes little sense when large publishers maintain editorial offices in numerous cities, with an ISBN identifier.

[Ab91]   Abdel-Hamid, T., and Madnick, S.E., *Software Project Dynamics: An Integrated Approach*. Prentice Hall (0-13-822040-9), 1991.

[Al92]   Alter, S., *Information Systems: A Management Perspective*. Addison-Wesley (0-201-51030-8), 1992.

[An93]   Anderson, B.E.W., and Nilsson, P., How to manage complexity in inter-organizational information systems (IOIS)—some preliminary conclusions. In *Decision Support in Public Administration*, P.W.G. Bots, H.G. Sol, R. Traunmuller (Eds.). North-Holland (0-444-81485-X), 1993, pp. 17–28.

[Ar93]   Arnold, R.S. (Ed.), *Software Reengineering*. IEEE Computer Society Press (0-8186-3272-0), 1993.

[Au91]   August, J.H., *Joint Application Design*. Yourdon Press (0-13-508235-8), 1991.

[Ba79]   Balzer, R., and Goldman, N., Principles of good software specification and their implications for specification languages. *Proc. IEEE Conf. Specifications Reliable Software*, 1979, pp. 58–67.

[Ba90]   Basili, V.R., Viewing maintenance as reuse-oriented software development. *IEEE Software* 7(1), 1990, 19–25.

[Ba92]   Banks, W.W., and Weimer, J., *Effective Computer Display Design*. Prentice Hall (0-13-401027-2), 1992.

[Ba94]   Baker, R.H., *Networking the Enterprise—How to Build Client/Server Systems that Work*. McGraw-Hill (0-07-005089-9), 1994.

[Ba94a] Barnard, J., and Price, A., Managing code inspection information. *Software* 11(2), 1994, 59–69.

[Be73]   Bell, D., *The Coming of the Post-Industrial Society*. Basic Books (0-465-09713-8), 1973.

[Be86]   Berztiss, A., The set-function approach to conceptual modeling. In *Information System Design Methodologies: Improving the Practice*, T.W. Olle, H.G. Sol, A.A. Verrijn-Stuart (Eds.). North-Holland, 1986 (0-444-70014-5), pp. 107–144.

[Be90]   Berztiss, A., *Programming with Generators*. Ellis Horwood (0-13-739087-4), 1990.

[Be90a] Berztiss, A.T., The specification and prototyping language SF. SYSLAB Report 78, Department of Computer and Systems Sciences, The Royal Institute of Technology and Stockholm University, Electrum 230, S-16440 Kista, Sweden, 1990.

[Be90b] Berztiss, A., Formal specification methods and visualization. In *Principles of Visual Programming Systems*, S.-K. Chang (Ed.). Prentice Hall (0-13-710765-X), 1990, pp. 231–290.

[Be90c] Berztiss, A.T., Software methodologies for decision support. *Information and Management* **18**, 1990, 221–229.

[Be91] Berthomieu, B., and Diaz, M., Modeling and verification of time dependent systems using time Petri nets. *IEEE Trans. Software Eng.* **17**, 1991, 259–273.

[Be92] Berztiss, A.T., Engineering principles and software engineering. In *Proc. 6th SEI Conference on Software Eng. Educ., 1992*. Springer-Verlag (LNCS No. 640; 3-540-55963-9 or 0-387-55963-9), pp. 437–451.

[Be93] Berard, E.V., *Essays on Object-Oriented Software Development, Volume I*. Prentice Hall (0-13-288895-5), 1993.

[Be94] Berztiss, A.T., Non-functional requirements in the design of software. In *Proc. 7th SEI Conference on Software Eng. Educ., 1994*. Springer-Verlag (LNCS No. 750; 3-540-57461-1 or 0-387-57461-1), pp. 375–386.

[Be95] Berztiss, A.T., Reverse engineering, reengineering, and concurrent engineering of software. *Internat. J. Softw. Eng. Knowl. Eng.* **5**, 1995, 299–324.

[Bi85] Birrell, N.D., and Ould, M.A., *A Practical Handbook for Software Development*. Cambridge University Press (0-521-25462-0), 1985.

[Bi89] Biggerstaff, T.J., and Perlis, A.J. (Eds.), *Software Reusability, Vols. I and II*. ACM Press (0-201-08017-6 and 0-201-58818-3), 1989.

[Bl92] Blum, B.I., *Software Engineering: A Holistic View*. Oxford University Press (0-19-507159-X), 1992.

[Bo81] Boehm, B.W., *Software Engineering Economics*. Prentice Hall (0-13-822122-7), 1981.

[Bo88] Boehm, B.W., A spiral model of software development and enhancement. *Computer* **21**(5), 1988, 61–72.

[Bo89] Boehm, B.W. (Ed.), *Software Risk Management*. IEEE Computer Society Press (0-8186-8906-4), 1989.

[Bo91] Boehm, B.W., Software risk management: principles and practices. *IEEE Software* **8**(1), 1991, 32–41.

[Bo91a] Bollinger, T.B., and McGowan, C., A critical look at software capability evaluations. *IEEE Software* **8**(4), 1991, 25–41.

[Bo91b] Bowles, J., and Hammond, J., *Beyond Quality: How 50 Winning Companies Use Continuous Improvement*. Putnam (0-399-13650-9), 1991.

[Br86] Brooks, F.P., No silver bullet—Essence and accidents of software engineering. *Proc. IFIP Congress 86*, pp. 1069–1076 [Reprinted: *Computer* **20**(4), 1987, 10–19].

[Br93] Brykczynski, B., and Wheeler, D.A., An annotated bibliography on software inspections. *Software Engineering Notes* **18**(1), 1993, 81–88.

[Bu93] Burrus, D. (with Gittines, R.), *Technotrends—How to Use Technology to Go Beyond Your Competition*. Harper Business (0-88730-627-6), 1993.

262   References

[Bw91] I can't work this thing. *Business Week*, April 29, 1991.
[Bw93] Al Gore: What business can teach the feds. *Business Week*, September 13, 1993.
[Bw93a] Health care has a bad case of 'cost disease'. Column by R. Kuttner in *Business Week*, November 15, 1993.
[Bw93b] The horizontal corporation. *Business Week*, December 20, 1993.
[Bw93c] Myths about older workers cost business plenty. *Business Week*, December 20, 1993.
[Bw94] On-ramps for the info superhighway. *Business Week*, February 7, 1994.
[Bw94a] Quality—How to make it pay. *Business Week*, August 8, 1994.
[Bw95] The Business Week 1000. *Business Week*, March 27, 1995.
[Ca86] Cameron, J.R., An overview of JSD. *IEEE Trans. Software Eng.* **SE-12**, 1986, 222–240.
[Ca89] Cameron, J.R., *JSP and JSD: The Jackson Approach to Software Development, 2nd ed.* IEEE Computer Society Press (0-8186-8858-0), 1989.
[Ca93] Carmel, E., Whitaker, R.D., and George, J.F., PD and Joint Application Design: a Transatlantic comparison. *Comm. ACM* **36**(6), 1993, 40–48.
[Ch76] Chen, P.P., The entity-relationship model: Toward a unified view of data. *ACM Trans. Database Syst.* **1**, 1976, 9–36.
[Ch89] Charette, R.N., *Software Engineering Risk Analysis and Management*. McGraw-Hill (0-07-010661-4), 1989.
[Ch90] Charette, R.N., *Applications Strategies for Risk Analysis*. McGraw-Hill (0-07-010888-9), 1990.
[Ch95] Champy, J., *Reengineering Management*. Harper Business (0-88730-698-5), 1995.
[Co86] Cohen, B.W., Harwood, W.T., and Jackson, M.I., *The Specification of Complex Systems*. Addison-Wesley (0-201-14400-X), 1986.
[Co86a] Conte, S.D., Dunsmore, H.E., and Shen, V.Y., *Software Engineering Metrics and Models*. Benjamin/Cummings (0-8053-2162-4), 1986.
[Co94] Conger, S.A., *The New Software Engineering*. Wadsworth (0-534-17143-5), 1994.
[Co94a] Collins, J.E., and Sisley, E.M., Automated assignment and scheduling of service parsonnel. *IEEE Expert* **9**(2), 1994, 33–44.
[Cr84] Crosby, P.B., *Quality Without Tears—The Art of Hassle-Free Management*. McGraw-Hill (0-07-014530-X), 1984.
[Cu88] Curtis, B., Krasner, H., and Iscoe, N., A field study of the software design process for large systems. *Comm. ACM* **31**, 1988, 1268–1287.
[Cw93] Redesigning design. *Computerworld*, November 22, 1993.
[Cw93a] Wake up, U.S. programmers! *Computerworld*, December 6, 1993.
[Cw94] Glass act. *Computerworld*, January 17, 1994.
[Cw94a] Junk my mainframe? *Computerworld*, May 30, 1994.
[Cw94b] USAir overhauls IS to cut costs. *Computerworld*, June 20, 1994.
[Cw94c] Legacy systems, legacy options. *Computerworld*, July 11, 1994.
[Cw94d] American Express claims re-engineering saves $1.8B. *Computerworld*, September 26, 1994.
[Da82] Davis, G.B., Strategies for information requirements determination. *IBM Systems J.* **21**, 1982, 4–30.
[Da90] Davis, A.M., *Software Requirements: Analysis and Specification*. Prentice Hall (0-13-824673-4), 1990.

[Da93]   Davenport, T.H., *Process Innovation: Reengineering Work through Information Technology*. Harvard Business School Press (0-87584-366-2), 1993.

[Da93a]   David, J.-M., Krivine, J.-P., and Simmons, R. (Eds.), *Second Generation Expert Systems*. Springer-Verlag (3-387-56192-7).

[De78]   DeMarco, T., *Structured Analysis and System Specification*. Yourdon Press (0-13-854380-1), 1978.

[De90]   De Waal, B.M.E., and Van Der Heiden, G.H., The evaluation of user-friendliness in the design process of user interfaces. In *Human Factors in Information Systems Analysis and Design*, A. Finkelstein, M.J. Tauber, R. Traunmueller (Eds.). North-Holland (0-444-882855-5), 1990, pp. 93–103.

[Di91]   Digital Corporation, *Digital Guide to Developing International Software*. Digital Press (1-55558-063-7 or 0-13-211228-0), 1991.

[Dr93]   Drucker, P.F., *Post-Capitalist Society*. Harper Business (0-88730-620-9), 1993.

[Dy92]   Dyer, M., *The Cleanroom Approach to Quality Software Development*. Wiley (0-471-54823-5), 1992.

[Eb94]   *1994 Britannica Book of the Year*. Encyclopaedia Britannica (0-85229-600-2), 1994.

[El91]   Ellis, C.A., Gibbs, S.J., and Rein, G.L., Groupware—Some issues and experiences. *Comm. ACM* **34**(1), 1991, 39–58.

[Fa85]   Fairley, R.E., *Software Engineering Concepts*. McGraw-Hill (0-07-019902-7), 1985.

[Fo93]   Groupware goes boom. *Fortune*, December 27, 1993.

[Fo94]   Getting beyond downsizing. *Fortune*, January 10, 1994.

[Fo94a]   Rate your readiness to change. *Fortune*, February 7, 1994.

[Fo94b]   The information age in charts. *Fortune*, April 4, 1994.

[Fo94c]   How H-P automates to grow and grow. *Fortune*, May 2, 1994.

[Fo94d]   Your company's most valuable asset: Intellectual capital. *Fortune*, October 3, 1994.

[Fo95]   The struggle to create an organization for the 21st century. *Fortune*, April 3, 1995.

[Fr81]   Freedman, D.P., and Weinberg, G.M., *Handbook of Walkthroughs, Inspections, and Technical Reviews, 3rd ed.* Little, Brown, 1982 [Reprinted: Dorset House (0-932633-19-6), 1990].

[Ga79]   Gane, C., and Sarson, T., *Structured Systems Analysis: Tools and Techniques*. Prentice Hall (0-13-854547-2), 1979.

[Ga82]   Gause, D.C., and Weinberg, G.M., *Are Your Lights On? How to Figure out What the Problem Really Is*. Winthrop, 1982 [Reprinted: Dorset House (0-932633-16-1), 1990].

[Ga89]   Gause, D.C., and Weinberg, G.M., *Exploring Requirements: Quality Before Design*. Dorset House (0-932633-13-7), 1989.

[Gh91]   Ghezzi, C., Jazayeri, M., and Mandrioli, D., *Fundamentals of Software Engineering*. Prentice Hall (0-13-820432-2), 1991.

[Ge94]   Gerhart, S., Craigen, D., and Ralston, T., Experience with formal methods in critical systems. *IEEE Software* **11**(1), 1994, 21–28.

[Gi91]   Gill, G.K., and Kemerer, C.F., Cyclomatic complexity density and software maintenance productivity. *IEEE Trans. Software Eng.* **17**, 1991, 1284–1288.

[Go85]   Gould, J.D., and Lewis, C., Designing for usability: Key principles and what designers think. *Comm. ACM* **28**, 1985, 300–311.

[Go91]   Gould, J.D., Boies, S.J., and Lewis, C., Making usable, useful, productivity-enhancing computer applications. *Comm. ACM* **34**(1), 1991, 74–85.

[Gr84]   Gremillion, L.L., Determinants of program repair maintenance requirements. *Comm. ACM* **27**, 1984, 826–832.

[Gr87]   Grady, R.B., and Caswell, D.L., *Software Metrics: Establishing a Company-Wide Program.* Prentice Hall (0-13-821844-7), 1987.

[Gr92]   Grady, R.B., *Practical Software Metrics for Project Management and Process Improvement.* Prentice Hall (0-13-720384-5), 1992.

[Gu80]   Guttag, J.V., and Horning, J.J., Formal specification as a design tool. *Proc. 7th Symp. POPL, 1980*, pp. 251–259.

[Gu92]   Guengerich, S., *Downsizing Information Systems.* SAMS Publishing (0-672-30153-9), 1992.

[Ha87]   Harandi, M.T. (Ed.), *Proc. 4th International Workshop on Software Specification and Design.* IEEE Computer Society Press, 1987.

[Ha88]   Harel, D., On visual formalisms. *Comm. ACM* **31**, 1988, 514–530.

[Ha90]   Harel, D., Lachover, H., Naamad, A., Pnueli, A., Politi, M., Sherman, R., and Shtull-Trauring, A., Statemate: A working environment for the development of complex reactive systems. *IEEE Trans. Software Eng.* **16**, 1990, 403–414.

[Ha90a] Hackman, J.R. (Ed.), *Groups That Work (and Those That Don't).* Jossey-Bass (1-555542-187-3), 1990.

[Ha90b] Hall, A., Seven myths of formal methods. *IEEE Software* **7**(5), 1990, 11–19.

[Ha93]   Hammer, M., and Champy, J., *Reengineering the Corporation: A Manifesto for Business Revolution.* Harper Business (0-88730-640-3), 1993.

[Ho90]   Hollocker, C.P., *Software Reviews and Audits Handbook.* Wiley (0-471-51401-2), 1990.

[Ho91]   Hou, W.C., Sheang, L.K., and Hidajat, B.W., *Sun Tzu: War and Management.* Addison-Wesley (0-201-50965-2), 1991.

[Hu83]   Huber, G.P., The nature and design of post-industrial organizations. *Management Science* **30**, 1984, 928–951.

[Hu86]   Huber, G.P., and McDaniel, R.R., The decision-making paradigm of organizational design. *Management Science* **32**, 1986, 572–589.

[Hu89]   Humphrey, W.S., *Managing the Software Process.* Addison-Wesley (0-201-18095-2), 1989.

[Hu90]   Huang, K.-T., Visual interface design systems. In *Principles of Visual Programming Systems*, S.-K. Chang (Ed.). Prentice Hall (0-13-710765-X), 1990, pp. 60–143.

[Hu91]   Humphrey, W.S., Recent findings in software process maturity. In *Software Development Environments and CASE Technology*, A. Endres, H. Weber (Eds.). Springer-Verlag (LNCS No. 509; 3-540-54194-2 or 0-387-54194-2), pp. 258–270.

[Hu91a] Humphrey, W.S., Snyder, T.R., and Willis, R.R., Software process improvement at Hughes Aircraft. *IEEE Software* **8**(4), 1991, 11–23.

[In92]   Ince, D.C., *An Introduction to Discrete Matematics, Formal System Specification and Z, 2nd ed.*, Oxford University Press (0-19-853837-7), 1992.

[Ja94]   Jayachandra, Y., *Re-Engineering the Networked Enterprise.* McGraw-Hill (0-07-032017-9), 1994.

[Jo86]   Jones, C.B., *Systematic Software Development Using VDM.* Prentice Hall (0-13-880725-6), 1986.

[Jo91]   Jones, C., *Applied Software Measurement.* McGraw-Hill (0-07-032813-7), 1991.

[Jo93]   Johansson, H.J., McHugh, P., Pendlebury, A.J., and Wheeler, W.A., *Business Process Reengineering: Break Point Strategies for Reengineering.* Wiley (0-471-93883-1), 1993.

[Jo94]   Jones, C., *Assessment and Control of Software Risks.* Yourdon Press (0-13-741406-4), 1994.

[Ka92]   Kataoka, Y., Morisaki, M., Kuribayashi, H., and Ohara, H., A model for input and output of multilingual text in a windowing environment. *ACM Trans. Information Systems* **10**, 1992, 438–451.

[Ka92a] Kandel, A. (Ed.), *Fuzzy Expert Systems.* CRC Press (0-8493-4297-X), 1992.

[Ka93]   Katzenbach, J.R., and Smith, D.K., *The Wisdom of Teams.* Harvard Business School Press (0-87584-367-0), 1993.

[Ke90]   Kemmerer, R.A., Integrating formal methods into the development process. *IEEE Software* **7**(5), 1990, 37–50.

[Ke93]   Kennedy, P., *Preparing for the Twenty-First Century.* Random House (0-394-58443-0), 1993.

[Ke93a] Kenis, D., and Verhaegen, L., The MacPolicy project: Developing a group decision support system based on the Delphi method. In *Decision Support in Public Administration*, P.W.G. Bots, H.G. Sol, R. Traunmuller (Eds.). North-Holland (0-444-81485X), 1993, pp. 159–170.

[Kn86]   Knight, J.C., and Leveson, N.G., An experimental evaluation of the assumption of independence in multiversion programming. *IEEE Trans. Software Eng.* **SE-12**, 1986, 96–109.

[Kr92]   Kriegel, R.J., and Patler, L., *If It Ain't Broke . . . Break It!.* Warner Books (0-446-51539-6), 1992.

[Kr95]   Kraut, R.E., and Streeter, L.A., Coordination in software development. *Comm. ACM* **38**(3), 1995, 69–81.

[Ku90]   Kumar, K., and Bjorn-Andersen, N., A cross-cultural comparison of IS designer values. *Comm. ACM* **33**, 1990, 528–538.

[La92]   Landsbaum, J.B., and Glass, R.L., *Measuring and Motivating Maintenance Programmers.* Prentice Hall (0-13-567827-7), 1992.

[Le93]   Lewis, J.P., *How to Build and Manage a Winning Project Team.* AMACOM (0-8144-5137-3), 1993.

[Li80]   Lientz, B.P., and Swanson, E.B., *Software Maintenance Management.* Addison-Wesley (0-201-04205-3), 1980.

[Li89]   Lind, R.K., and Vairavan, K., An experimental investigation of software metrics and their relationship to software development effort. *IEEE Trans. Software Eng.* **15**, 1989, 649–653.

[Lu91]   Luqi, The role of prototyping languages in CASE. *Internat. J. Softw. Eng. Knowl. Eng.* **1**, 1991, 131–149.

[Ma85] Martin, J., and McClure, C., *Diagramming Techniques for Analysts and Programmers*. Prentice Hall (0-13-208794-4), 1985.

[Ma88] Martin, C.F., *User-Centered Requirements Analysis*. Prentice Hall (0-13-940578-X), 1988.

[Ma90] Mayrhauser, A.v., *Software Engineering: Methods and Management*. Academic Press (0-12-727320-4), 1990.

[Ma92] Marca, D., and Bock, G., *Groupware: Software for Computer-Supported Cooperative Work*. IEEE Computer Society Press (0-8186-2637-2), 1992.

[Ma93] Marine, A., Kirkpatrick, S., Neou, S., and Ward, C., *Internet: Getting Started*. PTR Prentice Hall (0-13-327933-2), 1993.

[Ma94] Markus, M.L., Finding a happy medium: Explaining the negative effects of electronic communication on social life at work. *ACM Trans. Information Systems* 12, 1994, 119–149.

[Mi87] Mills, H.D., Dyer, M., and Linger, R., Cleanroom software engineering. *IEEE Software* 4(5), 1987, 19–25.

[Mu87] Musa, J.D., Iannino, A., and Okumoto, K., *Software Reliability—Measurement, Prediction, Application*. McGraw-Hill (0-07-044093-X), 1987.

[My93] Myers, K.N., *Total Contingency Planning for Disasters*. Wiley (0-471-57418-X), 1993.

[Ny93] Now it's Japan's turn to play catch-up. *New York Times*, November 21, 1993.

[Op92] Opper, S., and Fersko-Weiss, H., *Technology for Teams—Enhancing Productivity in Networked Organizations*. Van Nostrand Reinhold (0-442-23928-9), 1992.

[Or94] Orlikowski, W.J., and Gash, D.C., Technological frames: making sense of information technology in organizations. *ACM Trans. Information Systems* 12, 1994, 174–207.

[Pa72] Parnas, D.L., On the criteria to be used in decomposing systems into modules. *Comm. ACM* 15, 1972, 1053–1058.

[Pa90] Parnas, D.L., Education for computing professionals. *Computer* 23(1), 1990, 17–22.

[Pa93] Paulk, M.C., Curtis, B., Chrissis, M.B., and Weber, C.V., Capability Maturity Model, Version 1.1. *IEEE Software* 10(4), 1993, 18–27.

[Pe77] Peterson, J.L., Petri nets. *ACM Comp. Surveys* 9, 1977, 224–253.

[Pe81] Peterson, J.L., *Petri Net Theory and the Modeling of Systems*. Prentice Hall (0-13-661983-5), 1981.

[Pe92] Peters, T., *Liberation Management: Necessary Disorganization for the Nanosecond Nineties*. Knopf (0-394-55999-1), 1992.

[Pe92a] Peyrefitte, A., *The Immobile Empire*. Knopf (0-394-58654-9), 1992.

[Pf87] Pfleeger, S.L., *Software Engineering: The Production of Quality Software*. Macmillan (0-02-395720-4), 1987.

[Po91] Potter, B., Sinclair, J., and Till, D., *An Introduction to Formal Specification and Z*. Prentice Hall (0-13-478702-1), 1991.

[Pr87] Pressman, R.S., *Software Engineering: A Practitioner's Approach, 2nd ed.* McGraw-Hill (0-07-050783-X), 1987.

[Pu92] Putnam, L.H., and Myers, W., *Measures for Excellence*. Yourdon Press (0-13-567694-0), 1992.

[Qe89]   QED Information Sciences, *CASE—The Potential and the Pitfalls*. QED Information Sciences (0-89435-285-7), 1989.

[Re85]   Reisig, W., *Petri Nets—An Introduction*. Springer-Verlag (3-540-13723-8 or 0-387-13723-8), 1985.

[Ri90]   Rich, C., and Waters, R.C., *The Programmer's Apprentice*. ACM Press (0-201-52425-2), 1990.

[Ro79]   Rockart, J.F., Chief executives define their own data needs. *Harvard Business Review* **57**(2), 1979, 81–93.

[Ro85]   Roman, G.-C., A taxonomy of current issues in requirements engineering. *Computer* **18**(4), 1985, 14–23.

[Ro88]   Rosson, M.B., Maass, S., and Kellogg, W.A., The designer as user: Building requirements for design tools from design practice. *Comm. ACM* **31**, 1988, 1288–1298.

[Ro93]   Roberts, W., *Victory Secrets of Atilla the Hun*. Doubleday (0-385-42448-5), 1993.

[Ru91]   Rumbaugh, J., Blaha, M., Premerlani, W., Eddy, F., and Lorensen, W., *Object-Oriented Modeling and Design*. Prentice Hall (0-13-629841-9), 1991.

[Sc92]   Scheer, A.-W., *Architecture of Integrated Information Systems*. Springer-Verlag (3-540-55131-X or 0-387-55131-X), 1992.

[Sc92a] Schnaidt, P., *Enterprise-Wide Networking*. SAMS Publishing (0-672-30173-3), 1992.

[Sc94]   Schlatter, U.R., Real-time knowledge-based support for air traffic management. *IEEE Expert* **9**(3), 1994, 21–24.

[Sc94a] Scheer, A.-W., *Business Process Engineering*. Springer-Verlag (3-540-58234-7 or 0-387-58234-7), 1994.

[Sh90]   Sheth, A.P., and Larson, J.A., Federated database systems for managing distributed, heterogeneous, and autonomous databases. *ACM Comp. Surveys* **22**, 1990, 183–236.

[Si60]   Simon, H., *The New Science of Management Decision*. Harper and Row, 1960 [Revised edition: Prentice Hall (0-13-616136-7), 1977].

[Si73]   Simon, H., Applying information technology to organization design. *Public Admin. Rev.* **33**, 1973, 268–278.

[Si94]   Singh, M.P., and Huhns, M.N., Automating workflows for service order processing: Integrating AI and database technologies. *IEEE Expert* **9**(5), 1994, 19–23.

[Sm90]   Smith, C.U., *Performance Engineering of Software Systems*. Addison-Wesley (0-201-53769-9), 1990.

[So92]   Sommerville, I., *Software Engineering, 4th ed.* Addison-Wesley (0-201-56529-3), 1992.

[Sp86]   Spector, A., and Gifford, D., A computer science perspective on bridge design. *Comm. ACM* **29**, 1986, 268–283.

[St94]   Stafford, C.D., and de Haan, J., Delivering marketing expertise to the front lines. *IEEE Expert* **9**(2), 1994, 23–32.

[Sw82]   Swartout, W., and Balzer, R., On the inevitable intertwining of specification and implementation. *Comm. ACM* **25**, 1982, 438–440.

[Ta92]   Taylor, D., *Global Software—Developing Applications for the International Market*. Springer-Verlag (0-387-97706-6 or 3-540-97706-6), 1992.

[Ta93]   Tapsoft, D., and Caston, A., *Paradigm Shift: The New Promise of Information Technology*. McGraw-Hill (0-07-062857-2), 1993.

[Th81]   Thayer, R.H., Pyster, A.B., and Wood, R.C., Major issues in software engineering project management. *IEEE Trans. Software Eng.* **SE-7**, 1981, 333–342.

[To79]   Tonies, C.C., Project management fundamentals. In *Software Engineering*, R.W. Jensen, C.C. Tonies (Eds.). Prentice Hall (0-13-822130-8), 1979, pp. 24–63.

[To90]   Toffler, A., *Powershift: Knowledge, Wealth, and Violence at the Edge of the 21st Century*. Bantam (0-553-05776-672295), 1990.

[Ve95]   Vessey, I., and Sravanapudi, A.P., CASE tools as collaborative support technologies. *Comm. ACM* **38**(1), 1995, 83–95.

[Wa86]   Waterman, D.A., *A Guide to Expert Systems*. Addison-Wesley (0-201-08313-2), 1986.

[Wa93]   Walz, D.B., Elam, J.J., and Curtis, B., Inside a software design team: Knowledge acquisition, sharing, and integration. *Comm. ACM* **36**(10), 1993, 63–77.

[We93]   Weller, E.F., Lessons from three years of inspection data. *IEEE Software* **10**(5), 1993, 38–45.

[Wi88]   Wing, J.M., A study of 12 specifications of the library problem. *IEEE Software* **5**(4), 1988, 66–76.

[Wi90]   Wiecha, C., Bennett, W., Boies, S., Gould, J., and Greene, S., ITS: A tool for rapidly developing interactive applications. *ACM Trans. Information Systems* **8**, 1990, 204–236.

[Wi92]   Wiederhold, G., Mediators in the architecture of future information systems. *Computer* **25**(3), 1992, 38–49.

[Wo95]   Wood, J., and Silver, D., *Joint Application Development, 2nd ed.* Wiley (0-471-04299-4), 1995.

[Yo92]   Yourdon, E., *Decline and Fall of the American Programmer*. Yourdon Press (0-13-203670-3), 1992.

Index

access control 132
accounting department 112
agricultural production 3
airline marketing 63, 72, 117
ambiguity 130, 136
American Express 7
antecedent of implication 252
Apple 218
ARPANET 225
artificial intelligence 62
artificial intelligence software 57
Asea Brown Boveri 6
audit trail 112
automatic company linkages 28, 203, 211
automatic teller machine (ATM) 77, 117
automation 27, 181, 211

bank 214
bottom-up development 71
bridge design 25
Brooklyn Bridge 103
business, day-to-day 18
business analysis 108, 257
business continuity 9
business manners 112
business merger 53
business reengineering 5, 45, 106, 207, 217
  and disruption 52
  and management 23, 207
  and profitable company 21
  and risk 216, 255
  and service sector 207

and technology 10, 202
and what it is not 6
acceptance of 212
steps in 22
business reengineering texts 255
business strategy 18, 107, 215
business tactics 18
business volatility 17

call/return paradigm 68
Canada 31
Cartesian product 154, 250
cause-effect 10
central processing unit (CPU) 79
change, approved 90
change request 90
charitable foundation 214
checks and balances 9
Cleanroom 257
Cobol 222
COCOMO 94
combinatorial explosion 98
comment count 240
communication 79, 220
  instant 17
communication breakdown 36, 87, 122
company 4
completeness 166
CompuServe 227
computer aided software engineering (CASE) 94, 257
computing, client-server 256
computing, host-based 225
computing, network-based 225, 256, 259